AF729949

DONNA SUMMER

Song by Song

DONNA SUMMER

Song by Song

MARC ANDREWS

FONTHILL

First published in Great Britain in 2026 by
Fonthill
An imprint of
Pen & Sword Books Ltd
Yorkshire – Philadelphia

Copyright © Marc Andrews 2026

ISBN 978-1-03619-421-5

The right of Marc Andrews to be identified as Author of this work has been asserted by him in accordance with the Copyright, Designs and Patents Act 1988.

A CIP catalogue record for this book is available from the British Library.

All rights reserved. No part of this book may be reproduced, transmitted, downloaded, decompiled or reverse engineered in any form or by any means, electronic or mechanical including photocopying, recording or by any information storage and retrieval system, without permission from the Publisher in writing. NO AI TRAINING: Without in any way limiting the Author's and Publisher's exclusive rights under copyright, any use of this publication to "train" generative artificial intelligence (AI) technologies to generate text is expressly prohibited. The Author and Publisher reserve all rights to license uses of this work for generative AI training and development of machine learning language models.

Typeset by Simon and Sons ITES Services Pvt. Ltd., Chennai, India.
Printed and bound in the UK by CPI Group (UK) Ltd, Croydon, CR0 4YY

MIX
Paper | Supporting responsible forestry
FSC® C013604

The Publisher's authorised representative in the EU for product safety is
Authorised Rep Compliance Ltd., Ground Floor, 71 Lower Baggot Street, Dublin D02 P593, Ireland.
www.arccompliance.com

For a complete list of Pen & Sword titles please contact

PEN & SWORD BOOKS LIMITED
47 Church Street, Barnsley, South Yorkshire, S70 2AS, England
E-mail: enquiries@pen-and-sword.co.uk
Website: www.pen-and-sword.co.uk
or
PEN AND SWORD BOOKS
1950 Lawrence Road, Havertown, PA 19083, USA
E-mail: uspen-and-sword@casematepublishers.com
Website: www.penandswordbooks.com

Acknowledgements

Thanks to Jay 'Hot Stuff' Slater at Fonthill Media for making this book happen.

Thanks also to Liam Peter Joseph @thedonnasummerarchive and Dave for record sleeves.

This book is dedicated to my father who taught me how to love to love Donna Summer and her songs. May they both rest in peace.

About the Author

Marc Andrews has been working as a music journalist for almost forty years. He began his career working as a journalist at 'pop Bible' *Smash Hits*, firstly in Australia (1988–1990), then at the UK edition of *Smash Hits* (1990–1992) and lastly as editor of the Australian edition (1992–1995).

He is the author of five other books: 2022's *Madonna: Song by Song* and *Kylie: Song by Song* (both published by Fonthill Media), 2012's *We Need to Talk: My Life as a Doggone Celebrity Journalist* as a Kindle exclusive for Amazon, 2011's *Pop Life: Inside Smash Hits Australia 1984–2007* with David Nichols and Claire Isaac (Affirm Press) and 2010's self-published novel *Revelations: 2 Weeks In Tel Aviv*.

His articles, interviews and reviews have appeared in numerous magazines around the world over the last four decades with stints working for *Mediaweek*, *The Daily Mail*'s MailOnline and *Classic Pop* magazine.

He has also been a contributor to Australian gay glossy *DNA* since 2001 and is currently on staff as their music editor.

He is also the author of two Australian fanzines: 1989's *Madonna: The Unofficial Story* and 1993's *Madonna: The Material Girlie Down Under*.

Since 2021 he has curated the Poptastic! site on Facebook, dedicated to chronicling the history of *Smash Hits*.

Based in London, he resides there with his husband, dogs and pop memorabilia. He is currently working on *Erasure: Song by Song* for Fonthill Media.

Contents

Introduction: The Donna Summer Story

> I was eight years old when I started singing in the choir. I knew that I was ordained to sing. I think a voice from heaven spoke to me very clearly when I was a young child and I knew that I had the gift of singing and would be a singer. When people would ask me as a child I would say, 'I know I am going to be famous, there's no question in my mind!'
>
> *Donna Summer, 1983*

She may have humbly titled her 2003 autobiography *Ordinary Girl*, but Donna Summer was truly an extraordinary talent. Born LaDonna Adrian Gaines on New Year's Eve in 1948 in Boston, she would become a true trailblazer in the music industry. Not only did she have an exceptional voice, but she also possessed a magnetic stage presence and a masterly gift for songwriting.

Some fifty years after she scored her first international hit in 1975, with the orgasmic 'Love to Love You Baby', Donna Summer is still regarded as the 'Queen of Disco' and her music is just as beloved as it was when it first hit the charts.

She came from what she described as a loving family 'with deep spiritual roots'. Her grandfather, Solomon Gaines, had been a Christian minister with one of the biggest churches in Fairfax, Alabama. She liked to point out that this quite literally made her father, Andrew, 'the proverbial son of a preacher man'. During the Second World War, her father had been a soldier in Germany and when he returned to Boston, took any job available, be it butcher, wallpaper hanger, or television repairman. He met and married Donna's mother, Mary Ellen Davis, whose parents had emigrated from Nova Scotia, Canada, with a mixed heritage of African, Indian and Dutch-Irish. Donna was the third of seven children—Jeanette, Ricky, Donna, Amy, Mary, Dara and Linda—initially living in a working-class housing project. When she was six, the family moved four miles outside of Boston to a partially integrated middle-class neighbourhood in Brookline.

At the age of 10, when the soloist for the local church choir fell ill, Donna's mother volunteered her daughter Donna (dropping the 'La') to fill in and sing 'I Found the Answer I Learned to Pray'. When Donna witnessed her parents, sisters and the church minister all crying, she knew this 'scary and wonderful moment' would be the start of something. After this, Donna's life became consumed by music and she was 'intrigued by the whole burgeoning Sixties scene'. At age 17, she joined an all-male white rock 'n roll band, the Crow, as their Black female singer. Her game plan, incidentally, was to 'be like Judy Garland and sing my way to a place that opened other doors'. In 1966, she experienced Janis Joplin live, afterwards deciding to emulate the 1960s icon's 'vocal freedom' and naturally relaxed stage presence. After getting involved in what she called 'a pretty heavy drug scene—the Janis Joplin part of my life', she abruptly stopped.

Around that time, Donna witnessed a woman being mugged, who died soon after. Donna came forward to testify against the three young perpetrators. Luckily, the Crow had received an offer to play in New York and Donna's parents had the good sense to get her out of Boston. Donna's vocal talent was duly spotted while performing with the band in NYC's Greenwich Village. She was offered a recording contract with RCA Records: minus the band. Donna even cut demos of three Aretha Franklin songs (*Respect, Dr. Feelgood* and another) for the label in August 1968, which, she noted years later, were 'on tape somewhere'.

Before anything could come of that, however, she was talent-spotted again, and cast in a featured role in the English, French, or German productions of the musical *Hair*. A near-kidnapping event in Manhattan convinced Donna to quickly get on a plane to Munich, and she ended up living in Germany for seven years. Unsurprisingly, she was a huge success in *Hair* (or *Haare*, as it was known in German). Her first hit single came from the show: 'Wasserman', a German- language version of the song 'Aquarius'. Other roles in other musicals followed, plus stints at the Vienna Volksoper in black opera *Porgy & Bess* and the musical *Showboat*. During this time, Donna fell in love with fellow actor Helmuth Sommer, got married and had a daughter, Mimi, born in February 1973.

'I played small parts in those musicals,' Donna remembered. 'I did other musicals and it was basically musical theatre—acting and singing, which was exactly what I wanted to do. Eventually, I met somebody and they recorded me and the rest is sort of history.' That somebody was actually two somebodies— Italian music genius Giorgio Moroder and his sidekick, English music genius Pete Bellotte— who had set up their own studio in Munich, called Musicland, in 1971. They wisely realised they had a vocal genius on their hands. After a patchy year or two, with some dubious releases that barely made it out of Europe, the trio finally hit the jackpot in 1975 with the sensual overload that was 'Love to Love You Baby'. Donna played the part of the disco seductress so well that the 'sex symbol' image stuck, something she later detested.

The sexed-up 'Love to Love You Baby' became a major international hit in 1975, thanks to some serious wheeling and dealing courtesy of Neil Bogart's Casablanca Records. Having moved back to the US, within three years from 1976 to 1979, Donna released eight albums. Even more incredibly, four of them were double albums. She became not just the Queen of Disco, but a Black sex symbol and a gay icon simultaneously. In mid-1977, her futuristic electro-disco single *I Feel Love* hit #1 in the UK and #6 in the US while literally changing the face of music, especially disco and electronic dance music. That same year, Donna long since divorced from her first husband, left an abusive relationship, before finally getting together with fellow musician Bruce Sudano, who would become the love of her life (and father of her other two children). That's when Donna Summer's career purple patch commenced, kicking off with 1978's *Live and More* album.

Yet just as Donna was riding her highest wave of success as the true Queen of Disco, with a run of four #1 US singles within a year—'MacArthur Park', 'Hot Stuff', 'Bad Girls' and 'No More Tears (Enough Is Enough)' with Barbra Streisand—the 'disco sucks' backlash, with its roots in racism and homophobia, kicked in. Suddenly disco music, the sound that had united the world across dancefloors, clubs and discotheques, became uncool and fell out of favour.

At the same time Donna became personally embroiled in a lawsuit against her long-time US record label, Casablanca. Alleging undue influence, misrepresentation and fraud in the agreements she had signed with them, the legal action came as Donna herself underwent a huge spiritual transformation, becoming a born-again Christian. Soon after she finally married Sudano and became pregnant with her second child, Brooklyn, born in 1981.

Exiting Casablanca and signing with Geffen, the label run by entertainment impresario David Geffen, Donna and her A-team producers/co-writers Giorgio Moroder and Pete Bellotte opted to quit disco and switch to what was, by then, the hip sound of new wave rock. Her 1980 *The Wanderer* album, the title track of which spawned a #3 US single, was rockier and a shock to her disco fans. The follow-up, *I'm a Rainbow*, was unceremoniously yanked from the release schedule by David Geffen as he considered it subpar and without any obvious hits. This effectively marked the end of Donna's working relationship with Giorgio Moroder and Pete Bellotte after almost a decade of unparalleled success.

By the time Donna came to record her 1982 self-titled album with legendary producer Quincy Jones she was pregnant with her third daughter, Amanda, born that same year. While the album spawned two hits—the funky 'Love is in Control (Finger on the Trigger)' and majestic 'State of Independence'—it didn't prove to be a huge commercial, or critical, success for Donna. She was also informed around this time that as part of her litigation settlement she still owed her old label, Casablanca, one more album.

1983 was a truly pivotal year for Donna Summer. Although the lead single from that year's *She Works Hard for the Money* album became a huge hit—a female empowerment anthem harking back to her hugely successful disco years— Donna's new-found Christianity rubbed up the wrong way against her devoted gay audience. After an Atlantic City concert that year she invited members of the audience afterwards to learn more about her faith. During the session, a conversation between Donna and a member of her audience who had AIDS reportedly became heated. 'It was Adam and Eve, not Adam and Steve,' Donna allegedly told her audience members. It was also reported she said, 'AIDS is the result of your sins.'

Almost overnight there was a blanket ban on Donna and her music within the gay community, previously her most ardent support group. Suddenly Donna Summer, the Queen of Disco and a gay icon, was no longer beloved by her audience of hardcore disco queens.

Donna's career, and chart momentum, never fully recovered. Both 1984's *Cats Without Claws* and 1987's *All Systems Go* failed to spawn a major hit. Donna retreated to life with her husband and three children, surrounding herself with predominantly like-minded Christian musicians and personnel in her life and on stage.

Leaving Geffen behind in 1989, Donna signed with Atlantic/Warner Bros records. Initially there was a brief return to form on the *Another Place and Time* album, produced in London by super successful British trio Stock Aitken Waterman, aka 'The Hit Factory'. Donna's final US top ten hit, 'This Time I Know it's for Real' also gave her a well-deserved #3 UK hit. That same year Donna also belatedly penned a formal apology to the gay community, but it would only be made public after her passing in 2012. 'It was never my intention to reject you, but to extend myself in love,' she wrote to the ACT UP organisation. 'Can't we just forgive each other for this past confusion?'

For some inexplicable reason, Donna opted not to record anything further with Stock Aitken Waterman. 1991's *Mistaken Identity* album, produced by Keith Diamond, was poorly received in the charts and by those fans who still remained loyal to Donna. It would be her final new studio album for 17 years, although she did have some major releases of note during that period.

Donna recorded a festive album, 1994's *Christmas Spirit*, while 1993's *The Donna Summer Anthology* and 1994's *Endless Summer* compilations revitalised her back catalogue. The following year, 'I Feel Love' and 'State of Independence' were remixed, both returning to the charts. 1981's lost *I'm a Rainbow* album was also eventually released in 1996 as disco music, and thus our 'Queen of Disco' became hip again.

Performing at an auspicious New York City AIDS charity concert in 1998, it also finally seemed as if Donna and her gay audience might have healed their rift. In 1999, via new label Epic, Donna recorded the *Live and More Encore!* album/TV concert, featuring two new singles, 'I Will Go with You' and 'Love is the Healer'. Another compilation, 2003's *The Journey: The Very Best of Donna Summer*, included three new songs, to tie in with the release of Donna's memoir, *Ordinary Girl: The Journey*. Yet for the most part, during the 1990s and 2000s,

Donna remained very much a stay-at-home mum, taking care of her family and becoming a painter of renown.

In 2008, her seventeenth and final studio album *Crayons* was a massive success in the clubs as its singles 'I'm a Fire', 'Stamp Your Feet' and 'Fame (The Game)' topped the US dance charts. A final single, 'To Paris with Love', another US dance #1, appeared in 2010, but would sadly be Donna's last new solo release during her lifetime. At the age of just 63, Donna tragically died in 2012 from lung cancer, yet her legacy and music live on. As time has passed, Donna's sublime back catalogue of seventeen studio albums (and other material) has stood the test of time, signifying what a true music legend she remains.

In 2020, Norwegian DJ Kygo issued an updated remake of 'Hot Stuff' and in 2021 her *I'm a Rainbow* album received a major makeover as *Recovered & Recoloured*. Two years later came the release of acclaimed HBO 'warts 'n all' documentary *Love to Love You, Donna Summer*, co-directed by her daughter Brooklyn. In 2024 Donna posthumously became the first female solo artist to be inducted into the Grammy Hall of Fame and receive a Grammy Lifetime Achievement award in the same year. In 2025 Donna's creative genius was further acknowledged when she was inducted into the prestigious Songwriters Hall of Fame.

Donna Summer not only influenced the careers of numerous female artists who have come after her, including superstars Madonna, Kylie Minogue and Beyoncé, but by co-writing the majority of her hits, she proved there was serious substance behind her glittering sequinned façade. She also demonstrated defiantly that black women need not be mere disco queens, but can be global popstars, rock stars and icons too.

This book tells the incredible musical journey of Donna Summer one song at a time...

1

The Musical Theatre Years (1968–1972)

'Wassermann'

Polydor Records: 249 266. Single release: October 1968 (West Germany).
Cast Recording: *Haare*
Writers: Galt McDermont, Gerome Ragni, James Rado. German translation: Walter Brandin
Producers: Werner Schmid, Bertrand Castelli

In 1968, the world's biggest entertainment sensation was hippy counterculture concept musical *Hair*. A mere few months after it became a huge hit, on both Broadway and in London's West End, a German-language version opened in Munich. Among the cast was 19-year-old future superstar Donna Summer. Billed by her birth surname as Donna Gaines, she belted out the show's opener, and biggest hit, 'Aquarius', known as 'Wassermann' for German audiences. Credited to 'Donna Gaines und Ensemble' the single reached #4 in the West German charts. The German *Haare* soundtrack also featured Donna sharing vocal duties on four other tunes: 'Luft (Air)', 'White Boys', 'Schweben Im Raum (Walking in Space)' and the show's 'Finale'. The following year, in 1969, The Fifth Dimension reached #1 in the US charts with a *Hair* medley, 'Aquarius/Let the Sunshine In'. In 1988, Donna performed the English version of 'Aquarius' at an AIDS benefit organised by UNICEF, also featuring her buddy, songwriter Paul Jabara (from the original Broadway cast of *Hair*). He would tragically die from AIDS in 1992.

'If You Walkin' Alone'/'Can't Understand'

Phillips Records: 388 410 PF. Single release: July 1969 (West Germany).
Writers: (sic) Donna Gains, Hans Hammerschmied
Producer: Hans Hammerschmied

Donna's second single, but her first solo single, was erroneously credited to Donna Gains. One of the breakout stars from *Haare,* in what was then West Germany, Donna's first proper solo single is a very sixties-sounding tune reminiscent of British star Petula Clark, but with some added distinctive funky soulful grit. This mono recording, which notably was Donna's first credit as a songwriter, appears not to have made a dent in the charts. The quirky B-side, 'Can't Understand', is something of a Teutonic attempt at sexy soul, with a dash of Bond theme. It's also not a million miles away from where 'Love to Love You Baby' would take her a few short years later. Donna's soaring unmistakable vocals on 'Can't Understand', which almost rival those on 1982's 'State of Independence', make this a more interesting listen and arguably a better A-side in retrospect.

'Black Power' (Peter Thomas Sound Orchester)

Marina Records MA39/MuZikBeater MB022. Compilation: October 1998.
EP release: May 2024. (Digital) Album: *Moonflowers & Mini-skirts* (1998)
Writers: Peter Thomas, Gil Francropolus
Producer: Peter Thomas

Despite its strident title, this 1969 oddity is more blacksploitation than *Black Power* ('black power, that's my name in the night'). Credited to Peter Thomas Sound Orchester, when this curio was eventually released on CD almost 30 years later it wisely added 'vocal: Donna Summer'. German composer Thomas provided music for German film/TV for over 50 years until his death in 2020. Lyrics for 'Black Power' were penned by his wife (the very non-Black) Cordula Thomas, using Gil Francropolus as an alias, who died in 2017. A four- track EP was digitally released in 2024 on MuZikBeater, a label founded by Thomas's son Philip to promote his father's legacy and catalogue. The EP comprises English, German and instrumental versions of 'Black Power', plus 'Minotti on the Run' (minus any vocals), which is just what you would expect the soundtrack for a German television show in the late 1960s to sound like. Donna certainly worked hard for her Deutschmarks here with her powerful, multilingual vocals.

Vid bit!

A scantily-clad Donna seductively swings and sings 'Black Power' in television crime miniseries *11 Uhr 20*, which aired in West Germany in January 1970. The 3:42 minute clip from the show—featuring consummate professional Donna continuing to sing, and swing, after a nightclub brawl, with a little of 'If You Walkin' Alone' tossed in—was uploaded to YouTube in 2024 and was directed by Wolfgang Becker.

'How I Feel'

Global Records: 6306 910. Album release: 1971 (West Germany).
Cast Recording: *The Me Nobody Knows*
Writers: Gary William Friedman, Will Holt
Producers: Peter Kißten

Long before she was feeling love, Donna was letting people know how she felt on this gripping state-of-the-world ballad. *The Me Nobody Knows* was a Tony winner for best musical about inner city kids in NYC, known as *Ich Bin Ich* in West Germany where it played in both Bremen and Munich. An English language version of this rock musical was sung by the German cast, including a certain 'Gayn Pierre', the stage name Donna briefly adopted. *The Me Nobody Knows* soundtrack, on which Gayn/Donna appears across a number of other show tunes, is catchily credited to 'The Me Nobody Knows Ensemble'. There was also an original German cast recording of *Ich Bin Ich*, but instead of voicing Catherine as Donna did in the English version, she became the character of Melba. Another song Donna sang on, 'Light Sings', became a minor pop crossover for The Fifth Dimension that same year.

'Sally Go' Round the Roses'/'So Said the Man'

MCA/Decca: MK 5060. Single release: January 1971
Writers: Zelma Sanders, Lona Stevens
Producer: Vincent Melouney

On her second solo single Donna (Gaines) covers American R&B girl group and one-hit wonders The Jaynetts' 1963 song which reached #2 in the US. It was recorded in London in 1970 when she was a '*Hair* refugee', staying with buddies from the *Hair* cast in Kensington. This remake has a sly funk feel with Donna in fine vocal form, hinting at what a huge star she so clearly is, but is also yet to be. There have been suggestions that the lyrical content of the song hints at lesbianism, but that's unlikely given the era in which it was originally written. The single's folky, haunting, if not unexpectedly poetic B-side, 'So Said the Man', was written by Vincent Melouney, Doug Parkinson and Johnny Dick, at the time members of a hard rock Australasian 'supergroup' of expats called Fanny Adams. Sadly, this tune, or single, wasn't to be Donna's big breakthrough, and she would have to return to the world of musical theatre to bide her time until stardom came calling.

'Oh, Segne Gott, Mein' Seel'/'Du Bist Das Licht In Der Welt'

Reprise Records: 61 743. Album release: 1972 (West Germany). Cast Recording: *Godspell*

Writer: Stephen Schwartz. German translation: Robert Gilbert
Producer: Norman Foster

Another cast recording by Donna, this time solely in German. By this time she was fluent in the language. Her father Andrew, incidentally, had been stationed in Germany as a soldier after the Second World War and when he didn't want his kids to understand what he was saying he spoke German to Donna's mother, Mary. Not anymore though, eh?! 'Oh, Segne Gott, Mein' Seel' was the German language version of Godspell's 'Bless the Lord', while 'Du Bist Das Licht In Der Welt' was 'Light of the World' in the original. Not only was 1972 an important year for Donna's career, but it was also during her time performing in *Godspell* that she fell in love with her Austrian castmate, the very blond Helmuth Sommer. She became pregnant with her first child, Mimi, born in early 1973, and got married. Yes, Donna Sommer was on her way.

'Time For Change'/'Somethin' I'd Like to Tell You'

Change: D-3000. Single release: October 1972
Writers: (A-side) Broder Brodersen/EFS and (B-side) Brodersen and Gayn Pierre
Producer: Broder Brodersen

Credited to Cool Drive Union, this funky, if workmanlike, one-off single was released by the conservative German political party CDU (hence the band name). It was recorded to support their youth organisation, 'Junge Union', with an election looming in West Germany after the chaos of that summer's Munich Olympics. On the A-side obtuse lyrics such as 'Let's walk together hand in hand/ Let's put an end to the red fire in the land' read very much like an anti-socialism manifesto. For the rockier B-side, 'I'd Like to Tell You', Donna (credited as Gayn Pierre) scored a writing credit and once again this guitar- and- piano led stomper is debatably stronger than the A-side. Curiously, it's not Donna pictured on the single cover, but her younger sister, Linda Gaines, perhaps because Donna wasn't keen to attach her image to this blatantly political release, or be photographed heavily pregnant. As it transpired, when the election was held in West Germany in November that year, the liberal SDP became the largest party in Parliament since the pre-Nazi Party days of 1930. Copies of this rare single now fetch over €250.

'Nice To See You' (Veit Marvos)

Ariola: 86 673 IT. Album release: October 1972. AKA: *Summernight*, *Funstreet*, *Shout It Out!* and numerous other titles through the decades
Writers: Veit Marvos, Richard Palmer-James
Producer: VM Productions

If you're keen to bend an ear to a confusing fusion of krautrock and pre-disco, here's your chance! The original eight-track album, credited to Veit Marvos and his Red Point Orchestra, featured background vocals by Donna, aka Gayn Pierre, but is a true 'buyer beware' moment. This collection of mostly painfully schlager-drenched tunes, with Donna's vocals pumped upfront—'Na Na Hey Hey', 'They Can't Take Away Our Music', 'Jeannie', 'Little Marie', 'Shout it Out', 'Funstreet', 'Back Off Boogaloo' and 'Do What Your Mother Do'—has been remixed, renamed and re-released numerous times across the years to capitalise on Donna's subsequent fame. Not surprisingly, the best known (not to mention best!) tracks are the album's three covers. 'Na Na Hey Hey' was originally a #1 US hit for Steam in 1969, then later a #5 UK hit for Bananarama in 1983, while 'Back Off Boogaloo' was a 1972 top-ten US/UK hit for Ringo Starr. The highlight, if that's the right word to use here, is a slick gospel soul rendition of 'They Can't Take Away Our Music', a 1970 hit for Eric Burdon and War, giving Donna's prominent vocals a chance to shine. Released as she waited out her difficult pregnancy, this dicey release in all its various permutations became a legal bone of contention for decades. Other editions of Veit Marvos's collection added German songwriter Ralph Siegel's cheery 'Nice to See You', while a 1975 single release of 'Nice to See You' stuck jam-session (minus vocals) 'Right On' as its B-side.

2

Lady of the Night (1974)

Lady of the Night
Groovy: LGR 8301
Originally released: February 1974 (Netherlands only)

Side A		Side B	
'Lady of the Night'	3:58	'The Hostage'	4:16
'Born to Die'	3:24	'Wounded'	2:43
'Friends'	3:31	'Little Miss Fit'	3:06
'Full of Emptiness'	2:26	'Let's Work Together Now	3:58
'Domino'	3:14	'Sing Along (Sad Song)'	3:20

'Denver Dream'

Lark Records: INS 7510. Single release: January 1974
Writer: Pete Bellotte
Producers: Giorgio Moroder, Pete Bellotte

Living in Munich as a young mother and supporting herself between nappy changes and naps as a backing singer for the likes of rock band Three Dog Night and Krautrock band Emergency, Donna was introduced to Munich's very own music/Moog maestro, Giorgio Moroder. 'I had already developed a minor reputation in Germany as a pop singer,' Donna remembered. 'By the time I started working with Giorgio, I had recorded several songs from the musicals I had been in that had become hits.' British-born Bellotte was Giorgio's assistant at the time, proving his worth by writing the lyrics for 'Son of my Father', a UK #1 hit for Chicory Tip in 1972. Pete remembers Donna entering the studio as a freelance singer one day, and while warming up he discovered what a mighty voice she possessed. 'I called her a few weeks later to sing a lead vocal for me on a demo of a song I'd just written called 'Denver Dream', which I then sent to a publisher friend of mine in Paris. A reply came two days later to say the record company, Delta France, would like to bring the song out, as it stood, with Donna's vocal.' Donna agreed and, after a misspelling of her name, it was also a group decision to anglicize her married surname of Sommer to Summer 'as part of my makeover from the ordinary Donna Gaines, onetime hippie of Greenwich Village, to the uptown sophisticated diva Donna Summer'. 'Denver Dream' is thus the very first record credited to Donna Summer. Yet all of this collective star-power still couldn't push a Boston homegirl's sorrowful singalong tune about Colorado sisterhood into the charts. To that end, 'Denver Dream' was never included on any Donna album, presumably due to its failure to chart in any territory. Despite its Americana title, it could have been a serious Eurovision contender.

'Something's in the Wind'

Lark Records: INS 7510. Single release: January 1974 (B-side to 'Denver Dream')
Writer: Giorgio Moroder, Pete Bellotte
Producers: Giorgio Moroder, Pete Bellotte

Here's another example of where Donna's B-side is more interesting, if not blowing harder with more hit potential, than its somewhat laboured A-side. A catchy tune is hampered by some heavy-handed lyrics, with Moroder presumably acknowledging this. Soon after, he called a halt to most of his English lyric-writing duties. This wasn't the last we'd hear of 'Something's in the Wind' though. Three years later, it was surprisingly resurrected and reworked on Donna's *I Remember Yesterday* album as the jaunty 1960s-sounding 'Back in Love Again'. The second time around, thankfully, it came with much improved lyrics and melody courtesy of Donna herself. 'Back in Love Again' was so good, in fact, that it was even released as that album's fifth and final single in April 1978, reaching #29 in the UK charts. Talk about shifting winds!

'The Hostage'

Groovy: GR 1207. Single release: June 1974
Writers: Giorgio Moroder, Pete Bellotte
Producer: Pete Bellotte

Not willing to give up easily, thankfully, the soon-to-be Moroder/ Bellotte/ Summer dream team returned for seconds six months later and were finally rewarded with some glimmers of chart success. 'Giorgio had written a schlager tune called "The Hostage" that we were going to record when the 1972 Olympic tragedy happened, after which no one in Germany would touch it,'

Donna recalled. 'It's actually written in the form of a morbid phone call from a husband to a wife.' Thanks to Dutch television championing this bizarre song, which leans uncomfortably into bad taste kitsch, 'The Hostage' did well ('A nice little hit,' according to Giorgio) in that territory, spreading to Belgium and Spain. While the subject matter was unquestionably a poor choice for a bouncy pop tune—a wife whose husband is kidnapped—'The Hostage' offered the best example to date of Donna's world class vocals. Spoiler alert: there's a funeral at the end. In 1990, Donna admitted 'The Hostage' was 'an awful song'.

Vid bit!

Donna's lip-sync performance on Dutch television show *Van Oekel's Discohoek* has been on YouTube for years. Starring Dolf Brouwers as his comedy character Sjef van Oekel, this parody show wove in 'The Hostage' (landline phone calls included), with Donna looking suitably worried in a green print frock (green was her favourite colour, fact fans!) as a grieving wife but flubbing her lip-syncing. Directors: Wim T. Schippers, Ruud van Hemert, Gied Jaspars, Wim van der Linden.

'Let's Work Together Now'

Groovy: GR 1207. Single release: June 1974 (B-side to 'The Hostage')
Writer: Pete Bellotte
Producer: Pete Bellotte

After the eerie eccentricity of its A-side, the B-side of 'The Hostage' was a lot more palatable. Once again, there's more of a focus on a folky German schlager feel than anything resembling disco. Written and produced solely by then 30-year-old Bellotte, it's a far more satisfying harmonising outing, showcasing some wistful harpsichord keyboard keys. A rousing tune lyrically about getting together 'for the children' and respecting our neighbours, 'Let's Work Together Now' also speaks about different faces, other races, new conditions, old traditions, all as one. It's hard to believe no one suggested making this hard-working nugget the A-side, instead of the more dubious, and tastelessly salacious, 'The Hostage'.

'Lady of the Night'

Groovy: GR 1208. Single release: November 1974
Writer: Giorgio Moroder
Producer: Pete Bellotte

'We made a series of recordings, beginning with "Lady of the Night", that were completely different from anything and everything I've ever done, or even heard before,' Donna mused years later. 'On this single, I like to think of that time as musical boot camp.' Reaching #4 in the Dutch charts, this would be the second single from her debut album, also titled *Lady of the Night*. It was somewhat unusually released in February that year in Dutch record stores, much earlier than its two singles in 1974. There were also top-ten entries for the 'Lady of the Night' single in Austria and Belgium, plus it squeaked into the West German top forty. Something of a Phil Spector 1960s throwback pastiche, the lyrics were less demure when it came to mentioning this lady's business—'an easy living girl with love for sale'—touching on the same theme, 'Bad Girls' would toot- toot- beep-beep five years later. This also accentuated soon-to-be signature Moroder flourishes, such as his chanting background vocals and electro-ripe synth lines. It's worth noting how, in Donna's 2003 *Ordinary Girl* memoir, her official discography commences with 1975's *Love to Love You Baby* album. No love from Donna for this 'Lady of the Night'!

Vid bit!
A bewigged, very lady-like, clip of Donna performing *Lady of the Night* on Dutch television show *TopPop* was restored for YouTube in 2017.

'Wounded'

Groovy: GR 1208. Single release: November 1974 (B-side to 'Lady Of The Night')
Writer: Giorgio Moroder
Producer: Pete Bellotte

The blueprint for the initial batch of Moroder/Bellotte/Summer singles appeared to be this: choose somewhat controversial, even questionable, subject matter for the A-side; then opt for a much more conservative topic, albeit more interesting vocally, on the B-side. It's fair to suggest the magic ingredient missing on this chugging rock stomper is Donna, who was still being excluded from the closed boys' club of songwriting. As soon as she joined the writers' circle on her next album, the hits started coming thick and fast, baby. And is it just us, or is the dreary hard rock guitar solo here about as useful and interesting as the one a decade later on 'She Works Hard for the Money'? Talk about wounded!

'Born to Die'

Writers: Giorgio Moroder, Pete Bellotte
Producer: Pete Bellotte

The second track on Donna's *Lady of the Night* debut album, 'Born to Die', is a sad sorry tale about a baby left on a doorstep. 'Was I born to die?' Donna trills at full throttle, 'without love in my life'. Saddled with a hard-to-love 1970s folk-rock style, via a chugging persistent guitar riff, 'Born to Die' hasn't aged particularly well, though that was probably transparent at the time too. It's yet another early example of Donna's world-class vocals outshining the second- rate material foisted on her by Giorgio and Pete. Donna later liked to describe her musical mentor Giorgio as 'very intense—he had dark curly hair, a thick moustache that drooped like an Italian gunman's in a spaghetti Western and eyes that could illuminate a sheet of music without a flashlight'. Luckily, there were brighter days ahead for both of them.

'Friends'

Writers: Giorgio Moroder, Pete Bellotte
Producer: Pete Bellotte

Stylistically similar to 'Born to Die', albeit veering sonically more towards pop than rock, 'Friends' has a simple, friendly chorus, the likes of which ABBA, who would win the Eurovision Song Contest that year with a pop-rock song, would covet. An ode to childhood friendship, turning to unrequited romance with the boy next door, Donna demands he be 'more than my friend'. Once again, lyrically and musically, Donna's vocals are the best thing about 'Friends'. Speaking of which, during the making of the *Lady of the Night* album Donna got a feeling there was a real growing bond and friendship with her two creative allies. 'I sensed right away Giorgio was a true original and his music had the potential for greatness. He was a master behind the console,' she mused. 'Along with Pete, he could do simplicity as easily as he could do grandeur, all with a marvellously unerring ear for production.'

'Full of Emptiness'

Writers: Giorgio Moroder, Pete Bellotte
Producer: Pete Bellotte

A timely ballad for Donna to showcase her gospel upbringing and roots, 'Full of Emptiness' is sad, yet seductively so, and the closest thing to what was to come next for Donna, Giorgio and Pete. Admittedly Pete's empty lyrics are somewhat pedestrian, something Donna, the gifted songwriter in waiting, would have been perfect at tackling, if not improving. The main claim to fame 'Full of Emptiness' now has is that it became the only track from the *Lady of the Night* album to make the upgrade to the *Love to Love You Baby* album in 1975. That meant that for future re-releases, especially on later CD pressings, 'Full of Emptiness' was dropped from the *Lady of the Night* track listing.

'Domino'

Writer/producer: Pete Bellotte

A 'tall, masked, mystic man', who appears only to be known as 'Domino', takes Donna by the hand. Is he the next in line to fall for her, or is he just playing the game, so to speak? 'Domino' is lamentably another album track steadfastly stuck in a regressive late 1960s sound, rather than the progressive 'discolicious' 1970s Donna would soon boogie in to. Another spoiler alert: a thoughtless crowd push 'Domino' away from Donna so she's left on her own to warble her cheesy, almost country, ditty. Aw, heck. Yet while the material on the *Lady of the Night* album may have often been subpar compared to her later releases, it was all a great learning curve for Donna. 'One of the most important aspects of my singing Giorgio encouraged me to expand was my approach to a song,' she recalled. 'I will approach a song as an actress approaches a script. I do not sing; I act. When I sing, I sing with the voice of the character in the song. Because of that, I don't have to make every song something from my perspective; rather it's something from the heart and the soul of the character who is doing the singing.'

'Little Miss Fit'

Writers: Giorgio Moroder, Pete Bellotte
Producer: Pete Bellotte

A year earlier in 1973, Dutch singer Debbie (real name Ria Schildmeyer) released the original version of 'Little Miss Fit' as a single in her home country, West Germany, and Denmark, produced by Martin Duiser and Fritz Muschler. She'd already charted with Giorgio's 'Everybody Join Hands' in 1972, yet this 'Miss' missed becoming a hit. Giorgio and Pete must still have had a soft spot for 'Little Miss Fit' in order to resurrect it for Donna. Almost like something you might hear blaring out at a beach taverna on some Greek island, this hard luck tale is a big miss from the start with its nonsensical lines 'there's a good, there's a bad, some are gay, some are sad'. Featuring a strident harpsichord, 'Little Miss Fit' is arguably the most forgettable (if not regrettable?) track on Donna's debut album. Meanwhile, another sound, the sound of that decade as it transpired, was calling. 'I was listening to disco, yes and no, in 1974 when we started to produce,' Giorgio told *Time* magazine in 2015. 'Finally, we said, "Okay, we have to have a sexy song!" That was the first disco sound I produced, but I was always interested in the idea of disco songs.'

'Sing Along (Sad Song)'

Writer/producer: Pete Bellotte

Speaking of sad, it appears the *Lady of the Night* album failed to chart in any territory where it was released, possibly due to being released some months before its two hit singles made any impact. The album's closing track offers more nursery rhyme lyrics ('Sing along with my song/If you've lost and you're alone') and a jolly, schlager-lite melody, akin to early ABBA, or the New Seekers. 'Lady of the Night' stands as the only Donna album from the 1970s without a hint of disco: that's not a good thing, by the way. Yet there was some innovative production and Donna's impressive vocals never falter. It's just a shame Giorgio and Pete hadn't yet given her wings to fly as a songwriter. 'My greatest gift as a singer/songwriter has always been telling stories,' Donna noted. 'That's why I was a natural for musical theatre and it is what first caught the eye, ear and imagination of Giorgio.'

'Virgin Mary'

Groovy: GR 1215. Released: September 1975
Writers: Giorgio Moroder, Pete Bellotte
Producer: Pete Bellotte

Released only in the Netherlands, the praying-to-be-controversial 'Virgin Mary' would be the last of Donna's pre-stardom singles. The lyrics of 'Virgin Mary' were, as Donna herself noted, 'more or less the same as "Lady of the Night" and "Denver Dream"—a bit melodramatic with a tilt towards the schlocky side of life'. Relatively lengthy for a single, clocking in at just over five minutes, this is a turgid, sluggish ballad until the chorus suddenly kicks up its platform boots in a swirl of unexpected disco strings. The lyrics, which actually mention 'a lynch mob frenzy', appear to indicate a misguided gang rape ('You're not what we thought'). Little wonder this single flopped and it's hard to believe, given such unpleasant material as this, that Donna's next single release would be 'Love to Love You Baby' and—hurrah!—her international breakthrough.

'Pandora's Box'

Groovy: GR 1215. Released: September 1975 (B-side to 'Virgin Mary')
Writers: Giorgio Moroder, Pete Bellotte
Producer: Pete Bellotte

'Working with Giorgio was a priceless opportunity for me to learn the craft of three-minute, maximise-the-lyrics, maximise-the-hook pop songwriting,' Donna later reflected, on her early days learning her craft. 'It was through Giorgio's teachings that I began to understand how to write radio-ready tunes that got across exactly what I wanted to say.' Flipping 'Virgin Mary' over, we discover that when we open up our love to Donna we also open 'Pandora's Box'. The fact there's a slight hint of sexual innuendo on this catchy, midtempo charmer is presumably why the decision was made to retain it and reuse it on the following year's *Love to Love You Baby* album. Alongside 'Full of Emptiness' from the *Lady of the Night* album, 'Pandora's Box' would be the other early Donna Summer track to make the great leap to international attention.

3

Love to Love You Baby (1975)

Love To Love You Baby
Oasis/Casablanca: OCLP 5003
Originally released: August 1975

Side A		Side B	
'Love to Love You Baby'	16:48	'Full of Emptiness'	2:22
		'Need-A-Man-Blues'	4:30
		'Whispering Waves'	4:50
		'Pandora's Box'	4:56
		'Full of Emptiness (Reprise)'	2:20

'Love to Love You Baby'

Oasis: OC 401. Single release: (US) November 1975
Writers: Donna Summer, Giorgio Moroder, Pete Bellotte
Producer: Pete Bellotte

The song that changed everything for Donna, baby! 'Early in 1975, I had been playing around with a song idea. I didn't have anything more than just the title,' Donna recalled. 'In fact, the line was originally written as "I'd love to love you", which I thought was so cool. When I gave it to Giorgio, he paused for a second and then said, excitedly, "Donna! I like this!" He walked around the studio looking like a mad scientist from some B-horror movie as he moved his hands to a silent recording he could already hear in his head.'

Donna's first credited co-write with Giorgio and Pete was also inspired by Jane Birkin and Serge Gainsbourg's steamy 'Je t'aime...moi non plus' from 1969. Originally released as 'Love to Love You' in the Netherlands in mid-1975, it went top twenty. Giorgio then took the track with him to the annual MIDEM Music Festival in Cannes, France, handing it to Casablanca's Neil Bogart who was looking for the next big thing. Released in the US on Giorgio's Oasis label, via Casablanca, 'Baby' was subsequently added to the title. Despite being banned on many radio stations for being too racy, people power pushed Donna's single into the charts.

The single reached #2 in Donna's homeland (kept out of the top spot by Paul Simon's '50 Ways to Leave Your Lover') while also hitting #4 in both the UK and Australia. Mild-mannered Canada, surprisingly, was the only territory where it went to #1. It's no idle claim though to call million-seller 'Love to Love You Baby' the sexy sensation that kickstarted Donna Summer's global career. Additionally, Donna's sophomore *Love to Love You Baby* LP lovingly converged the formats of album, 12-inch single and 7-inch single all into one. Neil had taken the single version home to play at his orgies, where loved-up guests kept pestering him to play it again, baby. He called Giorgio demanding the original version be extended to 17 minutes to fill one side of an album. For the expanded version, Giorgio asked Donna to 'improvise and make it sound sexy'. They dimmed the lights, lit some candles and Donna provided suggestive moans, oohs and aahs. 'Love to Love You Baby' has since, in all its various guises and mixes, become one of the most readily identifiable hits of all time, not to mention one of the most culturally resonating. Notable cover versions have come courtesy of Bronski Beat/Marc Almond, No Doubt and Kylie Minogue. Beyoncé sampled it for her 2004 single 'Naughty Girl' (#3 US) granting Donna, Giorgio and Pete co-writing credits. Pete Bellotte called it 'our gamechanger', yet Giorgio realised Donna was not comfortable singing their sexy song, even if she later told reporters she had been channelling Marilyn Monroe and fantasising about her handsome new boyfriend, artist Peter Mühldorfer. 'Her parents did not like it,' Giorgio explained much later. 'I remember I met them once and they were not happy with me. They thought I was the devil corrupting their beautiful girl.'

The BBC once estimated there were twenty-three orgasms on 'Love to Love You Baby' while *Time* magazine counted twenty-two. For Giorgio, it was also 'the start of my career'. 'If truth be known, I didn't think it was so great when it was finished,' Donna later declared of 'Love to Love You Baby'. 'It was nice, but I didn't think it was so hot. But when it became a big hit, honey, I LOVED that record!' Pete, meanwhile, revealed in an interview that the two songs providing inspiration for the music to 'Love to Love You Baby' were the middle section of The Crusaders' 1975 track 'Sugar Cane' and the hi-hat from The

Hues Corporation's 1974 #1 US hit 'Rock the Boat'. 'We appropriated those two things and that gave it this early disco sound, which was quite different,' he admitted. He also remembered how the song got extended.

> Neil called us from the States one night saying, 'We're definitely going to release this record. I'm having a party at my house and it's turning into an orgy—and they want to hear "Love to Love You Baby" playing all the time. I've got someone on the record player just lifting the arm up each time and putting it on again and again. And that's given me the idea to copy "*In-A-Gadda-Da-Vida*" by Iron Butterfly and do a whole side of one song. I need you guys to do that as fast as possible...' As we had a six-minute song with a click track, all we had to do was copy the click track for 16, 17 minutes and we could drop in anything we wanted, at any part of the song, and it was all in time. That was revolutionary. All because of Iron Butterfly and sex at Neil Bogart's house!

Love to love that, baby!

Vid bit!
While there's no dedicated music video for 'Love to Love You Baby', Donna performed her risqué single numerous times on television shows around the world. In 2023, an animated music video (by Sharon Liu) was released in celebration of what would have been Donna's seventy-fifth birthday. While the intention was good, this rather lifeless and sexless clip doesn't do the song any favours (though we want a sparkly sequined disco outfit like that for our next disco party).

Remix fix!
In 1975, disco pioneer Tom Moulton produced a superlative white label mix, which at over 19 minutes is even longer than Donna's album version. It's since enjoyed a second life on the internet (and gives Giorgio his own cameo too!). Before Casablanca was shut by parent company PolyGram in 1984, 'Love to Love You Baby' was re-released as a 12-inch. On the A-side was the 'Come on Over to My Place Version' (the original full-length album version), with the B-side the 'Come Dancing Version' (the original edited down by half to 8:10). Giorgio also finally remixed his 'baby' in 2013, but more of that later.

'Need-A-Man-Blues'

Writers: Giorgio Moroder, Pete Bellotte

'I've got these need-a-man-blues and I need a man so bad!' Donna swoons and it's also driving her mad, sadly. This spacey synth tune builds nicely on what 'Love to Love You Baby' has already delivered, displaying a real creative development from the previous year's output by Giorgio and Pete. Worthy of being a single in its own right, that wasn't to be the case, as a follow-up Donna Summer album was issued just a few short months later in March 1976. In 1984, unapologetically gay trio Bronski Beat released a haunting synthpop ballad with the same title (and hyphens!) as 'Need-A-Man-Blues' for their *The Age of Consent* debut album, clearly influenced by Donna's song. The Bronski album also featured their slow/fast remake mixing 'Love to Love You Baby' with 'I Feel Love' for a #3 UK hit in 1985.

'Whispering Waves'

Writers: Giorgio Moroder, Pete Bellotte

Against a backdrop of recorded wave sounds, Donna emerges wistfully by the shore of the seas searching for the memory of her beloved man. 'Whispering Waves' is undoubtedly the best example on *Love to Love You Baby* of Donna's supreme vocal prowess, despite having to warble through cliched lyrics such as 'seagulls seem to cry my pain'. A decent chill-out tune, this would also have laid to rest, for once and for all, rumours that Donna was actually a drag queen! While this passionate romantic tale of lovers holding hands across the table might lead you to believe all was sweet and right in Donna's love life, her relationship with then boyfriend, Peter Mühldorfer, proved to be a toxic and violent one. In 2023's *Love to Love You, Donna Summer* documentary, he admitted hitting Donna during alcoholic rages and not being able to deal with her growing success. This led Donna to a later suicide attempt, although she stayed with Peter for a few further months. In 1976, 'Whispering Waves' was briefly released as a single with 'Could It Be Magic' on the B-side, but soon after flipped.

'Full of Emptiness (Reprise)'

Writers: Giorgio Moroder, Pete Bellotte

With just two seconds snipped off the running time from the original version (which as previously noted was a holdover from the *Lady of the Night* debut album), 'Full of Emptiness' returns to close Donna's 'Love to Love You Baby' orgiastic opus. It's a post-coitus comedown with noodling keyboards, courtesy of Giorgio, and breathy sleepy vocals from Donna. Bet this would have cleared the room at Neil Bogart's orgies! Incidentally, Casablanca wasn't Neil's first choice of name for his fledgling record label. He originally planned to call it Emerald City Records, after *The Wizard of Oz*, but after discovering the name was already taken he shifted to another favourite flick, *Casablanca*, starring Humphrey Bogart. By 1977, Giorgio's Oasis subsidiary label was fully integrated as part of Casablanca Record & FilmWorks.

4

A Love Trilogy (1976)

A Love Trilogy
Oasis/Casablanca: OCLP 5004
Originally released: March 1976

Side A		Side B	
'Try Me, I Know We Can Make It'	17:55	'Prelude to Love'	1:07
		'Could It Be Magic'	5:19
		'Wasted'	5:10
		'Come with Me'	4:20

'Could It Be Magic'

Oasis/Casablanca: OC 405. Single Release: January 1976
Writers: Barry Manilow, Adrienne Anderson
Producers: Giorgio Moroder, Pete Bellotte

Inspired by Chopin's 'Prelude in C Minor, Opus 28, Number 20', this Barry Manilow composition was originally recorded as a bubblegum number by a studio outfit he was part of called Featherbed with lyrics by Tony Orlando. It flopped, so Barry reworked 'Could It Be Magic' with lyricist Adrienne Anderson as a stirring ballad. Released as his solo single in June 1975, it became a US top-ten hit. A mere six months later, Donna cannily unveiled a magical disco remake as her follow-up single to 'Love to Love You Baby'. She also tweaked the 'Could It Be Magic' lyrics from 'sweet Melissa' (a nod to Barry's bestie, singer Melissa Manchester) to 'sweet Peter' (her then boyfriend Peter Mühldorfer). While the single just made the UK top 40, it missed the US top 40, peaking at a disappointing #52, although it was a top-ten hit across Europe. In 1992, British boy band Take That scored a #3 UK hit with a stomping version closer to Donna's version than Barry's.

Vid bit!

In 1999 Barry Manilow was headliner at the Gay Men's Health Crisis benefit with Donna guesting on a duet of *Could It Be Magic*. No footage exists, sadly. In 2004, however, Barry and Donna again performed it live on stage in Las Vegas, rough footage of which exists on YouTube. At one point Barry stops singing because he simply can't believe how good Donna's vocals are. It's a shame this magical duet was never properly recorded and released.

Remix fix!

Donna's album version ran for 5:20, with the single version chopped to a less magical 3:15. A 'full version' at 6:26, beginning with 'Prelude to Love', was finally released on CD in 2012, the year Donna died, on Ben Liebrand's *Grand 12 Inches 9,* through Sony Music.

'Try Me, I Know We Can Make It'

Oasis/Casablanca: OC 406. Single release: March 1976
Writers: Donna Summer, Pete Bellotte, Giorgio Moroder
Producers: Giorgio Moroder, Pete Bellotte

Considering her album is called *A Love Trilogy*, you might have expected there to be three songs contained here, but actually the title appeared to be a play on the fact this was actually Donna's third album. Side A is a continuous mixed medley of four songs: 'Try Me', 'I Know', 'We Can Make It' and, then (all strung together as one), 'Try Me, I Know We Can Make It'. Yes, it was the 1970s and the wild disco era, so why not try something… adventurous? While this may not have been another 'Love to Love You Baby', there's a real charm and elegance to 'Try Me, I Know We Can Make It'.

This sexy symphony of surging disco strings and synths is truly best experienced in its full, almost 18-minute, version. Some fans have suggested this might be Donna's best album A-side, even surpassing the extended 'Love to Love You Baby', especially when it comes to lovemaking. You make the call on that one! The single version of 'Try Me, I Know We Can Make It', meanwhile, was snipped down to just over four minutes. While it peaked at just #80 in the US and failed to chart in the UK, it did become a #1 on the US dance charts. Knowing now that Donna had a failed suicide attempt the same year *A Love Trilogy* was released only adds further poignancy to her 'Try Me, I Know We Can Make It' title.

Vid bit!

Again, it's worth trawling through YouTube for some of the television appearances Donna put in to promote 'Try Me, I Know We Can Make It', although some claim to be an 'official video'.

'Wasted'

Oasis/Casablanca: OC 406. Single release: March 1976 (B-side to 'Try Me, I Know We Can Make It')
Writers: Pete Bellotte, Giorgio Moroder
Producers: Giorgio Moroder, Pete Bellotte

Although the chart positions and sales for the *A Love Trilogy* album were somewhat less than its predecessor, as a collection of songs *A Love Trilogy* feels inherently more cohesive than the two previous Donna Summer albums. It's as if the Moroder/Bellotte/Summer love trifecta were truly getting their disco groove on. The fact the trio were able to release an album every six months or so proves just how determined they were to capitalise on their breakthrough and not waste the opportunity. Amid surging strings, futuristic synths and a regimented disco beat on 'Wasted', Donna is in full 'lover spurned' mode, although it's unlikely she would ever have written herself the line 'Guess I'm not too brainy'. In some ways, Pete/Giorgio's lyrics could even be interpreted as their commentary on Donna's tormented relationship with then boyfriend Peter Mühldorfer. He had quickly replaced husband Helmuth Sommer in Donna's affections, although she didn't officially get divorced until 1976. 'Wasted' was also the B-side to the second *A Love Trilogy* single, 'Try Me, I Know We Can Make It'.

'Prelude to Love'

Writers: Donna Summer, Pete Bellotte, Giorgio Moroder
Producers: Giorgio Moroder, Pete Bellotte

Not so much a 'Prelude to Love' as a knowing nod to what's to er, come next on the album with 'Could It Be Magic' (a pre-lube?) and another plundering of Chopin's 'Prelude'. Horny Donna was also back begging for more. 'Baby, it's been so long,' she coos enticingly. 'I've waited so long and now that I have you, I want you to come, come, come, come into my arms.' This brief one-minute interlude then segues seamlessly into the following track, making for another long LP side, not to mention late evening, of magic between the sheets. Musicians featured here, and now part of Giorgio and Pete's regular house band, were by this time being credited as Donna accompanied by 'The Munich Machine', including drummer of note Keith Forsey. The collective also included Thor Baldursson, responsible for the stellar string arrangements like the gorgeous work he did here.

'Come with Me'

Writers: Pete Bellotte, Giorgio Moroder
Producers: Giorgio Moroder, Pete Bellotte

Album closer 'Come with Me', like 'Wasted' before it, landed minus any songwriting input from Donna. Amid irrepressible strings and an 'ooh ooh ooh' chorus our gal promises to lead her lover 'there', which was most definitely on brand for the newly-appointed sexy Queen of Disco. Donna's backing vocal team comprised Madeline Bell, Sue Glover and Sunny Leslie, collectively known as 'The Midnite Ladies'. American Bell had already fronted British hitmakers Blue Mink, who scored top-five UK hits with 'Melting Pot' and 'The Banner Man'. She'd also sung background for Dusty Springfield, The Rolling Stones and Elton John. Sue and Sunny were British sisters and early members of Brotherhood of Man. In 1974, Sunny managed a UK top-ten hit with her version of 'Doctor's Orders', while Carol Douglas had the hit elsewhere. The Midnite Ladies also provided good backing vocals on Donna's other 1976 album release, while 'Come with Me' later showed up as the B-side to the forthcoming 'Spring Affair'.

5

Four Seasons of Love (1976)

Four Seasons Of Love
Casablanca: NBLP 7038
Originally released: October 1976

Side A		Side B	
'Spring Affair'	8:32	'Autumn Changes'	5:30
'Summer Fever'	8:08	'Winter Melody'	6:30
		'Spring Reprise'	3:53

'Spring Affair'

Casablanca: NB 872. Single release: August 1976
Writers: Donna Summer, Pete Bellotte, Giorgio Moroder
Producers: Giorgio Moroder, Pete Bellotte

'Ooh, something's coming over me!' In March 1976, Diana Ross released 'Love Hangover', a sexy disco song that not so much looked to Donna's 'Love to Love You Baby' for inspiration as borrowed heavily from it. Soaring to #1 in the US, it was a reminder to Donna and co that they couldn't just rest on their laurels. With that in mind, Donna's first concept album, *Four Seasons of Love*, rolled in. Duly inspired by Vivaldi's *The Four Seasons*, the basic storyline followed a romance from its spring awakening to its inevitable winter doom (and a little welcome early spring sunshine again afterwards). Donna, Giorgio and Pete were clearly on a hot, seasonal roll. Ahead of the album by two months came its jaunty, funky, uplifting, disco-soaked first single, 'Spring Affair'. Although the single version at 3:39 just missed the US top 40 at #43, the longer album version raced to #1 on the disco chart, bolstered by Donna's skin-tight, sex-drenched appearance on the *Soul Train* television show. The single also went top ten in Italy and Canada. Later, 'Spring Affair' became the B-side for the album's second single, 'Winter Melody'. Two decades later in 1996 segments of 'Spring Affair' were heavily sampled for the track 'Super Disco' on Étienne de Crécy's inventive cult dance *Super Discount* album with Alex Gopher.

'Summer Fever'

Writers: Donna Summer, Pete Bellotte, Giorgio Moroder
Producers: Giorgio Moroder, Pete Bellotte

Introducing the first hint of rock guitar to Donna's disco landscape, it's shocking that a track as outstanding, and chart-ripe, as 'Summer Fever' was never accorded a single release. Awash in Donna's sexy pillow talk, this was not just a little creative foreplay on her own surname, but sung entirely in falsetto. This is presumably the tie-in to the album cover's back shot with Donna recreating Marilyn Monroe's iconic 1955 *The Seven Year Itch* movie pose. Donna actually used Marilyn as inspiration for 'Love to Love You Baby' and in the press would often be referred to as the 'Black Marilyn'. 'I was told to act like I was sexy. I would always use Marilyn Monroe as my idea of what I thought was sexy,' she confessed years later. 'At some point I did a take-off of Marilyn Monroe, which we called the Black Marilyn, and that was the influence. Marilyn did some nude photos, but she had an innocence about her sexuality which I like. Even though people thought she was not that smart, she was actually a very smart woman and very well-read, but that was her act.' In Australia, 'Summer Fever' received extra exposure when used by the Seven television network as its summery theme promo. Donna at her sizzling best!

'Autumn Changes'

Writers: Donna Summer, Pete Bellotte, Giorgio Moroder
Producers: Giorgio Moroder, Pete Bellotte

Flipping the *Four Seasons of Love* album over and the season, not to mention the mood, has most definitely changed as Donna points out 'something is wrong'. The disco beat continues, thankfully, although there is a slight sly hint of a Caribbean groove in the memorable 'Autumn Changes' bridge. As an album consisting of four dance tunes, they all topped the disco chart in the US, again solidifying Donna as the Queen of Disco. In *Interview* magazine in 1976, she was asked about the title. 'Queen of Discos? I though Gloria Gaynor was the Queen of Discos? Disco Queen, huh? Well, I dunno, I may be, like you said, the new Queen of Discos, but lemme tell ya since I got to be Queen, I ain't been alone with my boyfriend for one minute!' Asked many years later if she still appreciated that title, Donna responded with a laugh, saying, 'It's nice to be the queen of something. It's the highest compliment. I don't give myself that name. If a person works hard and they become a diva of the theatre, or opera, like Maria Callas, it's a compliment to her because she took her creative abilities to the highest level.'

'Winter Melody'

Casablanca: NBD 100. Single release: January 1977
Writers: Donna Summer, Pete Bellotte, Giorgio Moroder
Producers: Giorgio Moroder, Pete Bellotte

Donna's year-long love affair comes to a chilly close as her 'Winter Melody' takes hold. The beats have slowed down considerably, though you could still dance through the bleak icy heartache. 'Emptiness and just a memory' is all that remains of the love that once was, as Donna realises she never knew love could hurt so bad. A disco ballad that would have been great for a slow(er) dance at the end of a long night, 'Winter Melody' was also the second and final single release from *A Love Trilogy*. The album version of 'Winter Melody' at 6:33 was truncated to 3:58 for the single version. It charted at #43 US, but a less wintry #27 UK, though every single track from *Four Seasons of Love* went to #1 on the US disco charts.

'Spring Reprise'

Writers: Donna Summer, Pete Bellotte, Giorgio Moroder
Producers: Giorgio Moroder, Pete Bellotte

Donna loved a 'reprise' on her albums and here's another (with more to come). Not wanting to leave on a downer, there's a touch of spring hope—basically a shortened version of 'Spring Affair', as if we've come full love cycle, like the seasons. Clever! *Rolling Stone* magazine's review declared, 'like Donna Summer's previous American releases, "Love to Love You Baby" and "A Love Trilogy", *Four Seasons of Love* is an extended exercise in ecstasy ... the songs build and break, surging on clean sweeps of violins, but because they ease off before reaching a climax, Summer and the orchestra are able to keep it up indefinitely without dissipating the record's vibrant energy.' Casablanca sold the album in trade ads as 'from the lady who brought you "*Love to Love You Baby*" and

"*A Love Trilogy*" comes the definitive love album ... Critics have called it "disco perfection"—*Four Seasons of Love* ... an album for all seasons.' Another ad called it, 'the definitive disco album' and 'the definitive love album' from 'the first lady of love'. Love to love that too, baby.

6

I Remember Yesterday (1977)

I Remember Yesterday
Casablanca: NBLP 7056
Originally released: May 1977

Side A		Side B	
'I Remember Yesterday'	4:45	'Black Lady'	3:47
'Love's Unkind'	4:24	'Take Me'	5:03
'Back in Love Again	3:54	'Can't We Just Sit Down (And Talk It Over)'	4:25
'I Remember Yesterday (Reprise)	3:02	'I Feel Love'	5:53

'Can't We Just Sit Down (And Talk It Over)'

Casablanca: NB 884. Single release: May 1977
Writer: Tony Macaulay
Producers: Giorgio Moroder, Pete Bellotte

As far as songwriting pedigrees go, they don't come much more regal than British composer Tony Macaulay. Some of his hits include classics such as 'Build Me Up Buttercup', '(Last Night) I Didn't Get to Sleep at All' and 'Baby Now That I've Found You'. His earnest break-up ballad 'Can't We Just Sit Down (And Talk It Over)' had already been released by soul singer Bill Brandon earlier in 1977, but wasn't a major success. 'Neil Bogart got us to do *"Can't We Just Sit Down (And Talk It Over)"*,' Pete recalls. 'None of us were that keen, but Bogart was doing so well for us that we recorded it.' By covering it and releasing it as Donna's new single, Neil's vision was patently to launch Donna's fifth album with something different, heartfelt and quite daring for her. Vocally, Donna is in fine form here on a touching rendition of this slow smouldering power-ballad, also recorded in 1977 by both television star David Soul and British singer Linda Lewis.

Released as a single by Donna in May 1977, a fortnight prior to her *I Remember Yesterday* album, 'Can't We Just Sit Down (And Talk It Over)' just so happened to have another track from her new album on its B-side. That turned out to be a revolutionary dance song which would change pop music, pop culture and her own career trajectory. Within weeks radio and club DJs had flipped the single over, flipped over what they heard and started incessantly playing this game-changing B-side that captured all the 'feels'. It didn't take long before Casablanca felt the love too, making it the official A-side by July. Truly a 'lost' Donna single, 'Can't We Just Sit Down (And Talk It Over)' did at least become a top-twenty R&B single in the US, and was featured in the Oscar-nominated movie (and its soundtrack) *Looking for Mr. Goodbar* alongside 'Prelude to Love' and 'Could It Be Magic'.

'I Remember Yesterday'

GTO: GT 107. Single release: September 1977
Writers: Donna Summer, Giorgio Moroder, Pete Bellotte
Producers: Giorgio Moroder, Pete Bellotte

Between March 1976 and October 1977, Team Donna released four concept albums with *I Remember Yesterday* the third in the series. Pete had read Anthony Powell's book *A Dance to the Music of Time*, which inspired him to make an album shifting through periods of time too. 'The idea of the album,' Giorgio explained, 'was, "Let's have the sounds of the '50s and '60s, Motown, then the '70s!"' Yet if anything, the album's title track and opener has more of a 1940s Andrew Sisters feel to it. Hence, backing vocal support came from Pattie Brooks, Petsye Powell, Marti McCall, Dani McCormick and, importantly, Brooklyn Dreams who, of course, would loom large in Donna's story, professionally and personally, in coming years. When Donna first met band member Bruce Sudano she 'knew instantly in my heart that I was going to marry this man one day'. The highlight of this track surely has to be Donna blissfully engaging in some jazz 'scat'-type singing. Not only was 'I Remember Yesterday' the first track on Donna's fifth album, but this bouncy pop disco tune also became the album's third single. It also had the somewhat unenviable task of being the European follow-up to *I Feel Love*, although in the US there were no further singles to encourage buyers to purchase the album instead. A UK #14 hit, 'I Remember Yesterday' made the top ten in Italy but was also a US disco #1 for three weeks, collectively along with 'I Feel Love/Love's Unkind/Take Me'. The Dutch version of the single stuck the 'I Remember Yesterday (Reprise)' on the B-side for a full remembrance service.

'Love's Unkind'

GTO: GT 113. Single release: November 1977 (UK)
Writers: Donna Summer, Giorgio Moroder, Pete Bellotte
Producers: Giorgio Moroder, Pete Bellotte

From the 1940s, we leap into the 1950s/1960s with a retro sound harking back to the golden age of girl groups and teen romances/crushes. With its 'wall of sound' arrangement and rousing heartbreak chorus, there's a close resemblance here to 1963's 'Then He Kissed Me' by The Crystals, which went top ten in both the UK and US. In 2012, the year Donna passed away, pop music journalist Alex Needham praised the recording in the *Guardian*. 'Part of Summer's strength was her versatility,' he wrote. 'The high concept of her album *I Remember Yesterday* was that each track would pastiche the sounds of a different decade, from the magnificent "Love's Unkind", her take on Phil Spector, to "I Feel Love" (which represented the future) and her voice is at home in any style Moroder and Bellotte can throw at her.' Released as the third/fourth European single, 'Love's Unkind' peaked at #3 in the UK, selling over half a million copies. In 1991, *EastEnders* actress Sophie Lawrence launched her short-lived UK pop career with a fairly faithful version of 'Love's Unkind', reaching #21 on the charts via Simon Cowell's IQ Records. Danish indie duo Ravonettes also took inspiration from 'Love's Unkind' for their 2009 single 'Bang!', while Scottish band Texas sampled it wholesale for their 2021 single 'Mr Haze'. Texas granted Donna, Giorgio and Pete co-writing credits, though their single only charted in Belgium.

'Back in Love Again'

GTO: GT 117. Single release: April 1978
Writers: Donna Summer, Giorgio Moroder, Pete Bellotte
Producers: Giorgio Moroder, Pete Bellotte

For an album of just eight tracks, to produce five singles is pretty damn impressive. If you've been reading through this book chronologically to this point then it won't be a surprise to you to read how 'Back in Love Again' was recycled from her 'lost' 1974 B-side, 'Something's in the Wind', the flipside of her very first single billed as Donna Summer, 'Denver Dream'. If you listen to both versions side-by-side one thing becomes very apparent: Donna was a much better lyricist than either Giorgio or Pete. Here, that same perky tune makes its reappearance as a Motown tribute to the sound of Diana Ross and The Supremes. There's even a knowing nod to that trio's 1964 'Baby Love' single, which reached #1 in the UK and US. Oddly, 'Back in Love Again' was selected for single release in the UK almost a year after the *I Remember Yesterday* album had been released and some six months after its successor *Once Upon a Time* had been released. The 'Back in Love Again' single managed a decent #29 place, bridging the gap before Donna's next single release in July 1978.

'I Remember Yesterday (Reprise)'

Writers: Donna Summer, Giorgio Moroder, Pete Bellotte
Producers: Giorgio Moroder, Pete Bellotte

At eight tracks, *I Remember Yesterday* had double the number on Donna's previous album and the most to date: a clear numerical sign that Team Moroder/ Bellotte/ Summer were keen to shift closer to pop and away from disco. That's also more than evident in the material contained on the genre-hopping 'I Remember Yesterday'. Again, as a mixed suite of four songs, this brings us back to where we started off all those musical memories of yesterday. At just over three minutes, it's a sleeker, slicker edit of the other 'I Remember Yesterday', and let's not forget that if we count the two 'I Remember Yesterdays' as one song, then all three of the tracks on Side A were issued as singles in various territories. That's how strong an album this is. In 1979, Tony Orlando recorded a funky disco version of 'I Remember Yesterday' for his *I Got Rhythm* album, released by Casablanca. 'I Remember Yesterday's opening bars were also sampled in rapper Skyzoo's braggy hood anthem 'I Shine' from 2008's *Corner Stone Classic Remixed* digital-only mixtape.

'Black Lady'

Writers: Donna Summer, Giorgio Moroder, Pete Bellotte
Producers: Giorgio Moroder, Pete Bellotte

Side two of 'I Remember Yesterday' opens like the theme from an early 1970s blaxploitation movie, but soon settles into something more like funky R&B, clearly influenced by the sound of Florida's KC & The Sunshine Band, who scored an impressive four US #1s in the two years from 1975–77. Lyrically, 'Black Lady' is the somewhat sinister tale of a 'mean, really bad' woman who appears to kill her prey like a black widow. 'The death was slow 'cos she won't let go,' Donna belts out in this busy disco affair, filled with a similar horn arrangement to 'I Remember Yesterday'. A year later, in 1978, cheap copycat act The Connection Group, featuring singer Dee Dee Smith, covered 'Black Lady' as part of their *The Best of Donna Summer* cover versions album. They released another album of Donna covers, *Disco Lady*, in 1979 (buyer beware!). Thanks to the success of its singles, predominantly 'I Feel Love', Donna's *I Remember Yesterday* album became her biggest seller to date, as well as her highest charting album at #3 in the UK (and second best to that point with #18 in the US). 'Black Lady' would also be the B-side to the 'Love's Unkind' single in some territories.

'Take Me'

Writers: Donna Summer, Giorgio Moroder, Pete Bellotte
Producers: Giorgio Moroder, Pete Bellotte

Back to more standard mid-1970s disco fare, 'Take Me' kicks off with typical sex queen Donna lyrics: 'Oh baby, I've got all this love, it's more than enough/Oh baby, I'm filled with desire, I'm caught in your fire'. Yes, this baby had the power to turn her on. It was time for someone to take her, make her their woman, use her and make her their own. With Giorgio's masculine chants, alongside a background of electronic bleeps and irresistible strings in the background, 'Take Me' returns Donna to the material which made her famous. Perhaps for that reason too it already sounded a tad passé compared to the rest of the album with its adventurous streak. Speaking of aural adventures, in 2011 hip-hop producer Elusive extensively sampled, if not deconstructed, parts of 'Take Me' for the track 'World on Wheels' on his *Hip Hop for Hipsters* album.

'I Feel Love'

Casablanca: NB 884. Single release: July 1977
Writers: Donna Summer, Giorgio Moroder, Pete Bellotte
Producers: Giorgio Moroder, Pete Bellotte

And, finally, Donna Summer changes the face of popular music—and it's soooooo good! 'The challenge was to figure out how a song would sound in 20 years,' Giorgio recalled. 'I thought the only way to do it would be to use a synthesizer and computers to do all the instruments. There's the bass, there's a snare, a kick, a hi-hat, all produced by synthesizers. It created a modern, mechanical feel. Then, you add the voice of Donna Summer and it's melodic and sexy. That's a big part of its success still—you have this metallic machine sound that becomes seductive.'

The first-ever entirely synthesized disco track (apart from Keith Forsey's kickdrum and Donna's voice), 'I Feel Love' became not just the most important song of the disco genre, but a masterpiece revolutionising both disco music and pop, and some fifty years later it is still influencing dance and club culture. Spun relentlessly at NYC's infamous Studio 54 club, its popularity took everyone by surprise. 'We really didn't know what we were doing at the time, it was just part of the album,' Pete insisted. 'We were very pleased with it, but I don't think we were sitting there thinking it was unlike anything else.' Returning Donna to the US top ten after a two-year absence, 'I Feel Love' did even better in the UK, topping the charts for four weeks, selling over a million copies and remaining her only #1 there. Wisely, Casablanca decided not to chop the 5:56 running time for a single version, only adding to its Moog mystique, although a promo version of around 3:46 was sent to radio stations and used later in numerous compilations. A 12-inch version at 8:15 was also issued on vinyl, later appearing on various CD/digital compilations.

Artists who have covered 'I Feel Love' include Bronski Beat/Marc Almond (whose hi-NRG version reached #3 UK in 1985), Messiah Feat. Precious Wilson (a rave take which went to #19 UK in 1992), Vanessa Mae (a classical dance take which went to #41 in 1997), Sam Smith (#76 UK in 2019), Blondie, Red Hot Chili Peppers, Madonna (live during her *Confessions* 2006 tour) and Kylie Minogue (live/studio during her *Fever2002* tour). Beyoncé interpolated 'I Feel Love' on her sexy MF *Summer Renaissance* in 2022 (giving Donna, Pete and Giorgio co-writing credits), while rappers ¥$, Kanye West and Ty Dolla $ign sampled it for 2024's 'Good (Don't Die)' without consent and were later sued by Donna's estate.

Asked if he was surprised by the continued impact and influence of 'I Feel Love', Giorgio insisted, 'at the beginning I thought, "Yeah, we have a great song!" Then Brian Eno gave it the stamp of approval and every few months I'd hear a remake or a song that had some elements of it. I still hear songs that have the same bassline with one note removed. A lot of people got inspired by it.' In 2011, 'I Feel Love' was inducted to the US Library of Congress's National Recording Registry as 'culturally, historically, or aesthetically important'. In 2025, *Billboard* crowned it the #1 best dance song of all time. Ahead-of-its- time, yet ultimately timeless, 'I Feel Love' proved to be a watershed moment in Donna's career, elevating the Queen of Disco to pop immortality. A true music superstar was born and you could feeeeeeeel the love!

Remix fix!

If 'I Feel Love' was the work of a European synth genius, then its remix was the work of an American synth genius. In 1978, gay keyboard mastermind Patrick Cowley supplied DJ remix service Disconet with his 15-minute remake of 'I Feel Love', which was like nothing anyone had ever heard before: the roots of disco, techno, house and EDM were all intertwined. The hi-NRG Cowley remix became so coveted among DJs that four years later Casablanca finally issued it as an official single in 7-inch and 12-inch formats. It was released on 20 November 1982, eight days after Cowley died of AIDS at the age of 32, hitting #21 in the UK. (For the 1995 mixes of 'I Feel Love' see Chapter 19).

Vid bit!

The original 'I Feel Love', and 1982 official remix, came without official videos, though there are plenty of television/live appearances by Donna, including her hilarious 'robot dance' performances, scattered across the internet.

'Down Deep Inside' (theme from *The Deep*)

Casablanca: CB 140297. Single release: August 1977
Writers: Donna Summer, John Barry
Producer: John Barry

During 1977, Donna released an incredible eight singles across three different albums: 'Winter Melody', 'Can't We Just Sit Down (And Talk It Over)', 'I Feel Love', 'I Remember Yesterday', 'Love's Unkind', 'Back in Love Again', 'Down Deep Inside' and then, finally, 'I Love You'. Before she released her second album that year (a double album, no less!) this one-off movie cash-in swam in. Not only was John Barry its co-writer, but he was also arranger, conductor and producer. 'Casablanca Records began to expand into the movie business,' Donna explained in her *Ordinary Girl* memoir. 'Neil and his new partner, Peter Guber, had arranged for me to work with John Barry, one of Hollywood's great music composers. Wow, an inexperienced girl like me in such elite company as the Oscar winner John Barry, being asked to cowrite the theme for the movie *The Deep*.'

A somewhat audacious blend of Donna's sexy lyrics and vocals ('deep down inside there's a place in me I'm yearning to explore') and Barry doing swimmingly with his best Moroder-lite impression, the single reached #5 in the UK, and did well across Europe, yet unfathomably didn't receive a release in the US. *The Deep* soundtrack also included a sluggish ballad version known as 'Down Deep Inside (A Love Song)'. An extended version was included on 1978's *Love and More* album. Although it didn't win, 'Deep Down Inside' was nominated for Best Original Song at the Golden Globes (Debby Boone's strident power-ballad 'You Light Up My Life' nabbed that, plus the Oscar, and was also the biggest hit of the decade in the US). The single B-side was John Barry's instrumental version of 'Theme from *The Deep*'. Casablanca's promo 12-inch featured Donna's track, the instrumental B-side, plus Beckett's genre-bending 'Disco Calypso'. There would be more movie magic coming Donna's way soon after this box office blockbuster too, thank God!

7

Once Upon a Time (1977)

Once Upon A Time
Casablanca: NBLP 7078
Originally released: October 1977

Act 1		Act 3	
'Once Upon a Time	4:02	'If You Got It Flaunt It'	4:43
'Faster and Faster to Nowhere'	3:34	'A Man Like You'	3:34
'Fairy Tale High'	4:25	'Sweet Romance'	4:31
'Say Something Nice'	4:44	'(Theme) Once Upon a Time'	0:48
		'Dance Into My Life'	4:10

Act 2		Act 4	
'Now I Need You'	6:09	'Rumour Has It'	4:57
'Working the Midnight Shift'	5:07	'I Love You'	4:43
'Queen for a Day'	5:59	'Happily Ever After'	3:51
		'(Theme) Once Upon a Time'	3:58

'Once Upon a Time'

Casablanca: VIP-2580. Single released: February 1978 (Japan only)
Writers: Donna Summer, Pete Bellotte, Giorgio Moroder
Producers: Giorgio Moroder, Pete Bellotte

1977 was the year the disco inferno caught fire and burned, baby, burned. In April, the most famous discotheque in the world, Studio 54, opened in New York, while in December the movie which came to define the era, *Saturday Night Fever*, hit cinemas. 1977 was also the year Donna released two classic disco concept albums with the second, *Once Upon a Time*, a double LP opus (her first). Like its title suggests, this was a disco fairytale about a working girl who falls in love and (spoiler alert!) lives happily ever after. With Donna having met Brooklyn Dreams' Bruce Sudano and realising she actually had met the man of her dreams (although they both had partners at that time), the story was also clearly art imitating life.

The original idea for 'Once Upon a Time' was credited to Al Bogatz (Neil Bogart's real surname was Bogatz), with the story concept by Donna and her two co-managers Joyce Bogart and Susan Munao. Joyce was Neil's second wife, whom he married in 1976, and also the manager of another Casablanca act, Kiss. Their son Evan 'E. Kidd' Bogart later won a Grammy in 2008 as co-writer of Beyoncé's 'Halo', the same year he co-wrote two tracks for Donna's final album, *Crayons*. Donna described her manager Susan Munao as 'a lioness in a Chihuahua's body', and said that although she was of Italian descent, 'swearing was her second language— divorced and on her own she threw herself into my career'. The thrilling, yet slightly distressing, disco overture 'Once Upon a Time' was released as a single in 1978 in Japan only with '(Theme) Once Upon a Time' as its B-side. That same year, 'Once Upon a Time' also became the B-side to Donna's 'MacArthur Park' single.

'Faster And Faster to Nowhere'

Writers: Donna Summer, Pete Bellotte, Giorgio Moroder
Producers: Giorgio Moroder, Pete Bellotte

Donna's 'nightmare/daymare/badmare/no matter which way-mare' is her rather bleak take on urban decay and a hustling city closing tighter around her ('oh there's violence lurking in the alleys where no one should dare go'). The segue from 'Faster and Faster to Nowhere' to the next track, 'Fairy Tale High', is unquestionably the album's least slick changeover. Oddly, on the following year's *Live and More* album, 'Fairy Tale High' switched places with 'Faster and Faster to Nowhere' in the sequencing, which does actually make more sense logically in the story. 'Faster and Faster to Nowhere' has been sampled twice over the years—on Italian hip-hop outfit's Colle Der Fomento's 'Più forte delle bombe' in 2005 and a year later by another Italian hip-hop act, Club Dogo, on 'La Notte Che Rovesciammo L'Ordine'. There must be something about the sinister piano riff on Donna's original track, which appeals to Italian rappers.

In 2023, auction house Christie's put Donna's handwritten lyrics for 'Faster and Faster to Nowhere' from September 1977 up for online auction as part of their 'The Collection of Donna Summer'. Written on two pages of München Hilton letterhead, it concludes with Donna's memorable 'it's a nightmare, daymare, it's a bad mare, no matter which way mare'. Expected to fetch S1,200, the lyrics sold instead for a whopping $10,710. Also up for grabs in the same 146-item lot were test shots of Donna with Barbra Streisand by Francesco Scavullo from 1979, a gold record for their duet and plenty more.

'Fairy Tale High'

Atlantic: ATL 11 057. Single Release: December 1977 (West Germany only)
Writers: Donna Summer, Pete Bellotte, Giorgio Moroder
Producers: Giorgio Moroder, Pete Bellotte

Donna's West German record company (Atlantic) opted for *'Fairy Tale High'* as the lead single in that territory, putting 'I Love You' on the B-side. With the single missing the chart altogether, they might as well have stuck with 'I Love You' as the A-side, as the rest of the world did. Giorgio himself was obviously a big fan of 'Fairy Tale High' and a snippet of it can be heard on his 'From Here to Eternity' single, released in September 1977 ahead of his solo album of the same name, which had been released some months earlier in July. That meant he gave Donna fans a preview of her new track months before it hit record stores. If you want to keep an ear out for it, check around the 3:52 mark to hear that bouncy 'Fairy Tale High' refrain. Perhaps Giorgio was simply into recycling years before anybody else (or anyone else noticed)! His own single reached #16 in the UK charts and was later included in the *Thank God It's Friday* movie, but mysteriously not on the soundtrack. French glamourpuss Amanda Lear voiced a re-recording of 'From Here to Eternity' for Giorgio's tribute album in 2000. Again, there were more handwritten lyrics at the Christie's online auction in 2023, with not many alterations to Donna's finished version of 'Fairy Tale High'. This went for a fairy tale $9,450! During Donna's 1980 television special, 'Fairy Tale High' was used in a fantasy sequence with seven- year- old Mimi guest starring. Donna reads her daughter a fairy tale in bed—the lyrics to 'Fairy Tale High'—and the next thing you know Mimi has morphed into Donna and is lip-syncing 'Fairy Tale High' on stage. Hello cuteness high!

'Say Something Nice'

Writers: Donna Summer, Pete Bellotte, Giorgio Moroder
Producers: Giorgio Moroder, Pete Bellotte

As a forerunner to Donna's next studio album, eighteen months away in 1979 with *Bad Girls*, the final track on side one (Act 1) is a rockier, edgier disco track boasting seriously dirty horns. 'Say Something Nice' also contains some of Donna's most effective, yet simplistic lyrics (rhyming 'if I were' with 'coat of fur' is commendably nice work). There's also another sassy sax solo from Dino Solera, who released an album melding classical music and disco—*Classically Dino Solera*—earlier in 1977, produced by Giorgio Moroder. Robert Christgau, reviewing the just under 70 minutes of the *Once Upon a Time* album for NYC's alternative newsweekly *The Village Voice*, called it 'the first disco opera'. The 'first two sides are uniformly strong but without real peaks', he added, before awarding it a B-grade. *Rolling Stone* magazine opted for three stars, declaring it a 'slightly more successful opus' than previous album *I Remember Yesterday*.

As with Donna's last album, there were only two singles released from *Once Upon a Time* in the US/UK, presumably to direct record buyers to the LP instead, which charted at #26 US and #24 UK. A not-for-sale promo single LP, *Selected Cuts from Once Upon a Time*, was also produced for radio airplay and press with a re-sequenced continuous mix of 'Queen for a Day', 'Fairy Tale High', 'Now I Need You' and 'Working the Midnight Shift' on side A and 'Rumour Has It', 'I Love You' and 'Happily Ever After' on side B.

'Now I Need You'

Writers: Donna Summer, Pete Bellotte, Giorgio Moroder
Producers: Giorgio Moroder, Pete Bellotte

After the staggering response to 'I Feel Love' it would have been churlish not to expect a synth-tastic successor. On the *Once Upon a Time* album that prestigious honour went to 'Now I Need You'. Keeping the sensual electronic template, but adding in soulful gospel elements, it's a yearning, surging slither of disco heaven. That no one thought to release this as a single is both a mystery and a travesty. DJs of note who have unofficially remixed 'Now I Need You' include David Morales and Ralphi Rosario. Not only does 'Now I Need You' possess one of the most haunting electronic endings of all time, but it was also my late dad's favourite Donna Summer song. Possibly the greatest album track from Donna's entire back catalogue, you need 'Now I Need You' now! Christie's 2023 'The Donna Summer Collection' auction included early draft lyrics for 'Now I Need You' with a number of noticeable differences from the completed recording. The line 'Since the day I sat and watched you die' and an alternate line of 'Since the day you left she cried', didn't make the cut, nor did another: 'I knew that I could learn to live without the pretty things you've given, I need you to guide my every step. I'm so afraid without you and when you stood there by my side, I never had to doubt you.' The lot eventually sold for $3,024. If anything in the Moroder/Bellotte/Summer canon can be considered a true successor to 'I Feel Love' it is the underrated, understated and under-appreciated 'Now I Need You'. Taking that trailblazing electronic blueprint and adding a layer of ethereal gospel, this spiritual disco hymn is staggeringly divine.

'Working the Midnight Shift'

Writers: Donna Summer, Pete Bellotte, Giorgio Moroder
Producers: Giorgio Moroder, Pete Bellotte

Donna's hard-done-by heroine is a working girl (are we meant to read that as having a double meaning?) just earning a living. Segueing smoothly from 'Now I Need You', 'Working the Midnight Shift' shifts magnificently into even more

Moroder Moog magic with a true double punch. Yet Donna herself was working the midnight shift a little too hard during the recording of the album, reflected in her lyric 'My body carries on but I'm dying inside'. Virtually the entire album was recorded in a reported three-day marathon session, with Donna being hospitalised straight after due to exhaustion. There are even photos of Giorgio pushing her in a wheelchair at Rome airport around this time. That wasn't his only talent though, obviously.

Unleashing his synthesiser creative juices in early 1978, Giorgio recorded and released his menacing soundtrack for the *Midnight Express* thriller. Not only did he win his first Oscar for Best Original Score the following year, but the movie's inescapable 'The Chase' (composed because director Alan Parker wanted a similar tune to 'I Feel Love') became a massive solo hit for him. Giorgio was no longer merely Donna's producer and co-writer; he had now become a star in his own right as he worked hard for his money. Fun fact—Australia's most famous gay club, The Midnight Shift, opened in 1981 and was named after this Donna song. Legend has it a prominent Sydney dealer chose the name as a homage to 'Working the Midnight Shift', which became the club's unofficial theme song.

'Queen for a Day'

Writers: Donna Summer, Pete Bellotte, Giorgio Moroder
Producers: Giorgio Moroder, Pete Bellotte

No doubt a favourite among Donna's humungous 1970s gay clone following, here we find Donna's downtown Cinderella putting on some rouge, wearing shoes made of glass and going out dancing (careful on that overcrowded dancefloor now, girl). In *Interview* magazine the previous year, gay television personality Lance Loud asked Donna if she'd ever been to any gay discos. 'Gay discos?!' Donna replied incredulously. 'Honey, I don't believe I've ever been in anything but gay discos. There ain't any other kind!' Taking an unexpected musical twist halfway through by switching from its percolating electronic footprint to a lush disco backdrop of strings and 4/4 drumbeats, the joyful 'Queen for a Day' ends side two on a high. Once again Moroder/Bellotte/Summer had indisputably raised the bar in the dance, dance, dance genre. Disco music seemed like it might even save the world, not to mention a few queens for a day and quite possibly some wild nights too.

In 1978, Britain's *New Musical Express* weekly *(NME)* called Donna's 'Once Upon a Time', 'remarkable by any standards', adding 'it set consistently high standards of composition and realisation throughout its four sides'. The weekly music paper also insisted its readers, 'test and try the sudden switch from electronic to electric instrumentation on "Queen for a Day"'. Also put up for bids in Christie's 2023 'The Collection of Donna Summer' online auction lot were Donna's handwritten lyrics for 'Queen for a Day', again scribbled down on München Hilton letterhead. This early draft bears an alternate title, 'Queen for One Day' and in this case, repeats the opening lines, 'Queen for a day/Queen for a night/Dressed head to toe so you'd never know it's me/it's me', deleting the next phrase, 'a King would stare'. This item went for $15,120 (not the $800 expected). A portion of the proceeds were donated to St. Jude Children's Hospital, the Save the Music Foundation and the Elton John AIDS Foundation: charitable organisations dear to Donna during her lifetime and still holding significance for her family. The auction eventually raised over $900,000!

'If You Got It Flaunt It'

Writers: Donna Summer, Pete Bellotte, Giorgio Moroder
Producers: Giorgio Moroder, Pete Bellotte

Come on now, get yourself together! Here comes that Summer fever again to unleash a sleazy, raunchy vibe that must have turned gay bars, if not all bars for that matter, into smouldering disco hot spots. Donna's sisters saunter to fever-pitch in the background like catty creatures Donna wants to teach a trick or two to. What's the bet Mama and Papa Gaines must have thought Donna and her soul sisters were flaunting themselves way too much for churchgoing folk? 'Everything you hear instrumentally was completed before Donna heard it. I had sung the melody for her on the tape and she took it from there,' arranger Bob Esty revealed some years later. 'It took about four weeks to do all the music, then Donna flew in from her tour of Italy and wrote the words to the songs. I didn't know what the lyrics were until she sang them. Then we added background vocals and Giorgio mixed it.' 'If You Got It Flaunt It', with its thrilling driving sax solo, features backing vocals credited to Midnight Dreams—Carlina Williams and Donna's sisters Dara Lynn Gaines and Mary Ellen Gaines. Former Ike & Tina Turner 'Ikette' Carlina also sang background for the Carpenters, Pink Floyd and Bonnie Raitt, and was a member of disco group Sunshine alongside Donna's sisters Mary, Dara and Linda.

'A Man Like You'

Writers: Donna Summer, Pete Bellotte, Giorgio Moroder
Producers: Giorgio Moroder, Pete Bellotte

Slinky seductress Donna gets more soulful on this record than she has in her career so far. While the cocktail disco setting floating around her is mostly muted and restrained, our preacher's granddaughter takes it to church. Preach, Donna, preach! The yearning slow dance 'A Man Like You' sounds very much like a love song written for Donna's beau Bruce Sudano by a 'sweet little 'ole loving girl'. It's little surprise then that the first thank you Donna gives on the sleeve notes of 'Once Upon a Time' is to 'the Brooklyn Dreams ... don't forget that all our dreams are Brooklyn Dreams'. *Rolling Stone*'s Stephen Holden heralded 'A Man Like You' as one of 'the strongest non-disco cuts of Donna's career', stating that it offered a clever pastiche of Gene Page's arrangement for 'Get Closer' by Seals and Crofts, a top-ten US hit in 1976.

'A Man Like You' was also the B-side to the Italian single release of 'Rumour Has It' and the B-side to 'Back in Love Again' in Germany. This mid-tempo smoocher was sampled in 2001 on French rapper Nakk Featuring X-Men's 'Ferme Ta Gueule' and in 2009 on DJ Whoo Kid and US rapper Lloyd Banks' 'Life Goes On'. There's a must-watch television performance of Donna singing 'A Man Like You' on *Burt Sugarman's Midnight Special* show in February 1978, wearing her finest white fur and backed by a huge band ensemble. The special ends with a funky jam session of 'I Feel Love', managing to be electronic, funky and gospel all at the same time.

'Sweet Romance'

Writers: Donna Summer, Pete Bellotte, Giorgio Moroder
Producers: Giorgio Moroder, Pete Bellotte

'Father dear, don't you hear me?' Bereft Donna sings with conviction about how she requires a heavenly conclave to help her find the man she had loved, then lost. 'Father, I've only got you, please won't you make him love me too?' Could this be considered Donna's first foray into melding disco with faith music? The church-like organ certainly lends a gothic religious feel to proceedings. In 1978, *Rolling Stone* magazine's Stephen Holden described 'Sweet Romance' as 'a pop/ soul tear-jerker with a catchy tune', adding that Donna is 'hilariously praying to "father dear" with a quasi-baroque harpsichord behind her'. Sampled numerous times by hip-hop artists such as Big Noyd, DJ Kay Slay, Akhenaton, IAMISEE and Savior Monroe, 'Sweet Romance' was used in the video game *Grand Theft Auto III* in 2001. A fictional band called Loudmouth cover 'Sweet Romance', played on radio station K-DST.

'(Theme) Once Upon a Time'

Writers: Donna Summer, Pete Bellotte, Giorgio Moroder
Producers: Giorgio Moroder, Pete Bellotte

A short piano, almost ballad, version—minus any vocals or Donna—of the album's title track. Perhaps the notion here was to remind us this record is still a fairytale and it is not over yet. We've still got one album side to resolve the story and, hopefully, to find Donna/Cindy's happily ever after.

'Dance Into My Life'

Writers: Donna Summer, Pete Bellotte, Giorgio Moroder
Producers: Giorgio Moroder, Pete Bellotte

After the first reprise of 'Once Upon a Time', it's Donna/Cindy at the crossroads, both musically and in this fairy tale. Donna wants a bit of rough play with a guy passing through her world, but of course since this is a disco concept album the message is just dance on ... and into Donna's life. With its stop/start switching between the lowkey, restrained verses and the upbeat unrestrained chorus, however, you imagine it would actually be quite hard to keep a crowd boogieing to this on the dancefloor. Gay American arranger Bob Esty (aka 'the man who created disco') played a significant role in the making of 'Once Upon a Time'. Although he is credited on the sleeve notes for percussion and back-up vocals, Donna gave him a special shout out as 'The Doctor Philosopher'. He'd already co-produced Donna's 'Last Dance' for the *Thank God It's Friday* soundtrack, recorded before 'Once Upon a Time', but held over until 1978 due to the movie's release. 'Donna sang the lead vocal, one side a night in four nights, in Giorgio's Musicland studios in a building called the Arabella House,' he remembered in 2013. Esty also produced and co-wrote Cher's two disco albums for Casablanca and produced Brooklyn Dreams' 1979 album *Sleepless Nights*. He later produced 'It's Raining Men' with Paul Jabara for The Weather Girls (which Donna famously turned down as 'blasphemous'), Barbra Streisand and gay porn star Jeff Stryker (2003's *Pop You in the Pooper*!). Esty passed away in 2019 at the age of 72 from cancer.

'Rumour Has It'

Casablanca: NB 916. Single release: March 1978
Writers: Donna Summer, Pete Bellotte, Giorgio Moroder
Producers: Giorgio Moroder, Pete Bellotte

A more conventional disco track than much of the material on the *Once Upon a Time* album, 'Rumour Has It' was greenlit as the first single, despite there being plenty of other solid gold contenders. It's also lyrically more positive than anything on the first three sides. That may explain why the album's two singles both came from the final, uplifting side, or is that just folks spreading rumours? The second *Once Upon a Time* UK/US single, 'Rumour Has It' sauntered up to #53 in the US, but reached #19 in the UK. The newsletter of the official Donna Summer Fan Club was also—perhaps somewhat inappropriately—titled 'Rumour Has It'. Rumour also has it there is a listing for a movie treatment called *Cindy* built around the *Once Upon a Time* premise and credited to Donna, Joyce Bogart and Susan Munao. Donna's gay glam squad for the *Once Upon a Time* album photoshoot included make-up artist Way Bandy who died of AIDS in 1986, hair stylist Yusuke Suga who died of AIDS in 1990 and photographer Francesco Scavullo who died in 2004 of heart failure. Scavullo's life partner, Sean M. Byrnes, was credited as stylist on Donna's album cover shoot. Art direction was by Stephen Lummel, who worked on a number of other Donna covers as well as notable releases for Cher, Brooklyn Dreams and Paul Jabara for Hollywood graphic studio and design company Gribbitt!

'I Love You'

Casablanca: NB 907. Single release: December 1977
Writers: Donna Summer, Pete Bellotte, Giorgio Moroder
Producers: Giorgio Moroder, Pete Bellotte

Although there is not the most seamless of segues from one track to the next, the ebullient 'I Love You' is nonetheless the album's apex, where 'he' finds 'her', much to her delighted disbelief. Once again, this underrated Donna single is a prime example of how her soulful pop pipes perfectly complimented a 'four on the floor' beat, akin to fellow 1970s dancing queens Gloria Gaynor, Thelma Houston and Sylvester. Unusually, as the album's first single, 'I Love You' was released two months after the album in December 1977, with tracks from Donna's previous album *I Remember Yesterday* and single 'Deep Down Inside' still in high rotation. Another top-ten hit for Donna in the UK (at #10), 'I Love You' just managed to squeak into the US Top 40 at #37, although it was another #1 disco chart hit. In 1992, 'I Love You' received more mainstream love when it was used as part of a *Saturday Night Live* skit starring Tom Hanks, Adam Sandler and Dana Carvey. In 2013, Japanese-Filipino singer Marlene covered 'I Love You'.

'Happily Ever After'

Writers: Donna Summer, Pete Bellotte, Giorgio Moroder
Producers: Giorgio Moroder, Pete Bellotte

With what sounds at times like the opener for a 1970s television variety show, we fairy tale fans finally reach the conclusion and—yay!—it's a proper happy ending ('look at me/right where I wanna be'). 'Happily Ever After' mercifully mirrored Donna's own personal joy as she and beau Bruce became a 'once in a lifetime' couple, eventually marrying in 1980. Let's also shower some happy praise on Donna's final, joyously giddy ad-libs. 'The word disco for me was always just a place where they played records,' Donna once explained.

> In Europe, they had discotheques everywhere. It wasn't a new thing or even a new kind of music. In discos in Europe they played everything—rock, pop, gospel music—even things like 'Oh, Happy Day' when I've been there. They played all these different records in a club on the same night, so there was never a separation of the type of music that went on in a disco.

'(Theme) Once Upon a Time'

Writers: Donna Summer, Pete Bellotte, Giorgio Moroder
Producers: Giorgio Moroder, Pete Bellotte

Defying expectations, this is not a disco track, more a spoken-word piece with moody instrumentation, which may seem a peculiar way to close a disco concept album. Donna also displays her impressive operatic chops in the final ten seconds. Besides writing the lyrics and coming up with the concept of the album with her co-managers, Donna also contributed her own fairy story of sorts, on the album's inner gatefold sleeve. Significantly different lyrically, it reads more like a poem, something Donna had been writing since she was a child. It's essentially the *Once Upon a Time* album storyline condensed to fifty-one lines, offering a more succinct ending—'And one day she did awake/And found herself somewhere else/Beside her a brand new face/Of someone that she loved'. The dancing is over, thus it's time for our favourite bedtime story, as Donna recites her fairy tale (read along on the album sleeve!) set in the land of Nevernever 'where all things unreal are real'. Listening now this seems a touch overwrought (those squealing guitars!), but Mimi must have loved how mommy set her very own fairy tale to music. *Once Upon a Time* would be Donna's final disco concept album and a good place to finish them as it would be hard to top this for sheer scope, musicality and ambition. In some media circles at the time Donna was even deemed 'the disco Pink Floyd' for her addiction to concept albums.

8

Thank God It's Friday/Live and More (1978)

Live and More
Casablanca: NBLP 7119-2
Originally released: August 1978

Side One

'Once Upon a Time	3:04
'Fairy Tale High'	2:20
'Faster and Faster to Nowhere'	2:09
'Spring Affair'	2:34
'Rumour Has It'	2:34
'I Love You'	3:38

Side Two

'Only One Man'	2:06
'I Remember Yesterday'	3:52
'Love's Unkind'	2:37
'My Man Medley: The Man I Love/I Got It Bad(And That Ain't Good)/Some of These Days'	6:25
'The Way We Were'	3:23
'Mimi's Song'	4:28

Side Three

'Try Me, I Know We Can Make It'	4:14
'Love to Love You Baby'	3:34
'I Feel Love'	6:56
'Last Dance'	5:32

Side Four

'MacArthur Park Suite: MacArthur Park/One of a Kind/Heaven Knows/ MacArthur Park (Reprise)'	7:47

'Last Dance'

Casablanca: NB 926. Single release: July 1978
Writer: Paul Jabara
Producers: Paul Jabara, Giorgio Moroder, Bob Esty

In the eighteen months between studio albums (October 1977's *Once Upon a Time* and April 1979's *Bad Girls*), Donna was one busy queen of disco. Besides her debut movie role, with soundtrack duties, there was a massive tour resulting in a live (and more!) album, complete with a bunch of new hits, including what would be her first #1. With *Saturday Night Fever*, a monster box office blockbuster, its accompanying Bee Gees soundtrack becoming the best-selling album in history to that point, and Studio 54, a pop cultural phenomenon, everyone wanted a slice of the disco pie. Casablanca attached itself to a movie project, *Thank God It's Friday*, giving their biggest star not only a breakout role, but two soundtrack cuts.

Paul Jabara was someone Donna knew from the *Hair* castings in NYC. 'When my first records were released, he wasn't satisfied with all of my breathy cooing,' Donna explained. 'He wanted me to sing out loud, in full voice. He trapped me in the bathroom in a hotel in Puerto Rico and sang "Last Dance" to me over and over again until I consented to do it. Thank God he did!' The triple-album *Thank God It's Friday* soundtrack was released in April 1978, a month before the movie hit US cinemas that May. With a budget of just $2.2million, *Thank God It's Friday* made over three times that amount, despite reviewers calling it 'dismal' and a 'bomb'. Critic Leonard Maltin even called it 'perhaps the worst film ever to win some kind of Academy Award'.

Recorded before *Once Upon a Time*, but released afterwards due to the timing of the movie's release, 'Last Dance' was Donna's big showstopper from her movie debut, typecast as 'aspiring disco singer' Nicole Sims. As the soundtrack went top ten in the US, 'Last Dance' reached #3 there, although it stiffed in the UK at #53. Credited only as arranger on 'Last Dance', Bob Esty was furious about Jabara—who also acted in the movie—taking a sole co-writing credit, saying he learned a 'bitter lesson' from it. That also meant Jabara took home the Oscar when 'Last Dance' won the Academy Award for Best Original Song in 1979 (the same year Giorgio won for Best Original Score for *Midnight Express*).

Although she didn't get an Oscar herself, Donna performed 'Last Dance' on the night (collecting the award with Jabara on stage). 'I was elated,' Donna recalled, but noted, 'Hollywood saw me as a singer and I was never going to shake that image by doing films like *Thank God It's Friday*. So I returned to the thing I did best, making music.' She also picked up her first Grammy award for Best Female R&B Vocal Performance for 'Last Dance'.

Numerous artists have covered 'Last Dance', including Jabara's mid-tempo version on his *Keeping Time* solo album in May 1978, plus a disco-esque take by US/Australian artist Marcia Hines (a childhood friend of Donna's) in 2006. 'Last Dance', now considered one of Donna's dazzling constellations of iconic seventies disco classics, is also a standard club closing number, yeah.

'With Your Love'

Casablanca: NB 926. Single released: July 1978 (B-side to *Last Dance*)
Writers: Donna Summer, Giorgio Moroder, Pete Bellotte
Producers: Giorgio Moroder, Pete Bellotte

Although it would wind up as the B-side to 'Last Dance' and a cut on the *Thank God It's Friday* soundtrack, 'With Your Love' is a true fan favourite and one of Donna's best deep B-sides. It's so good it could have been a A-side in its own right, but with the quality of single releases Donna was putting out, this unstoppable electro-disco number was relegated to 'almost forgotten' status. Donna is in fine lyrical form (why were her songs with 'love' in the title so good?), as Giorgio devises another impressive Moog'n'strings setting. A promo 12-inch mix of 'With Your Love', coming in at 7:32 (compared to the original's 4:10), finally appeared on 1987's fabulous *The Dance Collection: A Compilation of Twelve Inch Singles*. In true Hollywood typecasting fashion, Donna's breakout role in *Thank God It's Friday* was as 'an aspiring disco singer', Nicole Sims. Another aspiring singer featured in the movie was Terri Nunn as Jeannie, part of the band Berlin who scored a US/UK #1 in 1986 with 'Take My Breath Away'. Co-written by Giorgio Moroder for the movie *Top Gun*, it went on to win an Academy Award for Best Original Song and is the piece of music Giorgio insists he is most proud of.

'Take It to the Zoo' (by Sunshine)

Writers: Bruce Sudano, Donna Summer, Joe Esposito
Producer: Arthur G. Wright

Donna appears on two tracks on the *Thank God It's Friday* soundtrack and received two songwriting credits too—this is the second, a euphoric disco stormer that truly gets down. 'One thing I shared with Bruce was music,' Donna remarked much later. 'When I found out he was a composer, I wanted to write some songs with him. Ever since "Love to Love You Baby", I'd wanted to do some more writing, but I felt inadequate because I couldn't read music, or play an instrument. With Giorgio I'd only written lyrics or come up with catchphrases like "Love to Love You Baby". I had to learn form and structure from Giorgio, but with Bruce I had finally met someone who could teach me how to put music to my words—how to use all my senses, how to visualise a song and how to say what I saw in a very real way.'

Thus Donna, beau Bruce and fellow Brooklyn Dreamer Joe Esposito contributed 'Take It to the Zoo' for Sunshine, a band comprising Donna's sisters Linda Gaines, Dara Bernard and Mary Ellen Bernard, plus Carlena Williams. It reached #1 on the US disco chart as part of a *TGIF* four-play with Donna's 'Last Dance', the movie title song by Love & Kisses and 'After Dark' by Pattie Brooks.

Donna also sings background vocals on 'Take It to the Zoo', produced by R&B legend Arthur G. Wright. A planned Sunshine album, *Watching Daddy Dance*, never got released (see Appendix), so Sunshine continued to work hard for their money as Donna's back-up singers.

'Je T'aime (Moi Non Plus)'

Casablanca: NBLP 7099-3. Bonus 12-inch single release: July 1978
Writer: Serge Gainsbourg
Producers: Giorgio Moroder, Pete Bellotte

It seemed only fitting Donna eventually covered the song which inspired her to write 'Love to Love You Baby'. After girl group Saint Tropez scored a minor 1977 hit with a disco rendition of 'Je T'aime', Casablanca granted Donna/ Giorgio/ Pete's version a proper release. After being pressed as a DJ promo-only 12-inch in 1977, the following year 'Je T'aime (Moi Non Plus)' was included as a bonus one-sided 12-inch single with the *Thank God It's Friday* soundtrack.

Running at 15:51, the explicitly 'sexiest single of all time' has a smooth groove BPM of 112. There was also a promo-only 7-inch single in Mexico which split the song into two parts, editing it down to 6:30 on both sides (Parte I et Parte II, *bien sûr*!). Yet Donna's simpering cover of Jane Birkin and Serge Gainsbourg's simmering 1969 duet was ostensibly released a year or two too late to capitalise on its similarity to 'Love to Love You Baby'. A virtual duet, as Donna and Giorgio trade whispery French pillow talk, 'Je T'aime' comes across as more playful than foreplay.

By 1978, disco had moved on from sexy hipsters to suburban mallrats, courtesy of The Bee Gees' total chart domination, Boney M, Chic and even ABBA, who went full disco mode with 'Summer Night City'. Instead, more chaste disco fare like 'You Make Me Feel (Mighty Real)', 'Love is in the Air', 'Night Fever', 'Le Freak' and Gloria Gaynor's 'I Will Survive'—the only song to win a disco Grammy—became huge hits in 1978. The full almost 16-minute version of 'Je T'aime' veers *un peu* unsexily towards disco muzak, a sign perhaps that this remake was foisted on Donna and co. by Neil Bogart. Fun fact! Jane Birkin was once married to John Barry, with whom Donna wrote *Deep Down Inside*!

'Only One Man'

Casablanca: NB 959. Single release: December 1978 (B-side to 'Heaven Knows')
Writers: Donna Summer, Bob Conti, Virgil Weber
Producers: Giorgio Moroder, Pete Bellotte

Kicking off side two of the *Live and More* album is 'Only One Man', also the B-side of the 'Heaven Knows' single later that year. Co-writer Bob Conti explained:

> The sound quality of the recording of 'Only One Man' isn't the best because it's a live version, but it is perfect for the song—it's live and it's raw… 'Only One Man' was the first time I wrote for someone else and I did write it for Donna to sing. I didn't have a melody in mind, just an idea that developed into a cute set of lyrics. One day when I was thinking about Donna being such a sex symbol and me being such a hedonist, that's how the concept of the chorus, 'there's only one man in my life and that's you, and you, and you, and you and you' came about. The rest of the lyrics filled in the blanks. Finally, we sat down with Virgil Weber, our keyboard player. He played some chords and Donna just started singing, 'I've got fire in my touch', and laid it back and it was beautiful.

Weber was the synthesizer player and musical director for Donna's tour and also co-wrote 'Mimi's Song' on the *Live and More* album with her, plus 'Only the Fool Survives' for 1987's *All Systems Go* album. Percussionist Conti played live with Donna from 1977, later co-writing 'Can't Get to Sleep at Night' with Bruce Sudano for Donna's *Bad Girls* 1979 album.

'My Man Medley'

Writers: George Gershwin, Ira Gershwin, Duke Ellington, Paul Francis Webster, Shelton Brooks
Producers: Giorgio Moroder, Pete Bellotte

Donna's medley of three pop/jazz standards comprised the Gershwins' 'The Man I Love' (1924), Duke Ellington and Paul Francis Webster's 'I Got It Bad (And That Ain't Good)' (1941) and Shelton Brooks' 'Some of These Days' (1910), running for almost six-and-a-half minutes. Intriguingly, Barbra Streisand recorded 'The Man I Love' in 1993 for her *Back to Broadway* album and a year later Kate Bush tackled it, turning it into a UK #27 hit. 'I Got It Bad (And That Ain't Good)' became a hit in a version with a vocal by Peggy Lee, although Cher, Doris Day and Nina Simone have all recorded covers of it. 'Some of These Days', which became a signature song for 1920s/1930s star Sophie Tucker, has also been recorded by Ella Fitzgerald, Judy Garland and Streisand herself.

'The Way We Were'

Writers: Marvin Hamlisch, Alan Bergman, Marilyn Bergman
Producers: Giorgio Moroder, Pete Bellotte

Written for Barbra Streisand as the theme song for her blockbuster Hollywood love story with Robert Redford, also titled, *The Way We Were*, it became a #1 hit, the biggest selling single of 1974 and won two Oscars (Best Original Score and Best Song). In 1975, Gladys Knight & The Pips released a more soulful version, reaching #11 in the US and #4 in the UK (where it did better than Streisand's original). With Donna now joining the league of music superstars and covering this Streisand standard with ease, her *Live and More* album debuted a unique logo created by designer/illustrator Tom Nikosey. He also famously created the *Saturday Night Fever* soundtrack logo.

'Mimi's Song'

Writers: Donna Summer, Virgil Weber
Producers: Giorgio Moroder, Pete Bellotte

Live and More was recorded at Los Angeles' Universal Amphitheatre, demolished in 2013 to make way for a Harry Potter attraction at Universal Studios. A heartfelt ballad written for her daughter Mimi, who even gets to say 'goodnight' to the audience on the record, this is even before the encore. 'She changed my life,' Donna said about Mimi.

> She's the best thing that ever happened to my life. I wasn't married, my husband was Austrian and I couldn't get my birth certificate, but then I was seven months pregnant when I got married. Mimi is definitely a child of love. With Mimi came a lot of decisions in my life that I was responsible for someone else other than myself. That preference took precedence over anything else I wanted.

In January 1979, Donna sang 'Mimi's Song' on stage at the United Nations as part of *The Music for UNICEF Concert: A Gift of Song* event in New York. The version that later appeared on the UNICEF LP, however, was from *Live and More*.

'MacArthur Park'

Casablanca: NB 939. Single release: August 1978
Writer: Jimmy Webb
Producers: Giorgio Moroder, Pete Bellotte

Is 'MacArthur Park' true poetry, pure nonsense, or melting somewhere in between? How ever you think you can take it, cooking up a disco recipe of this unorthodox Jimmy Webb tune (originally a #2 US/#4 UK hit in 1967 for actor Richard Harris) was a bold, audacious and risky baking session.

'MacArthur Park' befittingly bestowed upon Donna her first US #1 single (and #5 UK). Giorgio and Pete had been looking for a golden oldie for Donna to cover, and 'MacArthur Park' was given a disco makeover surpassing all versions before it.

For Donna's part, when she was singing 'MacArthur Park', she said she, 'imagined a great love story and sang the song as if it were a great love story. Being in a great love story right now myself, as far as I'm concerned, I could relate to it. I felt like I was able to do it some kind of justice.' Written in four sections, or movements, like a cantata composition, Giorgio takes credit for unearthing 'MacArthur Park'. 'I was driving on the Hollywood Freeway and I hear this song, "MacArthur Park", and immediately thought of doing it with Donna Summer,' he said years later. 'In fact, I immediately called Neil Bogart of Casablanca Records to see if he could find the tapes because there was no record in the record shops. He had an old 8-track, so I took it off of that and it really became her first big #1 song. Even before I recorded it, I knew it would be perfect for her.' In 2017, Pete Bellotte said recording it, 'was the first time I'd ever seen Donna challenged with a song and she's an amazing singer'.

Donna's cover of 'MacArthur Park' became one of disco's finest moments—an oddball, quirky oldie transformed into a tune of epic proportions someone would want to leave their cake out in the rain to. Donna even gamely added the word 'Chinese' before 'checkers' in her version. Her remake has been sampled numerous times over the years with the best-known being Pet Shop Boys on their 1999 tribute to disco, 'New York City Boy' (#14 UK), co-produced by David Morales. In 2015, the *Guardian* newspaper, reassessing Giorgio's career, declared Donna's 'dazzling version of Jimmy Webb's "MacArthur Park" slays Richard Harris's original rendition'. The *Financial Times*, in a 2020 piece scrutinising the history of 'MacArthur Park', called Donna's version 'pure, exuberant disco, Giorgio Moroder produced and quite marvellous. Summer never sang better and makes it sound as if the song was written for the dancefloor.' Can we also add we still have a thing for that closing horn riff too?

In 2024, Tim Burton's huge box office sequel *Beetlejuice Beetlejuice* started and ended with Donna's 'MacArthur Park'. The song's writer Jimmy Webb told *Variety* magazine at the time that he, 'loved Donna Summer's vocal—she really sang the heck out of it and then I kind of thought, "Well, you know, disco's not so bad!" because the song went to #1. It's the only #1 I ever had in the United States.' Jimmy also explained his somewhat cryptic lyrics. 'The fact is I saw everything I wrote about in the song for a fact,' he divulged. 'I saw it in the real world, in MacArthur Park on Wilshire Boulevard, which is where I used to go to have lunch with my girlfriend, Susie Horton.' At the 2026 Winter Olympics, figure skater Alysa Liu sensationally used 'MacArthur Park' for her gold-medal winning free skate routine.

'One of a Kind'

Writers: Donna Summer, Pete Bellotte, Giorgio Moroder
Producers: Giorgio Moroder, Pete Bellotte

The true showpiece on the *Live and More* double album was the 'more' material all packed onto Side Four as the 'MacArthur Park Suite'. Between two bookends of the masterly 'MacArthur Park' and its single successor 'Heaven Knows' was sandwiched 'One of a Kind'. Here's Donna in full belter mode, which, as she knew, is what made people sit up and not just listen but also take her seriously, especially since she loved playing the clown and being the comedian. 'Donna was very inventive with voices,' Pete Bellotte said years later with a laugh. 'We had to curtail it sometimes. She'd do all sorts of funny voices.' A one-of-a-kind promo version of the track, extending the five-minute album version to over seven minutes with additional disco strings, handclaps and horn blasts, finally got a Canadian-only release on 2024's *Simply Summer* compilation, but is freely available elsewhere online. The internet suggests that 20 years later, in 1998, 'One of a Kind' was sampled in Aquarius' 'We Can Make It' (UK #20), but it's more of that horny horn riff which wraps up 'MacArthur Park'.

'Heaven Knows' (with Brooklyn Dreams)

Casablanca: NB 959. Single release: December 1978
Writers: Donna Summer, Pete Bellotte, Giorgio Moroder, Greg Mathieson
Producers: Giorgio Moroder, Pete Bellotte

By late 1978, Donna was a roll of classic disco hits as the irresistibly catchy 'Heaven Knows' glided in as if on a boogie fever roller-skating rink. It's also another example of why producer Bob Esty was bitter, due to Casablanca failing to credit him appropriately. The single version of 'Heaven Knows' combined Donna's vocal from the *Live and More* album, produced by Giorgio and Pete, with the backing track from Brooklyn Dreams' album version, produced by Bob. The final single credit omitted any mention of Bob's name, or heavenly hard work. Hitting #4 in the US and #34 in the UK, 'Heaven Knows', which is essentially a duet between Donna and Brooklyn Dreamer Joe 'Bean' Esposito, did best in Canada at #3.

'On Donna's 1978 double album *Live and More,* the fourth side is called "MacArthur Park Suite" and in the middle of it is "Heaven Knows",' Joe later explained. 'Neil said that sounded like a hit record. Donna asked, "Would you like to sing a duet with me?" I said, "Yeah. I'd love to!" We did it and it became a big hit. It was crazy. Once we got involved with her, then things really started to happen, including my involvement with *Flashdance*.'

Released a month after Donna's version in January 1979, the 'Brooklyn Dreams with Donna Summer' version, produced by Bob Esty, appeared on their *Sleepless Nights* album through Casablanca. Fascinatingly, Esposito takes lead on this version with his bandmates singing back-up while Donna sings second lead. On the sleeve notes of their album Brooklyn Dreams wrote, 'Thanks to Donna Summer who has given us more than we ever dreamed'. Heavenly dreams, even! Covers of 'Heaven Knows' include those by British boy band Bad Boys Inc on their sole album in 1994, R&B artist Faith Evans in 2003 from *The Fighting Temptations* soundtrack and Japanese-Filipino singer Marlene in 2013. 'Heaven Knows' was also sampled by French electronic critics' darlings Justice in 2007 on the track *DVNO (Justice Remix)*.

9

Bad Girls (1979)

Bad Girls
Casablanca: NBLP-2-7150
Originally released: April 1979

Side One	
'Hot Stuff'	5:14
'Bad Girls'	4:55
'Love Will Always Find You'	3:59
'Walk Away'	4:27

Side Two	
'Dim All the Lights'	4:40
'Journey to the Centre of Your Heart'	4:36
'One Night in a Lifetime'	4:12
'Can't Get to Sleep at Night'	4:45

Side Three	
'On My Honour'	3:34
'There Will Always Be a You'	5:07
'All Through the Night'	6:01
'My Baby Understands'	4:03

Side Four	
'Our Love'	4:51
'Lucky'	4:37
'Sunset People'	6:27
Deluxe Edition (2003)	
'Bad Girls (demo version)'	4:00

'Hot Stuff'

Casablanca: NB 978. Single release: April 1979
Writers: Pete Bellotte, Harold Faltermeyer, Keith Forsey
Producers: Giorgio Moroder, Pete Bellotte

1979 was Donna's sizzling apotheosis, triggered by 'Hot Stuff', her first of three #1 US singles, and two #1 double albums before the year was done. Little wonder that in April, when Donna released 'Hot Stuff', she appeared on the cover of *Newsweek* magazine alongside the headline 'Disco takes over' (not for much longer though sadly, as it turned out). 'Hot Stuff' was written for Donna by Pete with two of his and Giorgio's Munich Machine musicians: Harold Faltermeyer and Keith Forsey. 'Hot Stuff' sagely pre-empted the fall of disco and the rise of new wave with a grittier, rockier, guitar-driven dance sound. German synth-pop wizard Harold Faltermeyer went on to have his own big eighties hit in 1985 with 'Axel F' from the *Beverly Hills Cop* soundtrack (which in the noughties became a #1 UK hit for, er, Crazy Frog!).

'I was flown into Los Angeles in 1979 to do the arrangements for Donna Summer's upcoming album,' Harold recalled in 2014. 'Then, all of a sudden, we found Neil Bogart requested a double album not a single album, so we needed more songs. I got the chance to go to the studio and start composing songs and was lucky enough to write a song which later on became Donna Summer's biggest hit. This was "Hot Stuff".' Pete Bellotte had moved to LA at the time of the making of the *Bad Girls* album. 'That was actually our biggest success ever,' he says of its lead single. 'In terms of performance money, "Hot Stuff" earns well over twice what we get from "I Feel Love".' Londoner Keith Forsey was an in-demand disco percussion player who became Giorgio Moroder's drummer (most famously on Donna's "I Feel Love"). The media-shy muso later became a successful record producer and songwriter, including collecting an Oscar in 1984, together with Giorgio and Irene Cara, for 'Flashdance…What a Feeling' from the *Flashdance* soundtrack. The following year, Keith co-wrote another eighties classic, the US #1 'Don't You Forget About Me' for Simple Minds from *The Breakfast Club* movie. Donna would pick up a Grammy, the inaugural Best Female Rock Vocal Performance, for 'Hot Stuff', while that searing 'Hot Stuff' guitar solo was played by session muso Jeff 'Skunk' Baxter. A former member of both Steely Dan and The Doobie Brothers, Skunk later had a second career as a conservative defence advisor.

At first, Skunk wasn't that keen to play on Donna's song, telling Giorgio, 'There's a million guitar players who can do this. If you want something different then I'm happy to do it, but I'd like to have some space.' Giorgio told him, 'Play whatever you want!' Having just moved house, Skunk didn't have his usual guitars so he bought a $35 guitar at the Hollywood Guitar Centre, then went to the studio. 'They played me the song,' he reminisced. 'I turned everything up to 10, plugged the guitar in and said, "Roll tape." That was it—one take.' *The Boston Herald* in 2012 wrote, 'for rock fans who hate disco, take another listen to Summer. Try the 12-inch version of *Hot Stuff*. The guitar solo by Jeff "Skunk" Baxter of The Doobie Brothers is absolutely scorching.' On 30 June 1979, when 'Hot Stuff' descended 1-2 and 'Bad Girls' moved up 5-3, Donna became the first woman to have two singles in the Hot 100 top three at the same time. Despite spending three weeks at #1 and 'Bad Girls' spending five, *Billboard* lists 'Hot Stuff' as Donna's biggest US hit. Donna was also, incidentally, ranked #24 on *Billboard*'s list of Hot 100 Artists of all time for their 50th anniversary in 2009. Pussycat Dolls incorporated 'Hot Stuff' into their 'Hot Stuff (I Want You Back)' from 2005, produced by former Bananarama/Shakespears Sister member Siobhan Fahey, and voiced by Tony winner Nicole Scherzinger. Hot love, baby!

Remix fix!

For more on the 2018 and 2020 remixes/remakes of 'Hot Stuff', see Chapter 22.

'Bad Girls'

Casablanca: NB 988. Single release: June 1979
Writers: Donna Summer, Bruce Sudano, Joe 'Bean' Esposito, Edward 'Eddie' Hokenson
Producers: Giorgio Moroder, Pete Bellotte

'Toot toot, aah, beep beep—talkin' 'bout the bad girls!' 'We wrote the song in about ten minutes,' Joe Esposito recollected, 'but it goes on the shelf for maybe two years. Then she needed one more song for her double album. The engineer said, "What about that song 'Bad Girls'?" It became the hit and title of the album and was an afterthought. To me it's almost like a gift from God. You just never know.' 'Bad Girls' was inspired by life on the strip, as Donna recalled in her memoir. 'I noticed "working women" always walking the streets. One day, a young secretary, Nellie Prestwood, who worked in the PR department at Casablanca, went out for lunch and was mistaken by a policeman for a prostitute. That was the incident that inspired "Bad Girls".'

When Neil Bogart first heard the song, demoed around 1977, he demanded Donna give it to another Casablanca artist, Cher. Donna refused, holding on to it for two years and almost forgetting about it until engineer Steve Smith from Rush Studio found the song among some studio tapes. He took it to Giorgio who loved it, then Donna added what she called, 'a little cherry on the top of this cake' with the 'toot toot, ahh, beep beep'. She told Giorgio this was the sound of getting the attention of a hooker, especially if you were in a car on Sunset.

When Neil heard the finished version, he relented and agreed to it being released. Oh, and Cher recorded an almost identikit song called 'Bad Love' with Giorgio Moroder in early 1980. Imitation is the sincerest form of flattery after all, right? The success of 'Bad Girls' helped Donna realise that when it came to songwriting she didn't need to be a female singer/songwriter like Joni Mitchell, Carole King, or even Aretha Franklin, whose style of personalised songwriting she found 'too painful'. 'In my songwriting, I preferred to create characters like the "bad girl" whose story I told in that song. Of course, it contains an essential element of a universal truth but is not about me. I always preferred to play the role of an observer rather than the lead.' In 2012, after Donna's passing, *The Boston Herald* wrote:

> her signature song, 'Bad Girls', encompasses everything that made disco great. It had textbook syncopated guitar, bold, brassy staccato horns, a whistle and that killer cry of 'Toot! Toot! Beep! Beep!' Underneath it all was a sexy whisper. The song is the perfect gateway drug from ABBA's pretty pop to Parliament's dirty funk.

Included as an enticing extra on 2003's 'Bad Girls' deluxe edition is the demo version of 'Bad Girls'. Avowedly more new wave than disco, with acoustic instruments filling the spaces of Giorgio's usual electronic ones, it's a rare gem of a then work in progress. While it contains a slew of lyrical variations on the released version, the basic barebones of the 'Bad Girls' we know and love are there. There's also a classic house piano feel, years before disco morphed into house, which, sadly (or should that be 'bad-ly'?), never made it to the finish line. If you've got a dime, spend it here! A home recording of 'Bad Girls', possibly from 1977, used in 2023's *Love to Love You, Donna Summer* doco, became available for streaming that year. In 2024, co-writer Bruce Sudano uploaded his own solo version.

'Love Will Always Find You'

Writers: Pete Bellotte, Giorgio Moroder
Producers: Giorgio Moroder, Pete Bellotte

While *Once Upon a Time* might actually be a better, if not her most cohesive album overall, *Bad Girls* is the bad-ass Donna Summer album stuffed with hot hits. The *Bad Girls* album is truly the pinnacle of disco bliss with nary a weak track. Even rock critic Robert Christgau was won over, awarding it an 'A-' rating and declaring, 'you tend to suspect anyone who releases three double-LPs in eighteen months of delusions of Chicago, but Donna is here to stay and this is her best album. The first two sides, four songs per, never let up.' At a tempo of 114 bpm, down from the 121 of album openers 'Hot Stuff' and 'Bad Girls', 'Love Will Always Find You' is Donna giving sassy sister vibe with the highlight being the brassy brass blasts.

Each of the sides on the *Bad Girls* album is a continuous mix, so 'Love Will Always Find You' was a natural fit, coming after the two huge hit behemoths of 'Hot Stuff' and 'Bad Girls'. It's a bit rocky, a bit funky and while maybe not strong enough to be a single on its own, still good solid album material on a record that was all killer, no filler! In 1980, a one-sided, mono flexi-disc of 'Love Will Always Find You' was released in Poland on the Tonpress label, a government-controlled publishing unit that licensed 'western' music. With 'Hot Stuff' and 'Bad Girls' clearly too 'corrupting' to be heard by the youth behind the Iron Curtain, the more restrained 'Love Will Always Find You' was selected. In 2023, DJ Glenn Rivera, who specialises in the 'Shades of Seventies', remixed 'Love Will Always Find You' as an eight-and-a-half minute 1970s disco epic.

'Walk Away'

Casablanca: NB 2300. Single release: September 1980
Writers: Pete Bellotte, Harold Faltermeyer
Producers: Giorgio Moroder, Pete Bellotte

Ostensibly, 'Walk Away' was Donna's first single of the 1980s and the post-disco era. It was also released just two weeks before Donna's new single, 'The Wanderer', on her new label Geffen. Clearly, there was some record company politics and serious showbiz subterfuge going on here. Casablanca even bizarrely stuck 1976's 'Could It Be Magic' on the B-side and initially promoted the single as a double A-side before US radio wisely opted to go with the more modern sounding 'Walk Away'. As it turned out Geffen won this round: 'Walk Away' stalled at #36 in the US charts while 'The Wanderer' soared to #3. As if that wasn't enough obvious subversion already, that same month, in September, Casablanca released a fairly redundant nine-track Donna Summer compilation album entitled *Walk Away (Collector's Edition—The Best of 1977–1980)* with a cover that resembles a tombstone. It reached #50 in the US charts while Donna's new Geffen album, also called *The Wanderer*, and released the following month in October, went to #13.

Things were getting dirty and it truly was time for Donna to walk away. Yet 'Walk Away's lyrics can almost be read as Donna giving the middle finger to Casablanca's Neil Bogart—'I'm sure that I'll get over you/It'll take me a while you see'. Amid all the litigation, however, Neil Bogart was seriously ill. Six months later he died, on 8 May 1982. On Donna's self-titled album that same year (released through Geffen), she paid tribute to Neil in the liner notes writing, 'why head for the mountaintop when you're reaching for the sky?' In 2023, a movie based on Neil's life, *Spinning Gold*, directed, written and produced by his son Tim Bogart, was released with queer singer/songwriter/actress Tayla Parx playing the role of Donna.

Remix fix!
The extended *Walk Away* interestingly includes extra vocals not on the album version.

'Dim All the Lights'

Casablanca: NB 2201. Single release: August 1979
Writer: Donna Summer
Producers: Giorgio Moroder, Pete Bellotte

'Donna wanted to write one day and said, "Come on, let's write something, get on the piano!",' Bruce Sudano recalled. 'I don't know what I said, but I probably didn't feel like it, so she went on the piano and figured it out by herself.' As its sole composer, Donna wrote 'Dim All the Lights', 'for my husband. I had had laryngitis, so I sounded like Rod Stewart and figured I could give it to Rod Stewart to sing,' she told a radio show in 1983. 'I ran into Rod and was so petrified I just couldn't say it. So, I wound up singing it myself and I'm glad because it was a hit for me.' Presumably, what she ran into Rod for was the

Music for UNICEF Concert held at the United Nations on 9 January 1979, some four months before the *Bad Girls* album was released.

While something of a neglected Donna hit nowadays, 'Dim All the Lights' is a very important part of the Donna Summer story for two good reasons. One is that it was Donna's very first self-penned single, reaching #2 in the US charts, stuck behind The Eagles' 'Heartache Tonight', then the following week behind the Commodores' 'Still'. Two is that it might have actually got to #1 if Neil Bogart hadn't decided to bring forward the release of her duet with Barbra Streisand, 'No More Tears (Enough Is Enough)' before 'Dim All the Lights' had a chance to ascend from #2 to #1. Donna, as you might imagine, was furious, calling it 'Neil's betrayal'. '"Dim All the Lights" meant something to me beyond chart position and sales,' she raged. 'It was the first hit song I had written the music and words to alone. My personal goal of achieving a number one song as a singer/songwriter had been short-circuited.' This was the straw which broke the camel's back and Donna wanted out of her professional relationship with Neil and Casablanca. She set about a long process of litigation, yet in the meantime she had already met mogul David Geffen and decided to move to his label instead.

In the UK, 'Dim All the Lights' reached #29. It went top five in both Canada and the Netherlands, but was certified gold for a million sales in the US. In 1995, the late Laura Branigan released a nu-disco cover of 'Dim All the Lights' as her final single. For the 2023 movie *Spinning Gold*, Tayla Parx, playing Donna, sang 'Dim All the Lights', found on the digital release of the soundtrack. 'Outside of being a songwriter, she was one of the earliest black pop/R&B stars,' Tayla said about Donna. 'Even today, it's very hard to be a Black pop star. There were so many layers to Donna Summer.'

During the 1999 *Live and More Encore* television concert, Donna not only told the story about originally planning for Rod Stewart to record 'Dim All the Lights', but she also then performed the first half of the song acoustically, like raspy-voiced Rod might have (even adlibbing 'Maggie, Maggie I'd never leave you!'—referencing Rod's hit 'Maggie May'), before reverting to disco Donna. 'Dim All the Lights' was also one of five songs nominated for Best Disco Recording at the 1980 Grammy Awards (the only year the award was given out), although Gloria Gaynor's 'I Will Survive' grabbed the gong. It's also legendary for the sixteen seconds Donna holds a note. In mid-2025, popette Sabrina Carpenter referenced her love for both 'Dim All the Lights' and the *Bad Girls* album, while announcing the title and cover of her *Man's Best Friend* album. There has also been a minor controversy over the years about Donna's somewhat dim-witted lyric here—'You know the moment's so right/Turn my brown body white'. Lights out, folks, nothing to see here!

Remix fix!

An unofficial 10:55-minute Hot Tracks remix by Robert Farrell for DJs at a speedy 127 bm combined Donna's 1979 version with Laura Branigan's

1995 version (plus samples from German band La Bouche's 'Fallin' in Love') to become a true collector's item.

'Journey to the Centre of Your Heart'

Writers/Producers: Pete Bellotte, Giorgio Moroder

Time to go on a journey for a funky smackdown with Donna prepped to explore the borders of your mind, plus the bottom of your soul, with a spritely sax break thrown in for good measure. In late 1979, German schlager singer Elke Best recorded the song as 'Kriegst Du Kalte Füße', which translates as 'Are you getting cold feet?' with the same double meaning it has in English. The German text was by Bernd Meinunger, who in 1982 co-wrote the Eurovision Song Contest winner 'Ein bißchen Frieden' (aka 'A Little Peace'). Best's amusing version was produced by Horst Hornung, husband of Ramona Wulf from German disco act Silver Convention, who scored a #1 US hit (and a Grammy) in 1975 with 'Fly Robin Fly', much to Giorgio's chagrin. The B-side to 'Hot Stuff', in Japan 'Journey to the Centre of Your Heart' was known as 'Ai No Tabizi' (with 'Hot Stuff' translated as 'Hotto Sutaffu'!). The word 'journey' wound up an important part of Donna's lexicon going forward, as almost 25 years later 'journey' would tie together her memoir and accompanying compilation album.

'One Night in a Lifetime'

Writers: Pete Bellotte, Harold Faltermeyer
Producers: Giorgio Moroder, Pete Bellotte

Gambler Donna's still searching on 'One Night in a Lifetime' but now realises what she's been missing—she wants to make it with you, tonight, obviously! The song also features some great vibrant backing vocals as Donna puts 'my last buck on you'. A song in English, co-written by a German, is likely why the lyrics seem a little, um, wonky at times (i.e. 'love is faster than lightning so grab it while you can'). A decade after the *Bad Girls* album, British synth-duo Pet Shop Boys approached Faltermeyer asking to work with them on what would become their 1990 album *Behaviour*. 'I got a call from Neil (Tennant),' he recalled. 'My more-or-less first question was, "You guys are so talented, why do you need a third producer and third opinion?" He said, "Because we want to do it all with vintage synthesizers and we love the work that you did with Donna Summer!"' Luckily, Faltermeyer still had all his old equipment and the album gave birth to 'Being Boring', considered the duo's finest recording. In recent years Faltermeyer has published his autobiography, a book on Bavarian cooking and written a musical, *Wake Up*, about the history of the Munich Oktoberfest.

'Can't Get to Sleep at Night'

Writers: Bruce Sudano, Bob Conti
Producers: Giorgio Moroder, Pete Bellotte

Written by Bruce with Bob Conti, here's yet another example of how Donna quickly brought her beau Bruce into her musical world. More like old-school disco, it also has the winning addition of Giorgio's quirky Moog flourishes. Once again restless and sleepless, Donna is (still!) suffering from heartache and in desperate need of her man after speaking to him on the phone sounding 'very far away but I love you'. Thematically, side two of *Bad Girls* explores what happens when those bad girls who've been longing for some hot stuff realise it's actually love they need in their lives, and their beds too, of course. '"Can't Get to Sleep at Night" was a song about a girlfriend I'd had years ago,' Conti explained.

> One night, I couldn't get to sleep and she was on my mind, so I wrote about it. Bruce and I worked on the melody together. Donna loved it, Giorgio and Pete dug it and that's how it became part of the *Bad Girls* album. Donna came to her band one day and announced, 'If anybody has any songs they want to submit for consideration on the new album, I'm open to hear what you got!' It was the first time she ever solicited us as a group for material and a great opportunity. Donna wanted to spread the love. It was such a thoughtful and gracious thing to do.

'On My Honour'

Writers: Donna Summer, Harold Faltermeyer, Bruce Sudano
Producers: Giorgio Moroder, Pete Bellotte

Side three of *Bad Girls* literally grinds to a halt here for Donna in full balladeer mode. A sombre, piano-led song finds Donna on her own again and, yes, the nights are still slow, bridging a link for the entirety of Side Two, if not insomnia too. There's a pronounced country music feel to 'On My Honour' including some barnyard-style instrumentation, plus some truly astounding vocals from Donna towards the end. If Donna hadn't been anointed the Queen of Disco already, and if you just heard this, you might think she was a country diva. Decades before Beyoncé turned her hand to the genre on the Grammy-winning 'Cowboy Carter', Donna was breaking down racial barriers in the conservative country music world.

The following year, Donna would make her mark in the country charts via 'Starting Over Again', recorded by country superstar Dolly Parton. The 'Starting Over Again' single released in March 1980 was recorded in December 1979, so presumably it was one of the batch of songs written for the *Bad Girls* album earlier in the year. Instead of singing her then hit single 'MacArthur Park' on television, Donna sang 'Starting Over Again'. Dolly's people saw it, asked to cover it and 'Starting Over Again' became the first #1 country hit co-written by a Black woman. The B-side to the 'Bad Girls' single, 'On My Honour' was briefly an A-side single in the UK with 'Bad Girls' on the B-side before switching. *Bad Girls* would become Donna's biggest-selling album, selling over two million in the US alone and an estimated four million globally. It would also be her final studio album for Casablanca. Christie's 2023 'Collection of Donna Summer' exhibition/sale included the original handwritten lyrics for 'On My Honour'. Now a part of the Smithsonian National Museum of African American History and Culture based on the winning bid from the Christie's auction, they paid $3,276 for it. Besides the lyrics they also got a drawing of a house by Donna. 'On My Honour' was later included in *Summer: The Donna Summer Musical.*

'There Will Always Be a You'

Writer: Donna Summer
Producers: Giorgio Moroder, Pete Bellotte

Donna puts on one of her eerie spooky voices to start this off as another love song, presumably written for Bruce. 'There was never any question Bruce and I were going to wind up together no matter how many people there were between us,' Donna wrote in her memoir. 'It was a fabulous time of coming together for us, even if there was still one major rival Bruce had to fight for my attention—my career!'

Over the years, Donna mentioned 'There Will Always Be a You' as one of the songs she was proudest of. In 2019, Bruce Sudano revealed it as the one Donna song that really connected with him, 'because she wrote that by herself on the piano for me ... it's an understanding of the depth of love that somebody has for you'. Although recorded at the end of the 1970s, this smoochy number is one that sets up a template for similar keyboard-led twinkly ballads in the 1980s, the likes of which would help transform Whitney Houston into the next decade's premiere Black female superstar. You might even hear some similarities here to Giorgio's two big Oscar-winners of the 1980s: Irene Cara's 'Flashdance...What a Feeling' and Berlin's 'Take My Breath Away'. Donna's last high note of 'you' is sure to give you goosebumps.

As the B-side to 'Dim All the Lights', this means both A and B sides were solely written by Donna. No wonder she was so proud of this particular release and so bitter when her burning wish to have a #1 single she had written herself was snatched away from her by record company politics. It would also be the B-side to the 'On the Radio' single in November that same year.

'All Through the Night'

Writers: Donna Summer, Bruce Roberts
Producers: Giorgio Moroder, Pete Bellotte

Not to be confused with Cyndi Lauper's hit ballad of the same name from 1984, Donna's 'All Through the Night' commences like a gospel sermon. 'You know, boy. You're so busy reaching for a dream that doesn't even exist that you can't even see somebody who's standing right here who loves you so much' sure sounds like Donna lifting the veil on her and Bruce's long dalliance before they both fully committed to being in a relationship. Donna now needs to feel the magic as her partner makes love to her mind. With an unforgettable chorus, what almost sounds like a gospel choir hanging out at an underground jazz club and Donna delivering a masterclass in vocal delivery, 'All Through the Night' is the real standout on side three of the *Bad Girls* album. It's since been covered by KC & The Sunshine Band, Bruce Sudano and Naomi Campbell.

'My Baby Understands'

Casablanca: NB DSBS/Columbia:1-11125. Single Release: October 1979
(B-side to 'No More Tears (Enough Is Enough)')
Writer: Donna Summer
Producers: Donna Summer, Jürgen Koppers

'For all the time I was with Casablanca,' Donna noted. 'I was asked to record music that never veered all that much from the initial boundaries that defined Donna Summer, Disco Queen. Because of it no one in America had any real clue I had an extensive and quite successful European background in live musical theatre, or that I could actually sing other types of music.' Written by Donna and produced by Donna with (recording engineer) Jürgen Koppers, making it the exception on the *Bad Girls* album, here's another example of the most beautiful voice God has ever given the world. A mid-tempo number, with more of a rockier edge to it than disco, it raises the bpms on this album's side to match Donna confessing how she is attracted by desire ''cos he's the master of the fire'. Hot stuff indeed!

You can also hear elements of the quickly developing new wave punk sound towards the end as Donna screeches 'my baby' amid a hectic squealing guitar. Donna was refusing to be confined to just one genre and letting the world know that. Side three of *Bad Girls* would certainly have come as a shock to any record buyers who had assumed this was merely a disco album. Luckily for them it would be business as usual, albeit with an eye to the future, on the final side of *Bad Girls*. Interestingly, side three is the only one of this album's original four sides that didn't produce a single. The world wasn't quite ready for a hit ballad from the 'Queen of Disco'. 'My Baby Understands' was the B-side to 'No More Tears (Enough Is Enough)' on Casablanca, while Barbra's title track from her *Wet* album was on the Columbia single. There's a must-see 30-second clip of Donna singing this while accompanying herself on piano on Instagram's Officialdonnasummer page. It was also sampled most notably by Ne-Yo, Jamie Foxx and Fabolous in 2008 on 'She Got Her Own'.

'Our Love' (Nuestro Amor)

Casablanca: 61 98 356. Single release: August 1980 (Spain)
Writers: Donna Summer, Giorgio Moroder
Producers: Giorgio Moroder, Pete Bellotte

If you ever needed another good reason why vinyl got its groove back, post CD and digital, look no further than side four of *Bad Girls*. With no gap between tracks, the original LP format of this iconic album offers an unmatched seamless aural electronic experience. If you were desperate for this album's electrodisco 'I Feel Love', or 'Now I Need You', you'll dig this! 'Our Love', with its rapid- fire kick and snare drum pattern, is pure Moroder Moog magic, matched with Donna shifting seamlessly between coy sweetness in the layered verses and bold defiance in the stripped-back chorus. That bleepy, percolating synth cold close is one of the best things Donna and Giorgio ever concocted, and a preview of Donna's next album. It's also worth noting that 'Our Love' (which became the B-side to 'Sunset People' when that was released in some territories) is the first track credited to just Donna and Giorgio (no Pete).

The *Bad Girl* sleeve notes seem to indicate that the true inspiration behind 'Our Love' was Donna's daughter Mimi. Quoting the song lyrics, she writes to Mimi, 'Sometimes when you're gone, I don't know why, I find the simple need to sit and cry. It's not that I'm lonely or that I'm blue, it's just that I need to be with you. Our love will last forever.' The Spain-only 'Our Love (Nuestro Amor)' single was released just a few weeks after Donna and Bruce tied the knot on 16 July 1980. Donna called it 'the happiest day of my life' and she was already pregnant with her second child, daughter Brooklyn, born on 5 January 1981.

'Our Love' also served as the template for New Order's iconic 'Blue Monday' in 1983 and earlier hit 'Temptation' in 1982. The band's Peter Hook has openly admitted in interviews, that 'we stole it off a Donna Summer B-side'. An album of eighteen remixes of 'Our Love' called *Classics Vol. 2 (Our Love Remixes),* credited only to Giorgio Moroder, appeared in 2021 with Simone Anés taking vocal duties. In 2005, *Classic Pop* magazine listed their top twenty Giorgio Moroder tracks, putting 'Our Love' at #10 citing its 'rapid-fire beat and ebullient synth'.

'Lucky'

Writers: Donna Summer, Giorgio Moroder, Bruce Sudano, Joe 'Bean' Esposito, Edward 'Eddie' Hokenson
Producers: Giorgio Moroder, Pete Bellotte

With Giorgio providing another solid synthesised soundscape (although some have complained about the 'fart noises'), Donna sings in a variety of voices including her falsetto on the chorus. The 'Lucky' lyrics are unluckily not the greatest ever conceived—a person called Lucky who likes to take you for a casual sex ride, aka 'Lucky comes easy'—but Donna sings them with such impassioned virtue it hardly matters. In a 14 June 1979 cover story for British pop magazine *Smash Hits*, Donna was interviewed about her style of music at the time. 'I don't think disco is bad,' she said boldly. 'As the years go on, more and more artists are making disco records. People have stopped fighting disco music. Musicians have realised that if disco is what people want that they'll give it to them. People wanna dance, they wanna move. They're tired of being tied down. Discos are indoor playgrounds where people go to wind down from their frustrations.'

She also made mention of how people 'shouldn't keep sticking artists into little categories anyways. If I were to record "The Way We Were", would you call that a disco song? C'mon now.' In the same interview, Giorgio Moroder is quoted as saying, 'I do wish people would stop thinking Donna's recording sessions are sex orgies. We work together like any team. I play with my synthesizer and Donna experiments with her voice.' The piece by Robin Katz finished by observing, 'Donna Summer intends to keep sizzling until she's the biggest superstar the '80s have ever seen.' In 2019, 'Lucky' got some lucky, lucky, lucky attention on the small screen when it was included in an episode of the second series of Emmy- winning *Big Little Lies. Radio Times* magazine wrote how 'this disco banger comes on the stereo system at the party'. Now that's a party we all wanna be lucky enough to get an invite to!

'Sunset People'

Casablanca: CAN 198. Single release: June 1980 (UK/Europe)
Writers: Pete Bellotte, Harold Faltermeyer, Keith Forsey
Producers: Giorgio Moroder, Pete Bellotte

Side four of the *Bad Girls* album is an electro spectacle that some 50 years later still sounds ahead of its time and startlingly contemporary. Ending the album on a true high point and doing it right are Keith/Pete's pointed observations about LA's Sunset strip, where all Donna's bad mamas (and all the other girls for that matter) work hard for their dollars. 'That's the thing about that song, it had the pulse of a car cruising,' Donna noted, 'and cruising is what you do on Sunset, right? To see and be seen, that's Sunset.' That pulse was also courtesy of drummer Keith Forsey.

A closing ode to LA nightlife—with shout-outs to the Rainbow Bar & Grill, the Riot House and the Whisky—'Sunset People' was released as a single in the UK (#46) and was a top-twenty hit in the Netherlands. Its bubbly synth feel is very similar to Sparks' 'The Number One Song in Heaven', which Giorgio co-wrote and produced, reaching #14 in the UK in 1979, and also featuring—guess who?—Keith Forsey. His contributions both open and close the *Bad Girls* album (the other being 'Hot Stuff'). 'Because of Neil's Svengali-like role, I had almost no life outside the tiny space (a house in the Hollywood Hills and an office on Sunset Boulevard) in which I ate, slept and socialised with Bruce when I could get away,' Donna recalled.

'Looking back, it's no surprise to me that one of the songs I sang was called "Sunset People". It was not just about the people on the strip, but the people who populated what my entire world had somehow become—that street.' *Rolling Stone* magazine at the time called 'Sunset People' 'the closest thing to a social comment' on the *Bad Girls* album, adding it 'just might be the disco culture's "A Day in the Life"'. In 2023, the magazine revisited *Bad Girls*, listing it as #283 on their list of 500 Greatest Albums of all Time. They also called 'Sunset People', 'the underrated highlight' and Donna's 'post-Steely Dan snapshot of LA malaise'.

Vid bit!

Director: Don Mischer

Donna takes us for a trip 'down on the strip' during her Emmy-nominated *The Donna Summer Special* for US television network ABC in January 1980. Donna even portrays a wannabe starlet who has a conflab with an unimpressed nun, a homeless woman stealing a Donna Summer poster, and an Italian with a large moustache. This must-view version of 'Sunset People', albeit way too brief, is also a live recording with a cold ending.

10

On the Radio: Greatest Hits Volumes I & II (1979)

On The Radio: Greatest Hits Volumes I & II
Casablanca: NBLP-2-7191
Originally released: October 1979

Side One		Side Three	
'On the Radio'	4:00	'MacArthur Park'	3:54
'Love to Love You Baby'	4:07	'Hot Stuff'	2:54
'Try Me, I Know We Can Make It'	3:24	'Bad Girls'	3:05
'I Feel Love'	3:20	'Dim All the Lights'	4:11
'Our Love'	3:43	'Sunset People'	4:32

Side Two		Side Four	
'I Remember Yesterday'	4:46	'No More Tears (Enough Is Enough)'	11:43
'I Love You'	3:12	'On the Radio (Long Version)'	5:50
'Heaven Knows'	3:30		
'Last Dance'	4:56		

'No More Tears (Enough is Enough)' (Duet with Barbra Streisand)

Casablanca: NB DSBS/Columbia: 1-11125. Single release: October 1979
Writers: Paul Jabara, Bruce Roberts
Producers: Gary Klein, Giorgio Moroder

Paul Jabara and Bruce Roberts wrote *No More Tears (Enough Is Enough)* for Barbra Streisand, although she initially rejected it. Jabara, who was also pals with Babs, orchestrated the duet after Jason Gould, Barbra's then 14-year-old son and a huge Donna Summer fan, talked his mother into it. Recorded in summer 1979, Donna said singing with Barbra 'absolutely thrilled me for a lot of reasons'. It was not just the experience of singing with Babs in the studio, but being embroiled in heavy litigation. 'No matter what was going on in my business affairs, my talent was still in act,' Donna proclaimed. 'I was stronger than before, well, sort of, and I was not going to be bossed around any longer.' Donna also hoped the song would 'stretch my commercial horizons and make a legitimate run as an across-the-board recording artist'. During the recording, Donna, who had 'partied all night' after the last performance of a sold-out eight-night run at LA's Universal Amphitheatre, tried for a high note but instead fell off her stool, passing out. 'I was really more tired from my eight-night run than I'd realised,' Donna explained. 'When I came to and opened my eyes a few seconds later, Barbra was still holding her note. I could have died! It was so long. It was only when she finished, she turned and asked, "Donna, are you all right?"'

The song was a US #1, the first #1 female duet and Donna's final #1, but the pair never sang it together outside of the original recording. Donna did later perform it with Australian artist Tina Arena, her sister Mary and UK boyband Westlife (see Appendix). In 2012, Barbra finally gave the song some credit, singing a short version and dedicating it to Donna. Now considered not just a disco classic, but a gay classic too, Donna and Babs's duet of 'No More Tears (Enough is Enough)' was re-released in 2017 as 'Enough is Enough' (see Chapter 23). Unique demos of the original 1979 sister disco studio session with D&B duelling/rehearsing together can also be found online.

'On the Radio'

Casablanca: NB 2236. Single release: November 1979
Writers: Donna Summer, Giorgio Moroder
Producer: Giorgio Moroder

In 1979 was Donna at the pinnacle of her success, more Queen of Pop than Queen of Disco. She was the biggest female solo star of the era and it looked as if she would continue to be, yet record company lawsuits, her commitment to born-again Christianity and alleged slurs on the gay community, her most fervent fanbase, would change all that. The 1980s would be a decade when Donna stepped back from stardom and her career suffered dramatically. Before that, however, came the quintessential Donna compilation *On the Radio: Greatest Hits Volumes I & II*, her third and final US #1 album. The other new track, alongside 'No More Tears (Enough Is Enough)', was the titular track and fan favourite. Originally written for husband Bruce Sudano, Donna was inspired to write the line, 'it must have fallen out of a hole' from a Steven Bishop record. Side four of her double album included the full 11:43 version of the Donna/Barbra duet, plus a 'long version' of 'On the Radio' running for 5:50.

The album opener version on side one ran for four minutes. It was also featured in the cult *Foxes* movie/soundtrack (starring Jodie Foster), produced by Giorgio Moroder, in an extended soundtrack mix of 7:34. Also included was Janis Ian's 'Fly Too High', Cher's 'Bad Love', Brooklyn Dreams' 'Shake It', plus Giorgio's instrumental version of 'On the Radio', running for 4:27. *The Village Voice*'s Robert Christgau ranked the *On the Radio* album 'A' (Donna's best ever from him) stating, 'the title tells us Summer wants to be a pop queen rather than a dance queen and the music tells us she's got a right—almost in a class with '60s Motown'. In 2025, *Billboard* said it really loud, ranking Donna the #34 best R&B singer of all time, calling *'On the Radio'* a 'must listen song'.

11

The Wanderer (1980)

The Wanderer
Geffen: GHS 2000
Originally released: October 1980

Side One		Side Two	
'The Wanderer'	3:44	'Cold Love'	3:37
'Looking Up'	3:56	'Who Do You Think You're Foolin''	4:17
'Breakdown'	4:06	'Nightlife'	4:00
'Grand Illusion'	3:54	'Stop Me'	3:43
'Running for Cover'	3:47	'I Believe in Jesus'	3:18

'The Wanderer'

Geffen: GEF 49563. Single release: September 1980
Writers: Donna Summer, Giorgio Moroder
Producers: Giorgio Moroder, Pete Bellotte

In early 1980, songwriters Bruce Roberts and Paul Jabara took Donna to meet David Geffen, convincing her he was the best thing in the music business. 'We told her he was a good guy and she signed with him,' Bruce recalled. Donna called David Geffen a 'genius and innovator' as well as 'the shrewdest businessman ever to hit Hollywood'. He reportedly signed Donna to a guaranteed $1.5 million advance per album. First up was *The Wanderer* album, preceded a month earlier by the irrepressible title track as lead single. Like a hybrid of 'Hot Stuff's rockier edge and 'Sunset People's bubbling synths, Donna injects her whispery coquettish charm in the verses, before sexing it up in that keeper of a chorus. It is very much

Blondie influenced, especially since that February their single was released from the *American Gigolo* soundtrack: 'Call Me', co-written and produced by Giorgio Moroder, which became 1980's top seller.

Reaching #3 in the US, 'The Wanderer' single was a big hit in most other territories around the world except for the UK where it stalled at #48. The title of 'The Wanderer' couldn't have been any more prophetic. Wandering from Casablanca to Geffen, this would also be Donna's last album with Giorgio and Pete to get a proper release. A deluxe edition of the album was released for its 40th anniversary on Donna's own label Driven by the Music. It included seven remixes of tracks from the album, but no demos or extra tracks, although if you got the vinyl edition the original disc was a wandering pink!

Vid bit!

Director: Not credited (wrongly attributed to Sharon Liu on many sources)
Donna's brand-new husband Bruce was the man she tapped to cameo as 'the rider' in her first proper music video (which Geffen appeared to think not important enough to warrant a director's credit a year before MTV's launch). And is that Giorgio's back we catch briefly at the beginning? A pregnant Donna gives good headphones in the recording studio in this fairly rudimental clip, but it does at the very least demonstrate her ability to sell a song on camera.

Remix fix!

The Figo Sound Full Mix on 2020's *The Wanderer* album re-release is arguably less successful than the other remixes since the original was closer to dance/disco than anything else on here. Figo is one of many aliases used by Italian producer Stefano Colombo.

'Stop Me'

Geffen: GEF 49563. Single release: September 1980 (B-side of 'The Wanderer')
Writers: Pete Bellotte, Keith Forsey
Producers: Giorgio Moroder, Pete Bellotte

The B-side of 'The Wanderer' single, 'Stop Me' might be even more post-punk than new wave in style. We would have loved to hear Blondie cover this! Someone at Geffen sure had a devilish sense of humour, programming 'Stop Me' on *The Wanderer* LP before album closer 'I Believe in Jesus'. 'I couldn't guess/If I only would have known I never would have been in this mess,' Donna sings, as if she's been taking anti-vocal lessons from German punkster Nina Hagen, The Pretenders' Chrissie Hynde, or Poly Styrene (from X-Ray Spex). So when did all of the messy litigation with former label Casablanca actually stop? After once describing the music business as 'being raped over and over again', matters were finally resolved with Donna allowed to leave Casablanca and move to Geffen.

'It took a long time for me to finalise my differences with Casablanca,' she wrote in her memoir. 'In the interim, I recorded *The Wanderer* album with Giorgio for Geffen Records.' Donna's middle daughter, Brooklyn Sudano, who co-directed the *Love to Love You, Donna Summer* doco, shared her thoughts about the litigation in 2023. 'She just wanted to be out of her contract and there were some changes at the label,' she mused.

> She sued to get out of it and to be able to move forward in the way she thought she wanted her career to move forward. It was at the peak of her career, so it was a really big risk for her to take. Neil Bogart and the whole team at Casablanca at that time were really like family to her. It was a really difficult time for her because she was so close to them. Thankfully, we have all mended bridges and she was able to mend bridges with them as well. It was that she wanted to be an artist in a different way than they wanted her to be. She wanted to grow and write more of her music, which she did, and be a little more in control of her own destiny.

'Looking Up'

Writers: Pete Bellotte, Giorgio Moroder, Donna Summer
Producers: Giorgio Moroder, Pete Bellotte

Here's the only Moroder/Bellotte/Summer composition on the entire *The Wanderer* album. 'Looking Up' is a perky, positive affair about change and finding happiness. 'I'm coming back to life' and 'I see my troubles far behind' are just two of the lyrical mood-benders. There's also a subdued guitar break about how rainy days now stay away, yet 'Looking Up' lacks something. It's new wave and rock, but without a hint of disco, which is probably what it needed. Released a few months after her marriage, things certainly were looking up in the personal space for Donna, who was also in the early stages of her pregnancy with daughter Brooklyn during the recording. Asked in 2020 what it was like to have tracks from *The Wanderer* remixed some forty years later, Bellotte, then in his late seventies, was surprisingly effusive. 'To have younger guys come in and do it the way they want to do it, in a completely different way than you ever thought of, is fantastic,' he beamed. Asked about disco's ongoing revival, he responded, 'People like to have uplifting dance music that makes you want to move and smile and that it's connected to disco is fantastic.'

Remix fix!

The Figo Sound Version from the 40th anniversary 2020 re-release of 'Looking Up' adds a shimmering disco swooshing sheen, enhancing Donna's spirited vocal and even more high-spirited backing vocals. Imagine how things would have been looking up had this been the version released back in 1980!

'Breakdown'

Writers: Pete Bellotte, Harold Faltermeyer
Producers: Giorgio Moroder, Pete Bellotte

One of two contributions by Faltermeyer to *The Wanderer* album, here Donna is back on more familiar synth-pop terrain. Yet again though that throbbing disco beat is missing, and, it has to be said, the magic is missing too. The lyrics to 'Breakdown' are fairly formulaic, about how lying and cheating lead to a breakdown. 'You shouldn't put all your trust in me,' Donna warns us. There's also yet another guitar solo, although 'Breakdown' is admittedly more soft rock than hard rock. It was Faltermeyer, however, who revealed that production on *The Wanderer* album had to be moved up, if not rushed, because Casablanca were releasing a competing greatest hits collection and another single from the *Bad Girls* album. 'We would have liked to do more tweaking and have more time for production,' he complained, 'but we just had to let it go.'

No sooner was the album in the can than a release date was given by Geffen: 20 September for the first single, the title track, with the album released a month later on 20 October. Casablanca still managed to get in ahead with 'Walk Away' released as a single on 1 September and *Walk Away: Collector's Edition (The Best of 1977-1980)* out a week later on 8 September. However, although it hasn't aged as well as Donna's classic seventies albums, critically and aurally, *The Wanderer* album received some rave reviews from some unexpected places when it was released. *The Village Voice*'s Robert Christgau ranked *The Wanderer* album as 'A-' (the same as *Bad Girls*), calling it 'synthetic perfection'. *Billboard*, meanwhile, crowed that with *The Wanderer* album Donna had 'got the best shot at being the premier woman rocker of the 1980s'. *The Wanderer* album could not, alas, repeat the enormous success of any of Donna's previous three albums at #1, peaking at #13 in the US and a lowly #55 in the UK. It was certified for gold for 500,000 sales in the US, but that must have been a disappointment to everyone, especially her new label boss David Geffen.

'Grand Illusion'

Writers: Donna Summer, Giorgio Moroder
Producers: Giorgio Moroder, Pete Bellotte

There are certain Donna songs that as a fan you either love or hate, with no in between, and this is one of them. 'Grand Illusion' arrives at a slower pace than the previous four tracks on *The Wanderer* album. Amid Giorgio's atmospheric synths Donna pulls a strange, albeit quirky, voice out of her playbox. While it sounds like something that fell off one of Giorgio's less-appreciated soundtracks, 'Grand Illusion' is hard to like and even harder to love with its odd disconnect between the music and the vocals. If Donna had sung this straight, instead of sounding as if she had just inhaled a deflated helium balloon, perhaps it might have worked. This album's nadir, 'Grand Illusion', upsold elsewhere as 'avant garde', was also the B-side to the 'Cold Love' single.

Remix fix!
A smoother groove Poolside Mix of 'Grand Illusion', again courtesy of Le Flex, was included on the 40th anniversary edition of *The Wanderer* album. While Donna's weird vocals remain intact (there was no chance of extracting the original acapella clearly!) it morphs 'Grand Illusion' into a more palatable affair, compared to the original's 1980 grand illusion.

'Running for Cover'

Writer: Donna Summer
Producers: Giorgio Moroder, Pete Bellotte

Switching record labels, suing her old one to the tune of $10 million, taking care of a seven-year-old, organising her wedding and being pregnant: it's a wonder Donna found any time at all to write songs. Nonetheless she composed two tunes on her own, with each of them closing a side of the original vinyl/cassette versions of *The Wanderer*. 'I didn't stop creating in spite of all the problems plaguing the business side of my career,' she explained. More like funky R&B Chaka Khan, Donna wails a cautionary tale about how she left her loved ones behind but felt incomplete living out on the street where the devil lurks, and has to go running for cover. The tempo doubles for the chorus, but it's not disco, more akin to a punk thrash. 'The devil's in the bar and it's already after dark,' Donna cautions. More like an early version of what came to be known as Christian rock, with another ubiquitous guitar solo, 'Running for Cover' was also the B-side to the album's third single 'Who Do You Think You're Foolin''. Getting their money's worth, 'Running for Cover' was sampled in 2007 by Italian hip-hop/crunk outfit Club Dogo on the eerie 'Dolce Paranoia' and hard-hitting 'M-I Bastard'. Both were taken from their *Vile Denaro* album that reached #11 in their homeland.

'Cold Love'

Geffen: GEF 49634. Single release: November 1980
Writers: Keith Forsey, Pete Bellotte, Harold Faltermeyer
Producers: Giorgio Moroder, Pete Bellotte

As proof of how in-demand Giorgio had become as a producer at this time, he co-wrote less than half of *The Wanderer* album. His overriding genius is sorely missed here too. Stepping up in his place though were Pete (five co-writes), Harold (two) and Keith (two). Donna, with five songwriting credits, finally equalled Pete as chief songwriter for the first time on an album. Side two opens with the album's second single, 'Cold Love'. With a chugging rock guitar riff and a new wave dance beat it's not a million miles away from Pat Benatar's 'Hit Me with Your Best Shot', released in September 1980, which became Pat's first US top ten hit. Donna is also in full shouty mode here, although by the time of the chorus ('another shot of rock 'n' roll love') it perks up considerably. This still doesn't sound like a big hit, however, and it wasn't. It's an odd choice for a single, yet when you look at what else is on *The Wanderer* album there's little else that might qualify as a potential big hit.

'Cold Love', minus a video, barely made the US top 40 (peaking at a cool #33) and an even colder #44 in the UK. It did, however, garner Donna a nomination for Best Female Rock Vocal Performance (won that year by Pat Benatar for *Fire and Ice*). She was, of course, the only Black woman out of five (alongside Stevie Nicks, Yoko Ono and Lulu). While David Geffen later blamed racism for the poorer sales and lower chart placings of *The Wanderer* and its singles, Donna also faced sexism from American rock stations. Not only was she Black, but a woman, and at the time there appeared little or no place for Donna on the radio.

After years of forgetting about 'Cold Love', Donna added it to her live shows in 2004. In a 2020 interview, Pete said he listened to *The Wanderer* again after many years and 'really enjoyed it and very pleased with it. I don't think there's much I'd want to change about it to be quite honest. With *The Wanderer* we were just trying to get it more into a pop/rock area.' As to whether there were any leftover songs from the album, Pete revealed, 'in our traditional way we never had enough songs for the album, we never had too many songs'. He noted how Donna's album was recorded at LA's Westlake Studios in studio #8, or as Pete laughingly called it, the *Thriller* studio, since Michael Jackson recorded his killer album there.

Remix fix!

The extended dance version (doubling the original's running time at over seven minutes) is actually more like something you might pogo to in a mosh pit than twirl underneath a glitterball to. You have been warned!

'Who Do You Think You're Foolin'

Geffen: GEF 49664. Single release: February 1981
Writers: Sylvester Levay, Jerry Rix, Pete Bellotte
Producers: Giorgio Moroder, Pete Bellotte

The third and final single from *The Wanderer* album came courtesy of Hungarian-German Sylvester Levay, the man behind seventies disco outfit Silver Convention. Like Moroder, he went on to become a major soundtrack composer. A tad like an ABBA B-side, again Donna's in strident, shouty mode on this track.

Only just squeaking into the US top 40 at #40, this made *The Wanderer* album a major sales and chart disappointment just a year after Donna had ruled both. Was she just too closely tied to the disco genre, which by 1980 had been almost banished from the charts and people's hearts, or was the post-disco material on *The Wanderer* sub-par and not a good fit?

Essentially, there's little on *The Wanderer*, apart from the title track, where Donna gets her seductive vocals on. It's mostly a cool, if rather sexless, outing. Dutch singer, songwriter and producer Rix also worked with Elton John, Boney M and Silver Convention (as the male voice on their records). He had a 1976 international solo hit with the bandwagon-jumping 'Disco Train', working alongside Sylvester Levay. Pete had worked with both Sylvester and Peter on Elton John's much-panned disco album, *Victim of Love*, released at the end of 1979, which was presumably when the trio wrote this track, which wound up on Donna's album. Rix passed away in 2016 at the age of 69.

Vid bit!

While there was no official video for 'Who Do You Think You're Foolin'' (Donna was busy being a new mum again!) view the internet clip of teens from the era grooving to it on *American Bandstand* in March 1981, introduced by host Dick Clark who gushes 'Oh, I love to hear this woman sing—this is the inimitable voice of Miss Donna Summer.'

Remix fix!

A roof-raising 'Fire Island' remix of 'Who Do You Think You're Foolin'' was a big hit in gay clubs when it was released in 2012 and is well worth a spin.

'Nightlife'

Writers: Pete Bellotte, Giorgio Moroder
Producers: Giorgio Moroder, Pete Bellotte

On *The Wanderer* album, Donna comes across like a rebel with two causes. She's rebelling against both her seventies Queen of Disco title and her 'sex goddess' label. She substitutes them instead with new wave sister and hot rock priestess, yet neither seems to come naturally to her. With a title like 'Nightlife', you may have assumed this would be a full-on disco/dance number, but it's closer to hard rock than any other genre (opening with a chunky rock guitar riff). It also sounds vaguely familiar to the material Donna first recorded with Pete and Giorgio back in 1974.

Donna tackling a new genre was not just a big deal, but the fact she was a Black female artist heading into rock terrain was also almost unheard of. Her only close rival in this domain was Tina Turner, still a few years away from her big career revival with 'What's Love Got to Do with It' in 1984. That meant

Donna was truly breaking new ground, if not being ground-breaking. American radio certainly shied away from Donna's seismic shift from disco to rock/new wave. Black female singers were either disco/dance, or urban/R&B, and Donna was neither. It's worth speculating whether this is the song in which Giorgio and Pete had to change the lyrics to fit Donna's new Christian faith. It does veer near with 'couples coasting singles searching' and 'action turning on reaction', both sounding like they may have been watered down from the original words. Also, just who is 'Debra waiting on the corner'? 'Nightlife' does at the very least possess one of Donna's best surprise endings before ramping back up again a few seconds later.

Remix fix!

The Le Flex Sunset remix from 2020's deluxe package of *The Wanderer* strips out all that raucous rock, lovingly reimagining 'Nightlife' as a sleek nu-disco anthem, more befitting of its 'Nightlife' title.

'I Believe in Jesus'

Writer: Donna Summer
Producers: Giorgio Moroder, Pete Bellotte

In September 1979, Donna became a born-again Christian. 'The day I had my conversion was the first day of the rest of my life,' she wrote in her memoir. 'I knew I was forgiven and free.' Donna started attending Bible-study classes to become spiritually centred. It would help immensely when her sister Dara's husband Gilbert, who had helped convert Donna, died in a car accident. This was part of a great period of death surrounding Donna: her sister Linda's child died of SIDS, then her sister's husband Andre was killed in a car accident a year later. Her brother's son Morgan accidentally shot and killed himself, her cousin Richard was shot by police and her Uncle Solomon was killed by a hit-and-run driver.

'In spite of everything my faith in God grew,' Donna noted. 'He was holding me up and carrying me through.' Ending her first album since becoming a born-again Christian, Donna didn't see the need to be subtle about her new-found faith. There's long been a school of thought that 'I Believe in Jesus' is Donna 'Bible-bashing' her audience. While there's little subtlety in the lyrical department, 'I Believe in Jesus' is arguably the only song on *The Wanderer* where firstly Donna allows herself to sing with pure joy, and secondly she sings like she used to do before her conversion. After the title track this may actually be the best song on the album, if only to hear Donna doused in gospel and preaching like she really means it.

While much on *The Wanderer* album seems forced, thought-out and sticking to a business plan (i.e. disco sucks but new wave rocks!), there is a genuineness and an ease to 'I Believe in Jesus' making it more than just Donna trying to convert the masses. It's real and actually quite beautiful, although that still wouldn't have quelled the dissent from her disco-loving fans at the time. Donna later received a Grammy nomination for Best Inspirational Performance for 'I Believe in Jesus' (won by B. J. Thomas with his version of standard 'Amazing Grace'). She would go on to win the category twice in 1984 and 1985, however, matching legendary gospel singer Mahalia Jackson as the only female to win twice. *Rolling Stone* pointed out that the musical backbone of 'I Believe in Jesus' was constructed from militant fundamentalist hymn 'Onward Christian Soldiers' and children's nursery rhyme 'Mary Had a Little Lamb'. In 2004, Grammy winner Todd Edwards liberally sampled 'I Believe in Jesus' for his garage house track 'Not to Worry'. A bootleg of Edwards' excellent 2024 'I Feel Love' remix also lives, unofficially, on the internet.

12

I'm a Rainbow (1981/1996)/ *I'm a Rainbow: Recovered & Recoloured* (2021)

I'm A Rainbow
Casablanca: 314 532 869. Mercury: 314 532 869-2.Chronicles: 314 532 669-2
Originally released: August 1996

'I Believe (In You)'	4:31	'Brooklyn'	4:35
'True Love Survives'	3:36	'I'm a Rainbow'	4:06
'You to Me'	4:39	'Walk On (Keep on Movin')'	3:49
'Sweet Emotion'	3:44	'Don't Cry for Me Argentina'	4:22
'Leave Me Alone'	4:04	'A Runner with the Pack'	4:06
'Melanie'	3:38	'Highway Runner'	3:27
'Back Where You Belong'	3:52	'Romeo'	3:13
'People Talk'	4:15	'End of the Week'	3:38
'To Turn the Stone'	4:20	'I Need Time'	4:23

'I Believe (In You') (Duet with Joe 'Bean' Esposito)

Writers: Harold Faltermeyer, Keith Forsey
Producers: Giorgio Moroder, Pete Bellotte

I'm a Rainbow was an eighteen-track double album colossus intended to recall the glory days of Donna's double albums for Casablanca. Recorded in early 1981 and due for release that October, it was brutally, in Donna's words, 'canned' by label boss David Geffen. It would take fifteen years before the almost 73-minute long *I'm a Rainbow* received an official release (now on CD, hence no vinyl 'sides' anymore). The album's disco/R&B opener *I Believe (In You)* niftily finds Donna reteaming with Brooklyn Dreams' Joe 'Bean' Esposito. These two truly blend well together as vocalists and it's a strong start to an album considered 'unreleaseable', at least by Donna's then record company boss.

In late 1981, Black British band The Real Thing covered and released this track as a single. Their funky take removed the unnecessary brackets in the title, but *I Believe in You* failed to chart. In 2021, Donna's estate released *Recovered & Recoloured*, editing the album down to ten tracks (all in remixed form): the title track, 'I Believe (In You)', 'Back Where You Belong', 'You to Me', 'Don't Cry for Me Argentina', 'Sweet Emotion', 'Brooklyn', 'Romeo', 'Highway Runner' and 'Leave Me Alone'. Licensed by her family's Driven by the Music label, an extra disc/LP included two further remixes of 'Brooklyn', plus remixes of 'I Believe (In You)', 'Highway Runner' and 'Romeo'.

Remix fix!

Nabbing two remixes on the *Recovered & Recoloured* release, Figo Sound return from their work on *The Wanderer* 40th anniversary edition. The longer 'Figo Sound Version' at 4:48 of 'I Believe (In You)' is on the first disc/LP, with the 'Figo Sound Radio Version' at 3:01 on the second. This mix was used as the priority track from the *Recovered & Recoloured* project.

'True Love Survives'

Writers: Donna Summer, Pete Bellotte
Producers: Giorgio Moroder, Pete Bellotte

Strap on your platforms and flares: it's the unofficial return of Donna as the 'Queen of Disco'. With a fearless Eurodance air about it, 'True Love Survives' is one of the strongest tracks on *I'm a Rainbow*, yet has surprisingly never been covered by anyone else. *I'm a Rainbow* also, ominously, marked the end of Donna's working relationship with Giorgio and Pete after a partnership of almost ten years that literally changed the face of music. 'Our musical relationship was really, really good,' Giorgio told *Variety* about working with Donna. 'She believed in what Pete and I were doing and co-wrote the songs with us, while I did most of the music. She was very much involved. It was less of a singer-producer relationship and more like three guys working on songs together. That camaraderie had much to do with the success of our music.' Pete later added, 'There are some people one never ceases to miss and Donna Summer is certainly one of those.'

'You to Me'

Writers: Pete Bellotte, Sylvester Levay
Producers: Giorgio Moroder, Pete Bellotte

Slowing things down for the album's first ballad, 'You to Me' really is everything. Although Donna wasn't involved in the writing of the lyrics—presumably that was British-born Pete's job—the line 'and no one's gonna steal the way God dreamed' sounds like something that may have had to be changed to accommodate

Donna's strong faith values. Although a number of its songs had been covered by other artists—via music publishers—bootleg copies of *I'm a Rainbow* circulated among diehard Donna fans for years before getting an official release.

Here's the first of two songs from the album which Donna's erstwhile rival Amii Stewart recorded for her self-titled 1983 album on RCA. Most famous for her storming 1979 US #1 disco cover of 'Knock on Wood', Amii's version of 'You to Me' is a great take on a song deserving so much better than it got. In 2016, the gossipy and great Stargayzing.com's David Munk called Donna's *I'm a Rainbow* 'the best album ever rejected by a major label'. Donna's 'lost album', as he terms it, 'holds up remarkably well and several even stand up impressively with the very best work Summer did with Giorgio Moroder and co-producer Pete Bellotte'. He also sagely notes how 'perhaps the biggest irony is the "Moroder sound" epitomised on *I'm a Rainbow* was far from over when the album was rejected; some of his greatest successes came just after, including Irene Cara's 'Flashdance (What a Feeling)' in 1983 and Berlin's 'Take My Breath Away' from (the movie) *Top Gun* a year later.' It's a common response among fans who have long been baffled, bewildered and bitter about Geffen nixing the *I'm a Rainbow* project in 1981. It was finally allowed out of the vaults fifteen years later due to a new appreciation of Donna's disco and post-disco era releases. Did 'You to Me' also inspire Carly Simon's 'Coming Around Again' hit in 1986? Hmmm.

Remix fix!

Oliver Nelson contributes a remix of 'You to Me' on *Recovered & Recoloured* with a running time of 3:39. Yet 2021's *Recovered & Recoloured* release is a rather baffling conceit. Why was it issued as a standalone album instead of a bonus with the original 1981 *I'm a Rainbow* album? Could it be because of *I'm a Rainbow*'s running time of just slightly less than 70 minutes (CDs can hold up to 80 minutes)? A CD version of the colourful pair would easily have made a double set, or on vinyl either triple/quadruple discs, while on digital/streaming it doesn't make one iota of a difference. Without the context of the original *I'm a Rainbow* album, the *Recovered & Recoloured* package has the dubious air of a frivolous, money-focused remix set, especially considering its original track listing was hacked back from eighteen to ten tracks. Listen hard and you make the call on that.

'Sweet Emotion'

Writers: Pete Bellotte, Sylvester Levay
Producers: Giorgio Moroder, Pete Bellotte

Closely following the template of eighties R&B with a mid-tempo beat and Donna in glorious plaintive vocal form, 'Sweet Emotion' even showcases a very of-its-era keyboard break. A year earlier, Stephanie Mills had a hit called 'Sweet Sensation' and there's a real similarity here in both title and style. In 1981, Stephanie won the coveted Grammy for Best R&B Vocal Performance for the effervescent 'Never Knew Love Like This Before' with her material co-written and produced by Mtume's Reggie Lucas. Two years later he would produce the debut album of an artist burning up with post-disco fever: Madonna.

1983 was also an important year for 'Sweet Emotion' as it transpired. With Donna's version unceremoniously yanked from Geffen's release schedule, disco songbird Amii Stewart added 'Sweet Emotion' to her 1983 self-titled album. Produced by Simon Boswell, Amii's take is almost an identikit version, making you wonder what David Geffen thought was so awful about it and the rest of the material on *I'm a Rainbow*. Moving to Italy in the early 1980s, her 1986 album *Amii* was mostly produced and written by Giorgio. If you want to hear what Donna with Giorgio might have sounded like in the mid-1980s, if they had still been working together, this is worth a listen. Album opener and lead single, with a big surprise tempo switch (like plenty of Donna's classic disco hits), 'Time is Tight' was written by Giorgio with Keith Forsey. Released in Germany and Italy, it reached #25 in the Italian charts.

Remix fix!
Back for remix duty after his stellar work on *The Wanderer* 40th anniversary bonus remixes in 2020, Le Flex offers a brief remix of 'Sweet Emotion' running at 3:46. Sadly, it slickly sticks so close to the original version (sounding even more early eighties than the original, if that's possible!) that you do have wonder what the sweet point of it was!

'Leave Me Alone'

Writers: Harold Faltermeyer, Keith Forsey
Producers: Giorgio Moroder, Pete Bellotte

Rumoured to have been intended as *I'm a Rainbow*'s lead single, 'Leave Me Alone' might be the song that has dated the most out of all the album's eighteen tracks. In a shrieky voice amid a bevy of squealing guitars and shouting background vocals, Donna insists she has 'got my rhythm', but there's little evidence of that here. This is where the experimentation went off the deep end. Perhaps Harold Faltermeyer and Keith Forsey assumed they were writing a cool sequel to 1979's 'Hot Stuff', yet this is tepid stuff at best. In 1989, Donna was asked about the *I'm a Rainbow* album, admitting some of the tracks 'sound dated because the technology has changed so much, though some of the tracks still sound great'. Asked many years later why he and Giorgio stopped working with Donna, Pete had just two words—David Geffen.

> Neil Bogart got into trouble with money. He was a brilliant record man with a wonderful ear for success, but he spent money like there was no tomorrow. So, Geffen came in. I remember saying at the time, 'Why does he want Donna, he hates disco?' We did *The Wanderer* with Geffen but he just didn't like the follow-up *(I'm a Rainbow)* at all.

Remix fix!

As the final track on the *Recovered & Recoloured* release, 'Leave Me Alone' gets the treatment from Ladies on Mars for a version called 'Independence Remix', which runs for 4:16.

'Melanie'

Writers: Donna Summer, Giorgio Moroder
Producers: Giorgio Moroder, Pete Bellotte

Another trademark Moroder track, sweet 'Melanie' was actually written about Donna's first daughter Mimi, with lyrics such as 'so young, so fair' as well as the telling 'she's glad for what she's had/her Mom and several dads'. Mimi's full name is actually Natalie Pia Melanie Sommer. With tracks like the thumping 'Melanie', and the punchy 'Romeo', capturing the new wave musical zeitgeist between seventies disco and eighties dance, it's worth considering what direction Donna's career might have gone in if this material had been heard back in 1981.

After the *I'm a Rainbow* album was aborted, so too was this new wave experiment. Instead, Donna was pushed down a more traditional R&B/ female Black singer route for most of the 1980s. In the interim, white female artists such as Madonna and Cyndi Lauper found huge success mining that sweet-spot between old school disco and the rise of synthpop. In many ways the album *Flashdance... What a Feeling,* which singer Irene Cara issued in 1983, could be viewed as the album Donna shoulda, coulda, woulda made. Mostly written and produced by Giorgio, catchy pop/dance efforts such as 'Why Me?', 'Breakdance' and lost classic 'Talk Too Much' give us an inkling of what might have been if David Geffen hadn't intervened and steered Donna elsewhere. Even *Billboard* magazine, in their review of Cara's album, opined that the ten-track album 'should also please fans nostalgic for the early Summer sound'. In 1982, 'Melanie' was covered by pianist Helen St. John who renamed her instrumental version 'Images' for her *Power to the Piano* album produced by Giorgio. That the astoundingly catchy and still contemporary sounding 'Melanie' was omitted from 2021's *Recovered & Recoloured* still beggars belief.

'Back Where You Belong'

Writers: Harold Faltermeyer, Keith Forsey
Producers: Giorgio Moroder, Pete Bellotte

A contribution from Harold Faltermeyer and Keith Forsey, 'Back Where You Belong' has an odd, if not somewhat confusing, lyrical tale to tell: 'I'm gonna leave you just because I want you back where you belong'. There's a sense here though that what we're hearing on 'Back Where You Belong' is more of an unfinished demo, although the stabbing background vocals courtesy of Donna and Michael Sembello, soon to have his own global hit with 'Maniac' from the *Flashdance* soundtrack, certainly elevate 'Back Where You Belong'. In her *Ordinary Girl* memoir, Donna summed up David Geffen as 'a world-class charmer'. She also wrote that 'the great thing about David is how he is always able to focus on exactly what he wants, go after it, and not give up until he gets his way, although in my case I was a real test of his endurance'. According to Giorgio, when they were getting to the end of the sessions on *I'm a Rainbow*, Geffen dropped in unannounced to listen to it. He wasn't happy when he did and decided not only to scrap it, but also to put Donna together with another producer (we'll get to that in the next chapter). After this imbroglio, the ever-loyal Donna persisted with Geffen for most of the 1980s. Geffen sold his label in 1990, earning himself a reported $800m. In 1996, four years after he officially came out as gay, Geffen co-founded the DreamWorks movie studio and is now considered the wealthiest person in showbiz—worth around $9 billion.

Remix fix!

On the *Recovered & Recoloured* album, there is a Jean Tonique remix of 'Back Where You Belong' with a running time of 4:21. Grooving like the vibe of an Ibizan day club, JT, aka French producer Antoine Roux, offers a perky, summery vibe reminiscent of Spiller's 'Groovejet (If This Ain't Love)' from 2000, which hit #1 in the UK.

'People Talk'

Writers: Donna Summer, Giorgio Moroder
Producers: Giorgio Moroder, Pete Bellotte

Sporting a speedy trademark Moroder synth sound, almost a throwback to the 'I Feel Love' days, lyrically 'People Talk' chides 'gossiping hacks stabbing their words with all of their stars in our backs'. Is this Donna taking aim at the 'grapevine of lies' she constantly had to endure as a celebrity in the public eye? When *I'm a Rainbow* was finally released some fifteen years later in 1996, *The Los Angeles Times* reviewed it, noting that along with Karen Carpenter's 1979 solo recording with Phil Ramone, they were both lost albums recently unearthed. Awarding it two stars out of four, reviewer Robert Hilburn wrote, 'it probably made sense for Summer to take a hiatus from the Moroder/Bellotte team at the time, because most of *I'm a Rainbow* sounds tired. Not all of it, though.' Hilburn added that 'like some of her earlier hits, "People Talk"—one of the strongest tracks on *I'm a Rainbow*—mixes marvellously the Moroder/Bellotte musical tension with a strong dose of ABBA-like bounce. As usual, Summer's vocal injects the recording with character and style.' He concluded that at least three other tracks—'Walk On (Keep on Movin')', 'To Turn the Stone' and 'Romeo'—'also deserve to be on any best-of Summer package'.

Remix fix!

Arranger and producer Don Charles worked on the 1996 release of *I'm a Rainbow* and, in 2021, revealed there was a different version of 'People Talk' with female background singers rapping, or better gossiping, during the instrumental break. This can now be found, and heard, as the 'Alternate Rap Version' on YouTube, running for almost a minute longer than the original version.

'To Turn the Stone'

Writers: Giorgio Moroder, Pete Bellotte
Producers: Giorgio Moroder, Pete Bellotte

A mid-tempo song about change on a cosmic scale, 'To Turn the Stone' was like nothing Donna had done or sung about before. It even included bagpipes, surely a first on a Donna record. The actual meaning of 'To Turn the Stone' is to become rigid, petrified, or even face death. Yep, this was no rehashed Donna Summer 'toot toot beep beep' tune. Perhaps for that reason, 'To Turn the Stone' has been the most covered of all the songs from Donna's *I'm a Rainbow* sessions. With music publishers shopping the songs from *I'm a Rainbow* to other artists, one landed in the lap of ABBA singer Frida, then frantically searching for material to record for a solo album. Producer Phil Collins evoked a Phil Spector wall of sound for Frida's dreamy recording of 'To Turn the Stone', the second single from her *Something's Going On* album. A major European hit in 1982, it failed to make a dent in the US or UK. Around the same time as Frida released her single, pianist Helen St. John recorded an instrumental version of 'To Turn the Stone' for her *Power to the Piano* album, produced by Giorgio. Joe 'Bean' Esposito must also have loved the moody 'To Turn the Stone', as he recorded it twice: firstly in 1983 for the synth-drenched *Solitary Men* album, credited to Joe and Giorgio, and secondly in 1989 for his Austrian-only single retitled (or perhaps incorrectly written as) 'To Turn To Stone'. Prophetically, with its lyrics waxing about eternal sands, *Summer: The Donna Summer Musical* used 'To Turn the Stone' for an emotive scene in which Donna receives her cancer diagnosis.

'Brooklyn'

Writers: Donna Summer, Pete Bellotte, Sylvester Levay
Producers: Giorgio Moroder, Pete Bellotte

In some interviews, Donna mentioned how David Geffen 'didn't think there was enough dance music on the record. It wasn't what he was looking for. It was like having a miscarriage. I don't go into the studio to have an album canned.' That miscarriage meant a song she had written for her baby daughter Brooklyn, born in January 1981, was also canned. Written straight from the heart of a mother to her 'still new to this world' child, Donna's lyrics celebrate 'Brooklyn summer magic/My sweet baby girl'. There's a reason the *I'm a Rainbow* album was a much happier and more positive affair than previous album *The Wanderer*, and a lot of that had to do with Donna and Bruce's new bundle of joy. If Mimi could have a song written about her (or two if we count 'Melanie', also on this album), then why not Brooklyn too (named after her father's band and where he was born)?

In the 2023 documentary *Love to Love You, Donna Summer*, which Brooklyn co-directed, she reveals that when she first discovered the song 'Brooklyn', she was struck by its power. She also points out that this song, written about her by her mother, was a statement of female empowerment and a ground-breaking moment for a Black woman in the public eye.

Remix fix!

Clearly there's a great fondness for Donna's 'Brooklyn' ditty among the Donna Summer family, as you might well imagine. 'Brooklyn' features three times on 2021's *Recovered & Recoloured*—more than any other track on the album!—all in various remixes by Ladies on Mars who contribute nine of the fifteen new versions on the double release.

'I'm a Rainbow'

Writer: Bruce Sudano
Producers: Giorgio Moroder, Pete Bellotte

While most of the *I'm a Rainbow* album remained frustratingly buried in the PolyGram vaults until 1996, two tracks were finally allowed out in 1993—the album's title song, plus a remix of Donna's version of *Don't Cry for Me Argentina*—as incentives for fans to buy the double CD compilation *The Donna Summer Anthology*. The positive response to this pair of lost treasures must have been just the kick PolyGram needed to finally unlock the vaults and release all of *I'm a Rainbow*. 'I always look at that song as a purely inspirational piece of music,' Bruce says of 'I'm a Rainbow'.

> It's one of those things where I sat down at the piano and this song came out. I live in wonderment of that song because most songs when I write them, of course, there's that seed of inspiration. I look at songwriting as part inspiration and part craft, but that particular song was just a flow that came out of nowhere for me. That song has a special place in my heart. That at some point Donna decided to record it and name her album after it was an extra added bonus. It's a special song for me because it was like a gift. All songs are for me, but that one especially.

Remix fix!

Former Madonna bestie/fave remixer Junior Vasquez opens up the *Recovered & Recoloured* set with a 4:16 edit of his Shiny Rainbow mix of 'I'm a Rainbow'.

'Walk On (Keep on Movin')'

Writers: Giorgio Moroder, Pete Bellotte
Producers: Giorgio Moroder, Pete Bellotte

Giorgio's take on the end of his relationship with Donna is quite pointed, if not perceptive. 'She went to Geffen and started to become more religious,' he told an interviewer. 'The last two albums we did I was not really happy with her. She didn't want to sing this line because there was this word. She wanted to sing a song about Jesus. What can you do? She was my main singer.' He then admitted to *Variety*, 'after all was said and done, actually, *I'm a Rainbow* was not a great album. I had to agree with that. Maybe what we, or Geffen, should have done at the time was release it as a single album, rather than the double album, which we intended. We could have taken it down to ten great songs.'

There has been a lot of discussion among fans about another 'walk' song being left off *I'm a Rainbow*. 'Walk Hand in Hand' had featured on some bootleg copies of the album but later was assumed to have been a track intended for her Quincy Jones-produced album. It was actually neither. 'Walk Hand in Hand' actually dates back to 1972 when Donna recorded a bunch of songs with Broder Brodersen in Germany, which wound up as propaganda for right-wing political party CDU. In 1982 the song was remixed for German vinyl compilation *Disco Round 2*. Brodersen's son Patrick explained that 'what you hear here is the original voice track on a completely new arrangement, recorded a few years later in Hannover with the band Eloy as session musicians. My father had the rights to the track and the recordings, produced the new version and published it on a few samplers.'

'Don't Cry for Me Argentina'

Writers: Andrew Lloyd-Webber, Tim Rice
Producers: Giorgio Moroder, Pete Bellotte

Donna was obsessed with 'Don't Cry for Me Argentina' from 1976's Andrew Lloyd-Webber/Tim Rice rock opera *Evita*. Often singing it live, Donna once said she felt it 'belongs to me now. It's almost like my song. I know it may sound presumptuous, but I don't mean to. I just feel such a connection to that song. I feel like so many things have transpired in my life and my career and I wind up back with the audience where it all begins.' Donna's take on 'Don't Cry for Me Argentina'—the power-ballad to end all power-ballads!—had already received an airing in 1993 with a slightly shorter, glossier and infinitely more modern remix by Giorgio on the double CD compilation *The Donna Summer Anthology*.

It was bad timing for Donna that just a few months after her version was finally released in 1996, the movie version of *Evita*, starring Madonna, opened to big box office and great reviews. Also released was Madonna's version of 'Don't Cry for Me Argentina', finally turning it into a US top-ten hit (with dance mixes much beloved by her gay fanbase). Yet while Madonna's take reached #3 in the UK, it couldn't match Julie Covington's original recording, which was a #1 hit there in 1977. In 1998, Donna notably performed 'Don't Cry for Me Argentina' at a benefit concert called 'An Evening with Donna Summer' for the Gay Men's Health Crisis (GMHC), America's oldest and largest not-for-profit AIDS organisation. Her *Evita* showstopper brought the gay crowds to their feet as Donna embraced its poignant lyrics for herself and her gay fans: 'the truth is I never left you', 'I kept my promise, don't keep your distance' and 'I love you and hope you love me.' The concert not only marked a significant healing point for Donna and her gay audience, but also raised $400,000 for GMHC. She kept her promise!

Remix fix!

Ladies on Mars do the business on 'Don't Cry for Me Argentina' with their Buenos Aires remix running at 5:37 on *Recovered & Recoloured*. Buenos Aires, incidentally, is also the name of one of the other songs from *Evita*.

'A Runner with the Pack'

Writer: Pete Bellotte
Producers: Giorgio Moroder, Pete Bellotte

You'd have to go all the way back to Donna's first album, 1974's *Lady of the Night*, to find another track Pete wrote for her all on his own. Clearly, there was a lot of running, if not jogging, going on with the boys in the studio as there are two songs on *I'm a Rainbow* with the word 'runner' in the title. Donna again puts on one of her talky 'voices', akin to what she does elsewhere on the album on 'Romeo', although 'A Runner with the Pack' doesn't, er, pack, the same impact. Yet the burbling, relentless synth-pop setting was all the rage in that era. In March 1981, Kim Carnes' memorable, synth-drenched US #1, 'Bette Davis Eyes', which became the biggest hit of the year in the US, looked to be Giorgio/ Pete's studio template for 'A Runner with the Pack', not to mention Donna's haughty vocal inspiration. Further to that, the same month *I'm a Rainbow* was originally scheduled for release, in October 1981, The Human League released their seminal synth-pop album *Dare*, featuring the US/UK #1 'Don't You Want Me'. Giorgio and Pete were thus very much on trend, if not indeed running with the pack. However, David Geffen wasn't having any of that. It's worth considering what would have happened to Donna's career if he hadn't yanked Donna's *I'm a Rainbow* album from the Geffen schedule. Would the Moroder/Bellotte/ Summer partnership have happily endured for many more albums, with Donna continuing to be as big a pop music presence as she was in the 1970s? Sadly, none of that came to pass, but at the very least we get a taste of what might have been with 'A Runner with the Pack', oh yes, just like that.

'Highway Runner'

Writers: Donna Summer, Giorgio Moroder
Producers: Giorgio Moroder, Pete Bellotte

Taking *The Wanderer* album blueprint of marrying rock and dance, 'Highway Runner' makes it somewhat more palatable. In 1981 this was another relatively new sound, which would go on to become an eighties staple. Lyrically, 'Highway Runner' is about a male wanderer with 'restless feet and a restless mind/ never wanna travel through the same place twice'. There's an extended synth instrumental section that nowadays seems like it didn't get out of the 1980s alive, while Donna's vocals have also been severely treated, which makes them seem steely, cold and mechanised, but perhaps that was the original idea. This synth-rocker first showed up in 1982 on the Full Moon/Asylum soundtrack to *Fast Times at Ridgemont High*. Donna was in fine rock company alongside such music luminaries as Jackson Browne (whose track 'Somebody's Baby' became a top-ten US hit), Sammy Hagar and Stevie Nicks with the soundtrack peaking at #54 on the US album charts. It's also worth noting Giorgio co-wrote/produced a UK top ten hit song for The Three Degrees called 'The Runner' in 1979.

Remix fix!
Ladies on Mars offer a 'Street Race' mix of 'Highway Runner'– in short form (3:12) and extended form (6:18) on the *Recovered & Recoloured* album—retaining some of the gritty guitar edge of the original but ramping up the dance beats to 124 bpm.

'Romeo'

Writers: Pete Bellotte, Sylvester Levay
Producers: Giorgio Moroder, Pete Bellotte

This is truly the one that got away! In 1983, sassy new wave dance tune 'Romeo' materialised on the *Flashdance* soundtrack. A music video was even created for it with the intention of 'Romeo' being a single, yet with 'She Works Hard for the Money' on the verge of being a major hit, 'Romeo' was the song that never was a single but probably should have been. The *Flashdance* soundtrack, which included the Oscar-winning title song sung by Irene Cara, Michael Sembello's 'Maniac' and Joe Esposito's 'Lady Lady Lady' was released, ironically, through Casablanca. It hit #1 in the US, selling over 20 million copies worldwide, which means 'Romeo' is probably the most heard Donna Summer song that was never a single, let alone a hit. Even Geffen knew it was the likeliest hit from an album they didn't like.

Donna summed up her experience on *I'm a Rainbow* as 'the record company wanted me to make different kinds of songs and records. They didn't think the old way was working. They thought my time with Giorgio had run out. *The Wanderer* album did very well, but when Giorgio and I went in to record the next album they stopped us midway because they didn't like it. They used one of the songs, "Romeo", on the *Flashdance* album, but they said the rest of the songs wouldn't make it. That's when they made me switch producers.' Because 'Romeo' was so well known and liked, Donna included it as part of her live sets in the early 1980s. In 1984, the *Flashdance* soundtrack was nominated for Album of the Year, which meant Donna was actually one of the creatives included. Can you guess which album did win? The biggest-selling album of all time (produced by Donna's next producer), Michael Jackson's *Thriller*. *Flashdance* did win the Best Score Soundtrack for Visual Media Grammy, which included Donna as one of the album's 'Various Artists'.

Vid bit!
Director: Adrian Lyne
An official video featured a collage of clips from the *Flashdance* movie, but alas no Donna.

Remix fix!
Once again Ladies on Mars offer two versions of the same Luv-NRG mix of *Romeo* on *Recovered & Recoloured*—a single-length edit at 3:45 and an extended remix at 6:47.

'End of the Week'

Writers: Pete Bellotte, Sylvester Levay
Producers: Giorgio Moroder, Pete Bellotte

Here's Donna's rock/pop tribute to the working week and working women, a theme she mined previously on 'Working the Midnight Shift' from 1977's *Once Upon a Time* album and one she would successfully resurrect again in 1983 for 'She Works Hard for the Money'. 'End of the Week' does have a rough, unfinished quality to it, as if this is more a temporary demo for something yet to be perfected in the studio. There's another squealing, if not unnecessary, guitar solo, which transforms into the (very 1980s) 'keytar' that doesn't add anything. So how did Serbian-German disco producer Sylvester Levay come to work with Donna? 'I knew Giorgio from Munich—the times when I had worldwide success with Silver Convention and Giorgio had launched Donna Summer,' he recalled in 2015. 'Later on, he moved to Los Angeles and eventually started to compose music for films. He always needed talents around him who would put his ideas into realisation. Harold Faltermeyer was one of these artists.' Donna was, intriguingly, a studio singer initially hired to record tracks for 1975's debut album *Save Me* by Silver Convention. The band were so named because 'Silver' was Sylvester's nickname. After signing a contract, she was then offered a solo deal with Giorgio and the rest is history. Although there were claims that Donna sang on Silver Convention's debut album, it appears she skipped those sessions. Roberta Kelly, who did sing on that album, also sang on Donna's *Love to Love You Baby* album.

'I Need Time'

Writers: Donna Summer, Giorgio Moroder, Pete Bellotte
Producers: Giorgio Moroder, Pete Bellotte

The final track on *I'm a Rainbow* could almost be a prototype for all the 1980s R&B power-ballads to come after, especially those from Whitney Houston, who would release her first record in 1985. 'I Need Time' is a fine showcase for Donna's powerhouse vocals, but just who is the person standing at Donna's door in a 'torn up yellow T-shirt and guitar in hand'? Most likely it was Bruce, perhaps back in the early days when he and Donna were both still playing hard to get. Unfortunately, time was indeed up for the Moroder/Bellotte/Summer three-way.

Although there would be a one-off recording by Donna and Giorgio a decade later, their working relationship was effectively over. Giorgio only ever had nice things to say about Donna afterwards, even if their career paths had diverged. 'She is—or was—an incredibly talented singer and not only for R&B,' Giorgio said in 2024. 'By singing in churches in Boston, she was able to improvise, but also from singing in musicals she had great discipline too.'

Donna Summer (1982)

Donna Summer
Geffen: GHS 2005
Originally released: July 1982

'Love is in Control (Finger on the Trigger)'	4:18
'Mystery of Love'	4:25
'The Woman in Me'	3:55
'State of Independence'	5:50
'Livin' in America'	4:41
'Protection'	3:35
'(If It) Hurts Just a Little'	3:52
'Love Is Just a Breath Away'	3:55
'Lush Life'	6:26

'Love is in Control (Finger on the Trigger)'

Geffen: 7-299982. Single release: June 1982
Writers: Quincy Jones, Merria Ross, Rod Temperton
Producer: Quincy Jones

Donna recalled in her *Ordinary Girl* memoir how David Geffen, 'had the idea to phone Quincy Jones to see if he would produce my next album. Quincy had the challenge, however, of producing the record during my time I was pregnant with my third child.' With Donna focusing more on her pregnancy, Quincy was additionally given the task of sourcing material for the album. Not only did he put the word out that he was looking for tunes for Donna, but he also found the time to co-write two. One of them, 'Love is in Control (Finger on the Trigger)', became not just the album's first track, but also the first single. Quincy, of course, had been a music industry legend for decades before he worked with Donna. Brit Rod Temperton had been the songwriter/keyboardist for 1970s interracial act Heatwave. After writing hits for Michael Jackson's 1979 album *Off the Wall*, he penned hits for George Benson and Patti Austin.

The closest thing to disco Donna had recorded since 1979, one of 'Love is in Control's co-writers was Merria A. Ross, a noted disco and film music composer who was also the songwriter in the group El Coco. In 1976, they scored a #61 US hit with 'Let's Get It Together' and a year later, in 1977, their 'Commotion' went to #31 UK and #44 US. Both are considered disco bangers! Donna's cutesy single, which appears to give a tiny nod to 'Bad Girls' in its intro, just squeezed into the US top ten at #10 (and #4 in the R&B charts), reached #18 in the UK and went top five in Canada, Finland, Norway, Spain and Switzerland. Some have complained the song's chorus doesn't feature enough of Donna's vocals, swamped by a sea of other voices, yet 'Love is in Control (Finger on the Trigger)' has become another of Donna's enviable arsenal of upbeat hits across the decades. As soon as Quincy completed Donna's album in April 1982, he began work on his next project, released in November that same year—Michael Jackson's *Thriller*. Temperton died in 2016 at the age of 66. Quincy Jones died in 2024 age 91.

Vid bit!

Directors: Jeff Lancaster and Chris Whorf

Donna gives good photoshoot as she wanders around an Alex Da Corte-inspired pop-art set dressed in a black dress barely containing her pregnant belly. There's also plenty of footage of her modelling the iconic blue dress with big gold belt as seen on the album cover. It's not the most exciting of Donna videos though, perhaps a reflection of the fact her team still didn't realise the power MTV had, or would have.

Remix fix!

A 2014 expanded reissue of the *Donna Summer* album featured three versions: 7-inch, a dance remix and an instrumental version featuring Ernie Watts on saxophone. Remixes were by Craig Kostich and Bruce Swedien. 2022's 40th-anniversary edition of *Donna Summer* included the 7-inch and dance remix.

'Sometimes Like Butterflies'

Geffen: 7-299982. Single release: June 1982 (B-side of 'Love is in Control')

Writers: Donna Summer, Bruce Roberts

Producer: Quincy Jones

'One afternoon at (David) Geffen's house, songwriter Bruce Roberts and I wrote a song called "Sometimes Like Butterflies",' Donna recalled proudly in her *Ordinary Girl* memoir. 'I didn't stop creating in spite of all the problems plaguing the business side of my career.'

A stirring piano-only ballad, 'Sometimes Like Butterflies' is a true singer's showcase (Bette Midler inspired Donna's vocals here), with lyrics that could easily be interpreted as Donna yearning to break free of Casablanca, Neil Bogart and her past ('butterflies were made to fly/I've got to be free"). In 1985, British singing legend Dusty Springfield covered 'Sometimes Like Butterflies' for a synth-drenched power-ballad single, which she self-produced. Reaching #83 in the UK, it would be her only release on the short-lived Hippodrome Records label. 'Sometimes Like Butterflies' was later included on 2022's 40th-anniversary edition of the *Donna Summer* album as a bonus, while in 2026 Israeli DJ Offer Nissim released a pounding official remix, endorsed by Bruce Roberts, on his *Let Me Tell You Something* album.

'Mystery of Love'

Writers: John Lang, Bill Meyers, Richard Page
Producer: Quincy Jones

American synth wizard Michael Boddicker adds his signature flair to the opening of 'Mystery of Love', borrowing heavily from Bach's 'Prelude and Fugue in C Minor, BWV 847' written around 1722. Boddicker was even voted most valuable synth player in 1982 and went on to be an invaluable part of Michael Jackson's *Thriller* the same year he worked on Donna's album. Slapping into a much more contemporary sound, the real mystery here is why the jubilant and joyful 'Mystery of Love' wasn't up for consideration as a single. Songwriter Richard Page went on to become something of a popstar himself as the frontman for the band Mr Mister, who scored two mid-eighties US #1 hits: 'Broken Wings' and 'Kyrie'. Lyricist John Lang had been in an earlier band with Page called Pages and co-wrote the two Mr Mister #1s.

Musician Bill/Billy Meyers soon after became a big-name arranger, responsible for the opening strings on Madonna's 'Papa Don't Preach' in 1986 and Destiny Child's cover of 'Emotion' in 2001. String arrangements on this were by Michael Omartian, who would become Donna's producer on her next album *She Works Hard for the Money*. Clearly there was a strong Christian connection between them, with Omartian a major figure in the contemporary Christian music field. Donna's own mystery bundle of love, Amanda Sudano, was born on 11 August 1982, less than a month after the release of the *Donna Summer* album.

Remix fix!

The Driven by the Music label's 40th-anniversary edition of the *Donna Summer* album included two bonus remixes of 'Mystery of Love' by Le Flex—an edit and an extended mix of the 'Summer Mystery' remix.

'The Woman in Me'

Geffen: 7-29805. Single release: November 1982
Writers: John Bettis, Michael Clark
Producer: Quincy Jones

You would have to be a little suspicious of a song called 'The Woman in Me' written by two men. However, Bettis is one of the world's most successful lyricists, having at the time written a string of hits for the Carpenters, including 'Yesterday Once More', 'Top of the World' and 'Only Yesterday'. A year earlier, in 1981, Bettis and musician Michael Clark wrote the sultry 'Slow Hand' for The Pointer Sisters, a #2 US and #10 UK hit. You can hear echoes of 'The Woman in Me' in two hits he later wrote—1985's 'Crazy for You' for Madonna and 1986's 'One Moment in Time' for Whitney Houston. Donna said she especially liked singing 'The Woman in Me' to her husband Bruce. 'It's like every woman wants a man that she's with not just to know what he knows about her,' she explained. ''Cos it's obvious what you know about a person. You know what you want, you know what you don't want basically, but there's a lot of things that you want each other to know that are much deeper and much further inside. People just tend to constantly overlook that. It's a very deep song to me.'

Reaching #33 in the US and #62 in the UK, 'The Woman in Me' was also subject to Casablanca's continued disruption tactics, despite the fact Neil Bogart had passed away. Released the same month as 'The Woman in Me' single hit stores was the Patrick Cowley remix of 'I Feel Love', literally days after Cowley had died of AIDS. Donna wisely realised that it was time to call a truce on her ongoing legal situation. Her attorney, Don Engel, worked out a settlement with the executives at PolyGram who had since bought out the remaining 50 per cent of Casablanca. In return, however, she had to deliver one more album to PolyGram/Casablanca. She worked hard to finish it in June 1983, less than a year after the release of the *Donna Summer* album. In the UK, a limited- edition blue vinyl 12-inch picture disc was produced for 'The Woman in Me' (Warner: U9983CT). Featuring 'Livin' in America' and 'The Wanderer' on the B-side, it is worth eyeballing/ogling it in all its blue-hued glory tucked away in this author's Donna collection in this very book.

Vid bit!

Director: Brian Grant

Could the entire budget of 'The Woman in Me' video have been blown (literally) on Donna's big eighties hair? A fairly *el cheapo* clip with Donna suitably coquettish and sultry as befitting the smoochy ballad, 'The Woman in Me' does seem as if it was made by someone who filmed stationary concerts. Grant, unsurprisingly, was also the director of Donna's 'A Hot Summer Night' long- form video from 1983. It's also obvious Donna was pregnant at the time as the camera never pans any lower than her chest. Thankfully, her next video, less than six months later, would work hard on bringing Donna into the great music video age. Phew.

'State of Independence'

Geffen: 7-29895. Single release: September 1982
Writers: Jon Anderson, Vangelis
Producer: Quincy Jones

This stately synth spiritual was released as the second single from 1981's *The Friends of Mr Cairo*, the second album by Jon and Vangelis. Jon was British rock singer Jon Anderson, lead singer of the band Yes, while Vangelis was a Greek composer specialising in electronic music who had scored a US #1 with the theme from the Oscar-winning movie *Chariots of Fire* earlier in 1981. Recorded while Anderson improvised uplifting spiritual lyrics, Jon and Vangelis' version of 'State of Independence' (at almost eight minutes long) failed to chart. It did not, mercifully, go unnoticed by 'the best ears in the business': Quincy Jones. 'Quincy also came up with the idea of recording the Vangelis-Jon Anderson song "State of Independence" as an epic with a cast of voices,' Donna remembered fondly. 'This trendsetting song helped pave the way for such future epics as "We Are the World".' The all-star choir was composed of Michael Jackson, Lionel Richie, Dionne Warwick, Stevie Wonder, Michael McDonald, James Ingram, Kenny Loggins, Christopher Cross, Quincy Jones, Brenda Russell, actress/singer/songwriter Dyan Cannon, Quincy's wife Peggy Lipton Jones, Donna's sister Dara Lynn Bernard and Donna herself.

The true highlight of Donna's self-titled album and released as the second single, 'State of Independence' reached #14 in the UK and #41 in the US, but was her second #1 in the Netherlands. 'Quincy knows everybody,' Donna laughed. 'A lot of those people I didn't personally know but they came when Quincy called. Everybody loved the song so much and were very happy to participate. It was an incredible experience to have all those people sing on my record. When all those voices light up and start singing you feel like, "This is it! This is the high point!"' British avant garde electronic outfit Art of Noise sampled 'State of Independence' for the 1:44 minute track 'Donna' for their *Into Battle with the Art of Noise* EP from 1983 (For the 1996 'State of Independence' re-release see Chapter 19).

Vid bit!

Director: Chris Balton
Earth mother Donna saunters across sunset beaches in a burgundy mumu and the streets of New York City in a lady in red ensemble. There's also a black beret look too. That the clip doesn't include the footage of Q (Quincy Jones) conducting the superstar choir singing—four minutes of which is available elsewhere—is truly an act of criminal negligence. There's also the cutest video ever on the internet of then 10-year-old Mimi performing the song with her mother live on stage in 1983 at California's The Pacific Amphitheatre from 'A Hot Summer Night' long- form video. They even wear matching dresses. It's the show closer and Donna also manages to slip in a spot of preaching towards the end.

'Livin' in America'

Writers: David Foster, Quincy Jones, Steve Lukather, Donna Summer, Rod Temperton
Producer: Quincy Jones

Look out, Q fans, here comes another superstar choir! The first of Donna's two songwriting contributions to the *Donna Summer* album is not so much a social critique of her homeland, but more a jingoistic take where someone hustling to pay the rent ends up 'playing all the aces and wound-up President'. Then there's a 'soap opera child with stars in her eyes' who 'served an agent now she's a movie queen'. This is also the second writing contribution on the album for Foster, Q and Donna. Steve Lukather was lead guitarist for the band Toto, who hit #2 in the US in 1982 with 'Rosanna', then #1 the same year with follow-up 'Africa'.

Most of the other members of Toto also played on the *Donna Summer* album—Steve Porcaro, David Paich, Greg Phillinganes and Jeff Porcaro. That choir group of nineteen singers consisted of Donna's sister Dara Lynn Bernard, Patrick Crotty Jr., Deirdre Dantzler Ribeiro, Michael Davis, Tonya DeWalt, Debra Green, R&B legend James Ingram, Q's then eight-year-old daughter Kidada Jones, actress Rashida Jones, soprano Shanté Lewis, Heather Mason, Greg Phillinganes, Dina Rich, Cynthia Spears, Deirdre Spears, Bernard Walton, Pamela Quinlan, Lynn T. Walton and Faith D. Wong. African-American arranger and legend H.B. Barnum, who had worked with Aretha Franklin, Little Richard and The Supremes, was the director of the choir. Little wonder that at one point Donna told the *LA Times* how her self-titled album sometimes felt like 'a Quincy Jones album that I sang on'. 'Livin' in America' was also the B-side to 'The Woman in Me' single. Donna sang 'Livin' in America' in early 1985 at Ronald Reagan's inauguration for his second presidency with the US Naval Academy Glee Club. Footage exists on the internet of Donna's spirited performance—virtually the only Black person in a sea of white faces—introduced by Merv Griffin as Reagan and wife Nancy are shown gleefully clapping along.

'Protection'

Warner Bros. Records: P-1688. Single release: December 1982 (Japan/Belgium)
Writer: Bruce Springsteen
Producer: Quincy Jones

Springsteen-does-ABBA? That sure is the rock disco meeting place for this song 'The Boss' wrote especially for Donna. Well, that was after he wrote another one first, which his manager convinced him was too good to give away. The one that got away from Donna turned out to be a top-ten hit for Springsteen in 1984, 'Cover Me', lifted from his iconic *Born in the USA* album. 'It was Q's genius to team me up with Bruce Springsteen,' Donna recalled. 'Quincy asked him if he would write a song for the new album. Shortly thereafter, "The Boss" showed up at my front door with a new song he'd written for me called "Protection". I loved it. I'd seen him many times at his concerts, swinging his guitar from side to side as he strutted across the room. Now there he was in my little music room humbly singing his song just for me. Wow, somebody pinch me! And my husband was his #1 fan. Wow, that was a day to remember.'

Originally planned as a duet between Donna and Bruce, 'Protection' not only features Bruce on guitar, but also on backing vocals, proving how much of a fan of Donna and her work he was. Springsteen's own version of 'Protection'—recorded in early 1982 with his E Street Band—is still unreleased. Bruce has, however, performed the song numerous times live, mentioning its connection to Donna, and explaining how he was very impressed with her singing and that the 'disco sucks' movement was 'just thinly veiled racism'. Released as a Donna single in Japan and Belgium at the end of 1982, 'Protection' failed to significantly chart in either territory but was nominated for a Grammy for Best Female Rock Vocal Performance in 1983. Pat Benatar won for 'Shadows of the Night'.

'(If It) Hurts Just a Little'

Writers: David Batteau, Dan Sembello, Michael Sembello
Producer: Quincy Jones

'Come on baby, come on sugar, come on honey!' Flashy future pop sensation Michael Sembello not only contributed backing vocals and guitar licks to '(If It) Hurts Just a Little', but he also co-wrote this tune. The late soul great James Ingram was also brought in to add his dulcet tones to this funky R&B jam. Sembello had previously worked for Donna and a year after this, in 1983, briefly tasted pop fame with his frantic dance single 'Maniac' hitting #1 in the US and being included on the *Flashdance* soundtrack. Danny Sembello, brother of Michael, later wrote hits for The Pointer Sisters, Chaka Khan and Patti LaBelle. He sadly drowned in 2015 at the age of 52. Songwriter David Batteau had written hits for The Manhattan Transfer and Seals & Crofts before he came to Donna's attention.

'(If It) Hurts Just a Little' was the B-side of 'Protection' in those select few territories where it was released as a single. *Très cool* French electro duo Cassius sampled '(If It) Hurts Just a Little' for their 1999 'Cassius 99 Remix' single. That 'come on baby, come on sugar, come on honey' chant basically constituted the entirety of the song, but—*mon dieu!*—why not, *non*? This French delicacy went to #7 in the UK and was included on their debut *1999* album released in—you guessed it!—1999. Cassius credited the Sembellos and Batteau as songwriters on that version, which rocked the roofs of house clubs for years afterwards. You may have been wondering what Giorgio Moroder was doing now he was no longer making beautiful music with Donna. In March 1982, he scored a hit with the moody 'Cat People (Putting Out Fire)' with David Bowie. Later that year, he completed a soundtrack for a new movie called *Flashdance,* which would bizarrely include a then unreleased Donna song, *Romeo*. 1983 would also see Giorgio's album with Brooklyn Dreams' Joe Esposito, *Solitary Men*, released, plus his *Scarface* soundtrack, reuniting him with Blondie's Debbie Harry.

'Love Is Just a Breath Away'

Writers: David Foster, Donna Summer, Rod Temperton
Producer: Quincy Jones

There are some pretty heavy-hitting names associated with 'Love Is Just a Breath Away', which is something of a fan favourite, despite its dated production. This was both Temperton and Foster's second writing credit on the *Donna Summer* album. As for Donna, with just two songwriting credits on this album –her lowest on any album since her 1975 international breakthrough—she blamed a difficult pregnancy and her ongoing legal situation. Also interesting to note is how husband Bruce Sudano was sidelined here, with no contribution in any way, perhaps apart from spousal support. The *Donna Summer* album reached a disappointing #20 in the US, but a slightly better #13 in the UK.

It is interesting to speculate how *I'm a Rainbow* might have done if it had been allowed to be released instead. Would Donna have shifted into this fairly straightforward pop/R&B, or been allowed to keep experimenting, especially in the electronic space and with the onset of house music, which had already started bubbling up from Chicago's Black and gay (and some Black gay) clubs, and which then went mainstream in the second half of the 1980s? 'Love Is Just a Breath Away' was also the B-side to 'State of Independence'. In 1985, soul/R&B singer Carol Lynn Townes released her bouncy, synth-pop version of 'Love Is Just a Breath Away' on her second album, *Satisfaction Guaranteed*, produced by Rod Hui.

'Lush Life'

Writer: Billy Strayhorn
Producer: Quincy Jones

'I used to visit all the very gay places!' Jazz standard 'Lush Life' has been covered by many of the greatest singers of all time, including Ella Fitzgerald, Sarah Vaughan and Nat King Cole. Written by Billy Strayhorn during the Great Depression when he was just in his early twenties, the world-weary lyrics of 'Lush Life' have taken on a genuinely timeless quality. In 2022 Jared Young, on respected music site somethingelsereviews.com, listed his top twenty versions of

'Lush Life', ranking Donna's higher than Ella Fitzgerald at #3 (but behind #2 Blossom Dearie and #1 Johnny Hartman and John Coltrane), writing, 'Donna sells it!' She sure does. 'Quincy—or Q as we called him—was ever positive, a real trouper. He hung in there until I could accomplish what we had set out to do,' Donna laughed. 'He challenged me to sing the most incredible jazz song, "Lush Life". After having to sing it so many times, I learned what the term "paying your dues" really meant.'

14

She Works Hard for the Money (1983)

She Works Hard For The Money
Mercury: 812 265 1
Originally released: June 1983

'She Works Hard for the Money'	5:19
'Stop, Look and Listen'	5:46
'He's a Rebel'	4:22
'Woman'	4:19
'Unconditional Love'	4:41
'Love Has a Mind of Its Own'	4:16
'Tokyo'	4:25
'People, People'	4:38
'I Do Believe (I Fell in Love)'	4:34

'She Works Hard for the Money'

Mercury: 812 370-7. Single release: May 1983
Writers: Donna Summer, Michael Omartian
Producer: Michael Omartian

Contractually obligated to deliver her old record label one more album (although Casablanca had by now been swallowed up by Dutch multinational PolyGram), Donna wasn't going to merely go through the motions. 'As long as I was going to do it, even though I wasn't in a particularly good frame of mind,' she wrote in her *Ordinary Girl* memoir, 'I set about making the best record I knew how to make.' The album's title track and lead single 'She Works Hard for the Money' was, according to Donna, 'based partly on my ongoing fascination with the working woman. I saw it as a follow-up to "Bad Girls" that also offered some insight as to how I was feeling about the whole music industry.'

The final song written for Donna's new album would become its impassioned first single and the big hit she so desperately needed. It was inspired by a Grammys afterparty for Julio Iglesias that Donna attended in February 1983 where she spotted ladies' room attendant Onetta Johnson (who gets namechecked in the lyrics) asleep. Donna scribbled the words 'she works hard for the money' on a piece of toilet paper her manager Susan Munao handed her. The next day Donna phoned her producer Michael Omartian and sang him the melody and some of the lyrics she had written at Chasen's nightclub the night before. 'He loved it and immediately put down a track in less than 24 hours,' she recalled. 'I went to his studio the next day and wrote the rest of the words to the song at the microphone.' Donna was actually overwhelmed by how big a hit it became. 'The song became an anthem for many working-class people and the single shot up the charts,' she chuckled. 'Because no one had anticipated its success, it threw everyone at both labels into a king-sized tizzy! PolyGram was upset because I was back on top and they had let me out of my contract. That meant whatever follow-up was to be it wasn't going to be for them. They had a top ten lame duck on their hands.'

Geffen Records were also upset because Donna had a hit with her old label and felt she should have saved the material for them, 'especially after it went on to become one of the biggest albums I'd had in a long time'. The song's memorable guitar solo was by Toto's Steve Lukather. The single hit #3 in the US but only #25 in the UK, although it went top five in Australia, Canada, Finland, France and Sweden. It ended up as Donna's biggest US hit of the 1980s. The *She Works Hard for the Money* album, meanwhile, peaked at #9 in the US and #28 in the UK. Onetta even agreed to be photographed for the back of the *She Works Hard for the Money* album cover.

Donna's feminist/working-class anthem was nominated for Best Pop Vocal Performance at the 1984 Grammys, ironically won by Irene Cara's 'Flashdance... What a Feeling', co-written and produced by Giorgio Moroder. That must have stung! 'A lot of my biggest songs have been about pain,' Donna pointed out once, 'even if their arrangements were upbeat and worked against it—'She Works Hard for the Money', 'On the Radio', 'Last Dance', 'Bad Girls', 'Enough is Enough'—the list goes on and on'. Kelly Clarkson also covered this now eighties classic on her talk show, with *Billboard* claiming she had 'brought back disco'.

Vid bit!

Director: Brian Grant

'She Works Hard for the Money' is notable not just for being the first video by a Black woman to be put in high rotation on MTV in the US, but also for Donna finally joining the music video age with gusto. The plot is simple—hard-working, working-class women in service jobs and sweatshops, who take to dancing their frustrations off in the streets in their uniforms, while Donna reminds us all to treat them right, alright? Director Grant already had some classic music videos on his resumé, including Olivia Newton-John's 'Physical', M's 'Pop Muzik' and Peter Gabriel's 'Shock the Monkey', when he worked hard for Donna's money. She was so impressed with his work that she tapped him not only to direct her next video, 'Unconditional Love', but also her HBO *Donna Summer: A Hot Summer Night* television special/concert/long-form video. In a further nod to 'She Works Hard for the Money', Donna had a cameo in 1984 as a waitress in Frank Sinatra's 'LA is My Lady' video; the song co-written and produced by Quincy Jones.

Remix fix!

2023's 40th-anniversary edition of *She Works Hard for the Money* added a club mix and instrumental of the title track alongside a club mix and instrumental of 'Unconditional Love'. A year later, in 2024, a new EP featuring four thumping remixes by DJ John Michael was released through Peloton via Mercury Records. Presumably they're best heard during workouts.

'I Do Believe (I Fell in Love)'

Mercury: 812 370-7. Single release: May 1983
Writer: Donna Summer
Producer: Michael Omartian

Although the final track on the 'She Works Hard for the Money' single, this was another new track when it appeared as the B-side for the album's title track single. Donna co-wrote all nine of the tracks on *She Works Hard for the Money* and two she composed by herself: 'Woman' and album closer 'I Do Believe (I Fell in Love)'. In case you were wondering if 'I Do Believe (I Fell in Love)' was yet another heartfelt love song written for her husband Bruce Sudano, then yup, you better believe it's true. The giveaway is the line 'Oh, Charlie B don't you run away', because his full name is Bruce Charles Sudano. However, it wouldn't be until 34 years later this lost Donna twinkly love song finally fell into wider consciousness. Used in season two, chapter nine, of Netflix's hit television series *Stranger Things*, set in the 1980s, it was in good company alongside other eighties ladies Pat Benatar ('Love is a Battlefield') and Olivia Newton-John ('Twist of Fate'). If you want to find the *Stranger Things* scene that Donna literally fell into, search for 'Billy's at the door'.

'I liked that song,' Bruce Sudano told *Pop Matters* in 2020, 'more than I liked it for me I liked it for Donna. I just thought it revealed an interesting part of her persona that frequently gets glossed over, because she embodied a lot of mystery in a lot of different ways. People felt like they knew her because she was so accessible in so many ways, but there were also so many layers to who she was. That song reflected that little bit of mystery she possessed.'

'Stop, Look and Listen'

Mercury: 818071-1. Single release: January 1984 (UK)
Writers: Donna Summer, Greg Phillinganes, Michael Omartian
Producer: Michael Omartian

As a teenage girl in the early 1960s, one of Donna's favourite pastimes was watching Diana Ross and The Supremes perform on television 'and seeing how hard they worked to get there—how much energy and time they had to put into their careers.' Like an updated Diana Ross and The Supremes tune, Donna's 'Stop, Look and Listen' tune gives a titular nod to their 1965 #1 'Stop! In the Name of Love'. Around this time, incidentally, the supremely talented trio recorded a ballad called *Stop, Look & Listen*, composed by Ed Cobb (who also wrote *Tainted Love*) and produced by Motown founder Berry Gordy. *Rolling Stone*'s reviewer noted that Donna's arrangement of 'Stop Look and Listen' is 'jauntily upbeat, despite the fact Summer is actually trying to rewrite "Sounds of Silence" (with lines such as "The prophets of the times are written on streetcar walls").'

The third UK single from the *She Works Hard for the Money* album, 'Stop, Look and Listen' managed to get to #57 in the British charts. The single cover, featuring a live shot of Donna open-mouthed and singing into a microphone— also used for the laserdisc of *A Hot Summer Night* concert special—might be the worst designed single of her career. The mix is a 3:43 edit of the 12-inch remix of 5:43, while other territories opted for a 4:09 edit of the album version. Without a video to give it a promo push, or the likelihood of Donna putting in an appearance on seminal British television show *Top of the Pops*, the single was ultimately doomed not to ride high in the UK charts. The Canadian release of 'Stop, Look and Listen' went with a better cover: Donna in a posed photo wearing black and holding a lace umbrella (because that was the sort of thing you did back in the 1980s, clearly).

Co-writer of the track, Detroit-born Greg Phillinganes, had worked with a who's who of the music world since beginning his career in 1976. In 2014, he served as musical director for the 2014 Women of Soul performance at The White House. In front of President Barack Obama and First Lady Michelle, soul sisters Aretha Franklin, Patti LaBelle, Ariana Grande and Jill Scott performed. When Donna had died two years earlier, President Obama had paid her tribute, saying, 'Michelle and I were saddened to hear about the passing of Donna Summer. A five-time Grammy Award winner, Donna truly was the "Queen of Disco". Her voice was unforgettable and the music industry has lost a legend far too soon. Our thoughts and prayers go out to Donna's family and her dedicated fans.'

'He's a Rebel'

Writers: Donna Summer, Jay Graydon, Michael Omartian
Producer: Michael Omartian

It was a meeting of brave Christian soldiers when Donna and Michael Omartian came together to work on what would be the *She Works Hard for the Money* album. Omartian was openly Christian, having been involved in faith music since the late 1960s and recording a number of Christian rock records, as well as producing Christian music albums for other artists. However, he was also heavily involved in non-Christian music, winning three Grammy awards in 1980 for his work with Christopher Cross. 'I met Donna Summer in 1980,' he recalled in 2012. 'She heard the Christopher Cross record and was very interested in working with me. I went to her house in Los Angeles to meet her and we sat in a large room with wood floors and no windows. There was a piano in the middle of the room and she asked me to play a song so she could sing. I really don't remember what the song was, but I almost fell off the piano bench when she started to sing. I was familiar with the "disco queen" stuff, but I never heard her really "belt" out a tune.' Listening now to the punky, thrashy new wave Christian rock that is 'He's a Rebel', it could almost be heard as Donna's response to The Sex Pistols' 'God Save the Queen'. 'Ooh, he's a rebel, written up in the Lamb's book of life,' she hollers, referencing Christian scripture. It's actually a section of the Bible containing the names of those chosen for salvation who will inherit eternal life. *Rolling Stone* sagely pointed out that 'He's a Rebel', with its *West Side Story* sense of drama, could also be about James Dean, not Jesus Christ. Little wonder 'He's a Rebel' won the Grammy for Best Inspirational Performance in 1984—it was Donna's first win, but not her last, in that category.

'Woman'

Mercury: DONNA 2. Single release: August 1983 (B-side of 'Unconditional Love')
Writers: Donna Summer, Bruce Sudano, Jay Graydon, Michael Omartian
Producer: Michael Omartian

Like a less catchy, yet funkier 'She Works Hard for the Money', 'Woman' is a similar call out to women, except this time it appears to be 'treat that man real good like you know you should'. This must be where the clash between a hint of feminism and Donna's conservative Christianity came out to play. The song also featured rhythm guitar by Ray Parker Jnr, who at that time was enjoying some solo success after leaving the band Raydio. The following year, in 1984, he would score a #1 US single with the theme from the movie *Ghostbusters* ('Who you gonna call?'), which he wrote and produced, and eventually became his signature song. That same year, Ray also appeared with actress Nell Carter duetting on Donna's hit 'Heaven Knows' on the television sitcom *Gimme a Break*. Parker would later also record for the Geffen label.

Guitarist/songwriter Jay Graydon is one of the few non-Black performers to win a Grammy in the R&B category (twice!). He got his gongs in 1980 for co-writing 'After the Love Has Gone' for Earth, Wind & Fire and in 1983 for co-writing 'Turn Your Love Around' for George Benson. He had also previously played guitar on Donna's *Bad Girls* album. 'Woman' was also the B-side to the single release of 'Unconditional Love'. Released a month after Donna's album in 1983 was the debut album from the woman who would go on to define pop music in the 1980s and beyond: Madonna. Reviewers couldn't help but notice the similarities between the newcomer and Donna Summer on the *Madonna* album. In *Smash Hits* magazine, journalist Dave Rimmer tellingly wrote that her electro-disco set was 'not bad—if she stopped trying to be "Madonna Summer" it could be great'.

'Unconditional Love'

Mercury: 814 088-7. Single release: August 1983
Writers: Donna Summer, Michael Omartian
Producer: Michael Omartian

This sprightly, bright reggae-lite tune was a true change of pace as the second single from the *She Works Hard for the Money* album after the chartbusting title track. The use of the word 'agape' (Greek for love) is just one of 'Unconditional Love's numerous quirks. The line 'a new kind of love and we call it agape' also refers to a type of non-sexual or Christian love and giving love entirely unselfishly. In many ways, it's a bold choice because at times there's more of 'additional vocals' Musical Youth on 'Unconditional Love' than there is Donna.

'Unconditional Love' still managed a respectable #14 UK hit, but was a disappointing #43 in the US. As further evidence of their, erm, unconditional love for each other, Donna provided additional vocals ('Hello? Hello?') on the track 'Incommunicado 'from Musical Youth's 1983 second album *Different Style!* through Geffen Records in the US. It was written by Donna's husband Bruce Sudano with Carlotta McKee and Gordon Grote and produced by Peter Collins. The story of what became of Musical Youth is indeed a cautionary music industry tale, with two of the five band members since passing away. In 1986, 'Unconditional Love' was thrashingly covered by pioneers of the Christian punk genre with the non-ironic name of Altar Boys. 'Unconditional Love' also featured in 2018's *Summer: The Donna Summer Musical.*

Vid bit!

Director: David Mallett

Donna appears as a straightlaced teacher trying to control an unruly Musical Youth, but then—spoiler alert!—peels off her dowdy dress to reveal a glittery disco era gown. The video was shot at London's King Athelstan Primary School and the Bonner Hill Road Girls School, the latter being demolished. Musician, DJ and film director Don Letts, who conceived and directed Musical Youth's video for 'Pass the Dutchie', called 'Unconditional Love' the death knell for the band, leading them from being a legitimate reggae act to an overly commercial pop act. Also view Donna and Musical Youth duetting on stage to 'Unconditional Love' during the *Hot Summer Night* special/concert with more of a calypso feel. Donna wears such a huge-ruffled dress it's a wonder she can move (but she still manages to shimmy on stage).

Remix fix!
The Club Mix of 'Unconditional Love' is actually more an extended version, adding two minutes or more to the single version's running time.

'Love Has a Mind of Its Own'

Mercury: 814 922-7. Single release: December 1983
Writers: Donna Summer, Bruce Sudano, Michael Omartian
Producer: Michael Omartian

The third, perfunctory funk single from the *She Works Hard for the Money* album was an uncredited duet with Matthew Ward who formed the band 2nd Chapter of Acts (1973–88) with his sisters Annie and Nellie. Ward is considered one of the pioneers of the genre originally called Jesus music, later renamed contemporary Christian music. He also contributed backing vocals on the album with 'Tokyo'. Was his name omitted from the single release because this was an interracial duet? Donna was clearly doing him a favour by introducing him to the non-secular mainstream. Ward later sang background vocals for LeAnn Rimes and Jordin Sparks.

'Donna and I co-wrote that beautiful song with Michael Omartian,' Bruce explained about the genesis of the song. 'We met Matthew through Michael and he just has an amazing voice. When Donna was in the studio working on the *She Works Hard for the Money* album, she gave me the track for "Love Has a Mind of Its Own" for me to write the lyrics. From the time of her giving me the track and the day of the recording, we had a husband-and-wife disagreement. She went to the studio that day having no idea if I would even show up or whether I had written the lyrics. I used the disagreement as an inspiration, wrote the lyrics, showed up in the studio, handed it to her and they sang the song.'

Peaking at just #70 in the US, the decision was made to release the more chart-friendly 'Stop, Look and Listen' in other territories as the third single from the *She Works Hard for the Money* album. There were also duelling Donna releases as Casablanca's re-release of *Love to Love You Baby* was issued in November 1983. 'Love Has a Mind of Its Own' did become the fourth UK single with 'People, People' on the B-side, but failed to chart.

'Tokyo'

Writers: Donna Summer, Bruce Sudano, Michael Omartian
Producer: Michael Omartian

Despite its title, there is little Japanese influence to be found or heard on this track, on which Donna lyrically weaves a convoluted tale about living her life in Tokyo after receiving a message. Just what exactly 'a double agent amnesty/ An Ian Fleming mystery' really means might be forever open to interpretation. Donna was a frequent visitor to the land of the rising sun, touring there four times during her lifetime. While Donna's co-writing on this album is a big deal—especially considering she had given birth to her third child just a few months earlier—what about her husband Bruce getting his name as co-writer on four of the tracks? *The Village Voice*'s Robert Christgau gave the *She Works Hard for the Money* album a 'B+' rating, stating, 'in which schlocky Michael Omartian replaces magic man Quincy Jones and Summer is born again.' Michael Hall, reviewing the album for *Rolling Stone*, wrote, 'as the title implies, Donna Summer is getting down to business. You may be surprised, though, at what sort of business she means. *She Works Hard for the Money*, in marked contrast to last year's grandly overreaching *Donna Summer*, functions as efficient entertainment, but, like Summer herself, it's all in service to the Lord. Summer and producer Michael Omartian are both gone-public born-agains who haven't lost their commercial bent, and that's their saving grace.' 'Tokyo' was sampled in 2006 by Italian rappers Club Dogo on their track 'You Know NA-MI.'

'People, People'

Writers: Donna Summer, Bruce Sudano, Michael Omartian
Producer: Michael Omartian

Another narrative song, this time about 'a runaway child', the strident 'People, People' was released as a single in the Netherlands and Bolivia only, but failed to chart in either territory. Donna said things started to go downhill at Geffen Records after the release of *She Works Hard for the Money* when Donna delivered her old label a big hit record. 'A rumour was printed I was homophobic, which caused unnecessary pain for my fans and for me,' she wrote in her *Ordinary Girl* memoir. 'David Geffen publicly denounced the story and urged me to do the same.' She didn't and her career suffered thereafter. So, people (people) it's time, finally, to address the pink elephant in the room—did Donna make homophobic statements in 1983 after one of her concerts or not?

The alleged incident supposedly happened after her concert in Atlantic City. Asking her audience if they wanted to stay after the show so she could spread the gospel, she quipped that the Bible spoke about 'Adam and Eve, not Adam and Steve'. During a discussion with an audience member who identified as having AIDS, Donna reportedly declared, 'I have seen the evils of homosexuality. AIDS is the result of your sins.' In her embrace of born-again Christianity, it seemed that Donna had not just abandoned disco and her sex symbol past; her apparent abandonment of her gay fans in the middle of the AIDS crisis was viewed as a grave betrayal. Two long years later, in 1985, she issued a statement to gay publication *The Advocate* insisting, 'since the very beginning of my career, I have had tremendous support and friendship from the gay community. It is a source of great concern to me that anything I may have said has cast me as homophobic. All I can ask for is understanding as I believe my true feelings have been misrepresented.' Two years later she placed an ad in a Fire Island AIDS benefit stating, 'anything attributed to me in the past that may have hurt the Gay Community I hereby repudiate as these are not my feelings and never have been'. In 1989, she wrote a letter to AIDS activist organisation ACT-UP, insisting she 'did not say God is punishing gays with AIDS. I did not sit with ill intentions in judgement over your lives ... can't we just forgive each other for this past confusion?'. That same year Donna told *The Advocate*, 'What I supposedly said I did not say and my reference to AIDS was really an innocent reference,' adding that she didn't fully understand what AIDS was at the time. In 1991, she sued *New York* magazine for printing the rumour as true (the case was settled out of court) and appeared on VH1's *Behind the Music* to refute the claims. In 1999, Donna addressed her gay fans/critics via *The Southern Voice* saying, 'I'm sorry if I said something that hurt you, that was not my intention. Even if it's a complete falsehood or misunderstanding, I'm sorry that you were hurt by it.' People, people, it's time to move on and let this go, toot toot, ah, beep beep!

15

Cats Without Claws (1984)

Cats Without Claws
Geffen: GHS 24040
Originally released: September 1984

Side One		Side Two	
'Supernatural Love'	3:33	'Oh Billy Please'	4:55
'It's Not the Way'	4:22	'Eyes'	4:45
'There Goes My Baby'	4:05	'Maybe It's Over'	4:43
'Suzanna'	4:29	'I'm Free'	4:29
'Cats Without Claws'	4:20	'Forgive Me'	4:30

'There Goes My Baby'

Geffen: 7-29291. Single release: July 1984
Writers: Benjamin Nelson, George Treadwell, Lover Patterson
Producer: Michael Omartian

Hoping to make chart magic strike for a second time, Donna teamed up with producer and co-writer Michael Omartian for their second album together. Sadly, it couldn't better, let alone match, the success they'd had the previous year with *She Works Hard for the Money*. The *Cats Without Claws* album came in for both a critical and commercial mauling. Released a whole two months ahead of the album was lead single 'There Goes My Baby', a cover of a 1959 US #2 single for pop/R&B vocal group The Drifters. The song's co-writer Benjamin Nelson was better known by his stage name of Ben E. King, The Drifters' lead singer, while George Treadwell was the band's manager and Lover Patterson their road manager. 'On the fourth day of working on the album, Donna said, "There's a song by The Drifters I've always loved!" and that was basically it!' Michael Omartian explained.

> We started with a real simple synth track and the positive responses we got from many, many people made us put in on the LP. One of the last things we had to do was to cut five songs because there was so much good material, but there was never any doubt about 'There Goes My Baby'.

FYI: those five songs have so far never been recovered (though one may have been B-side 'Face the Music'). Donna's version of *There Goes My Baby* puts a female spin on The Drifters' classic but peaked at just #21 in the US— ominously her last US top-40 hit for five years—and a lowly #99 in the UK. *Smash Hits* reviewed the 'There Goes My Baby' single with scribe Dave Rimmer complaining: 'If Donna Summer hadn't made, in *She Works Hard for the Money*, one of my favourite records of last year, then this rather flat, mid-paced and half- hearted song might not have come as such a crushing disappointment. But it did.' 'There Goes My Baby' might also be the first (and last?) Donna Summer record that never warranted a remix or extended version.

Vid bit!
Director: Ian Leech
'There Goes My Baby' opens with a one-minute black and white dramatic theatre piece between Donna and husband Bruce Sudano. The main part of the video is set during the Second World War, with Donna waiting for Bruce to come back from his military service as she struggles to cope with her husband far away in a war zone. She sends letters, he doesn't respond, the other solders come home and then—surprise!—Bruce is back and they are reunited. After the memorable 'She Works Hard for the Money' video this was a major comedown. If nothing else, Donna looks great in her 1940s outfits and Bruce really did have the looks to be a movie matinée idol. Director Leech obviously made an impression on Donna with his music video for The Stray Cats' '(She's) Sexy & 17', but after directing 'There Goes My Baby' he appears to have never made another music video.

'Maybe It's Over'

Geffen: 7-29291. Single release: July 1984 (B-side to 'There Goes My Baby')
Writer: Donna Summer
Producer:Michael Omartian

The B-side to 'There Goes My Baby', and the middle track on side two of the *Cats Without Claws* album, 'Maybe It's Over' is the only solo songwriting contribution out of its ten tracks by Donna. It's not a new song either as it was originally written for her sisters, recording under the name of Sunshine.

Back then, the title was the more definite 'It's Over', recorded in 1979 for Sunshine's album, *Watching Daddy Dance*, which ultimately was shelved and never released due to Donna's ongoing legal wrangle with Casablanca Records. That it magically reappeared some five years later, after that legal battle had ended, tends to suggest the material Donna left in the Casablanca vaults was also finally returned to her. Was it worth the wait? What the production may lack, Donna's unmatchable vocals make up for. Omartian adored giving his audience early indicators of what the coming track would be, and this being a ballad it's signposted by a ponderous saxophone within the first ten seconds of 'Maybe It's Over'. Speaking of things being over, *Cats Without Claws* ominously became Donna's first album not to go gold in the US since 1975.

'Supernatural Love'

Geffen: 9 29142-7. Single release: October 1984
Writers: Donna Summer, Bruce Sudano, Michael Omartian
Producer: Michael Omartian

Should the perky 'Supernatural Love' have been the first single from *Cats Without Claws*? Perhaps so, but as the second single it stalled at #75 in the US charts and failed to chart anywhere else. Quizzed by the late Paula Yates in a British television interview in 1984 on just what 'Supernatural Love' is, Donna replied, 'everything in my life has a double meaning'. On *American Bandstand*, Donna told host Dick Clark that working with husband Bruce and producer Michael Omartian was a family affair. 'We work together and sometimes Michael and I write a song and my husband writes the lyrics and we get together and collaborate. We're a family—we sing that (Sister Sledge) song all the time.' During Christie's 2023 exhibition/auction of 'The Collection of Donna Summer', the single cover design for 'Supernatural Love', credited to photographer Harry Langdon and Art Hotel, with notes for the designer, was estimated to go for up to $800. In the end it sold for a whopping $17,640.

Vid bit!

Director: Irv Goodnoff
Some fans consider the 'Supernatural Love' video the worst of Donna's 1980s career. Donna and husband Bruce cavort about in little more than loincloths, while her hair couldn't possibly get any bigger (was it this which caused a hole in the ozone layer?). Just when you thought it couldn't get more eighties, Donna and Bruce are both transported to 1984, where Donna's outrageous matching make-up and hairstyle appear to have been borrowed from Boy George. Bruce also seems to have more eyeliner than Donna. Yet here they were as an interracial couple playing an interracial couple, which in 1984 was still a big deal. Donna's parents are also in the video, sitting at a table. We have a soft spot for the ridiculous dance/

chase sequence, although it's clear Bruce is no great actor (or dancer). After this supernatural fiasco Donna wouldn't make another music video for three long years.

Remix fix!
Donna's old pal Jürgen Koppers—who also mixed three of the tracks on the *Cats Without Claws* album—did the honours on the original extended dance mix of 'Supernatural Love'. There's also a slightly different UK mix but still the same length of 6:12. On the *Cats Without Claws (40th Anniversary)* American remixer, Jason Arnold's ShyBoy Remix stripped 'Supernatural Love' of its clunky eighties production, making it glisten brightly like a gleaming mirrorball.

'It's Not the Way'

Warner Bros. Records: U 9103. Single release: May 1985 (UK) (B-side to 'Eyes')
Writers: Donna Summer, Michael Omartian
Producer: Michael Omartian

Cats Without Claws is definitely a Marmite release for Donna Summer fans— you either love it or hate it. It was a more personal album, showcasing Donna's desire to bring gospel and religion to the masses, yet without any obvious big hits it was doomed to be a hard sell. It also becomes clear that Michael Omartian was no Giorgio Moroder. This rather disposable, fluffy tune features more squealing guitar noises and some of Donna's most opaque lyrics—'your heart's like an elevator' and 'your love is like a nasty habit'. In the end, 'It's Not the Way' was never considered a single contender, winding up the B-side to the 'Eyes' single. You have to wonder if any of those five songs chopped from *Cats Without Claws* might have been a better replacement for 'It's Not the Way', but that wasn't the way! It's also worth considering that *Cats Without Claws* came exactly a decade after Donna's first album, 1974's *Lady of the Night*. To put it another way, that's eleven studio albums in ten years at the same time as Donna had two marriages, three children and two record labels. Little wonder she disappeared from the music biz for three years after *Cats Without Claws*. The PopMatters website, in a retrospective of Donna albums in 2012, wrote, 'the breakneck tempo of "It's Not the Way" afforded Summer a chance to incorporate some gospel flourishes', but deemed the entire *Cats Without Claws* album 'a bit stylistically eclectic'.

'Suzanna'

Writers: Donna Summer, Michael Omartian
Producer: Michael Omartian

'Suzanna you better watch your mouth/Suzanna bad things are coming out', Donna informs us as she goes freeform style. There is a decent tune buried somewhere on 'Suzanna', but it keeps getting defeated by Omartian's overly busy, so-very-eighties, thudding production. 'On the last album, we began writing together and found we really enjoyed the procedure,' Omartian said after the completion of the *Cats Without Claws* album.

> I have a 24-track studio at home and Donna and I would spend about five or six hours a day working there. She's really gifted with melodies, so we put together a tune with drum machines and then put it away. Two weeks later we'd take it all out, review it and select what we wanted. Word gets around, so we also received lots of material—about 100 cassettes of tunes—from friends and publishers. I had someone listen to all of it for me, but in the end, it worked out our collaborations were going so well Donna wanted to keep the writing between herself, her husband Bruce and me.

Donna's long-time percussionist and band member Bob Conti had a different take on Donna's musical output at this stage. In an interview some years later, he claimed, 'Donna wasn't committed to just making great music anymore, but about making a great religious statement through the music and that was enough for me to move on.' *Cats Without Claws* would be the second and final studio album Donna would make with Michael Omartian, despite their intimate Christian 'agape' connection. In 2000, however, Donna reteamed with Omartian for *Child of the Promise*, a religious album (see Chapter 21).

Remix fix!
Ladies on Mars provided a 4:31 remix on the *Cats Without Claws (40th Anniversary)* reissue, adding an updated disco groove, shedding new light on Donna's 'not nice' lyrics.

'Cats Without Claws'

Writers: Donna Summer, Michael Omartian
Producer: Michael Omartian

Cue cat noises on the tape! With its constant tempo changes, Donna delivering a spoken word performance during the pseudo-religious verses and a central chorus metaphor that doesn't really make much sense, 'Cats Without Claws' sadly lives up to its title. Interestingly, the original album title was *Framed*, which may have been one of the five songs eventually cut from the track list. When it came time to do press for the *Cats Without Claws* album, Donna passed a lot of the PR duties to the other main man in her life: co-writer and producer Michael Omartian (with three kids at home it's easy to understand why). Asked about the album's title track, Omartian insisted it was:

> a very visual song, like a movie-type theme, using sound effects like you would behind pictures. It's taken from scenes of New York City life—gangs, drugs, street people—who are trying to be tough but are really like anybody else. They've got barks worse than their bites and they've really been decided, tricked into this negative life. They're like cats without claws.

Billboard's album review noted, 'several songs are religiously themed, most notably Reba Rambo's "Forgive Me".' *The Village Voice*'s Robert Christgau gave the album a B rating, adding a note of caution: 'what made the last album was two undeniably singular singles. This time she leads with a cover, which Ben E. King sang better a quarter-century ago.' *People* magazine went even further on the attack, deeming the *Cats Without Claws* 'unimaginative material'. In 2021, however, there was a positive reappraisal of the *Cats Without Claws* album by medium.com's Gregory Cox, who called it an 'overlooked gem'. He also wrote that 'as a result of lacklustre singles, forgettable music videos and a controversial rumour, *Cats Without Claws* suffered', but he insisted it 'deserves more attention'.

'Oh Billy Please'

Writers: Donna Summer, Michael Omartian
Producer: Michael Omartian

Donna's choice for the first *Cats Without Claws* single, 'Oh Billy Please' (which really did grammatically require a comma after the word 'oh') ended up not being a single at all. Geffen decided that going with a cover version of 'There Goes My Baby', was the safest option. That may have just robbed Donna of another big hit, as the more you listen to 'Oh Billy Please', the more it lodges in your ears and refuses to leave. Perhaps the reason Geffen execs voted against it was not because it's a bad song, but because it suffers from Omartian's 'kitchen sink' approach to production. Here, once again, he tacks on another unwanted squealing guitar. Was there really nothing more inventive Omartian could have thought of? Imagine 'Oh Billy Please' with the kind of lavish, glossy production Giorgio Moroder gave to Irene Cara's 'Why Me' in 1983, or in 1984 to both Freddie Mercury's gripping 'Love Kills' and Limahl's dreamy theme song to *The Neverending Story*. That is truly what the bulk of the material needed on the *Cats Without Claws* album—a visionary musical genius.

Remix fix!

Ladies on Mars provided a tasteful, if not completely pleasing, 4:03 remix on the *Cats Without Claws (40th Anniversary)* edition, emphasising Donna's unforgettable vocal hook on 'Oh Billy Please'. Can we just say the bonus disc of new remixes might just constitute the best Donna Summer album never to get a release in its own right? Oh, yes, it's that good!

Donna pictured at her home in Munich after the premiere of *Haare (Hair)* in 1968. Just 19, the then Donna Gaines left her home in the US to move to what was then West Germany to star in a production of *Hair*, called *Haare*, learning the language phonetically, before learning to speak it. 'I went into the show a teenager and I came out a woman,' Donna said. 'It was my university, my finishing school and my playground all rolled into one.' (*Alamy stock photo*)

25-year-old Donna pictured in 1974, the year her single 'The Hostage' was released. 'I had a really good song, a disco thing about kidnapping,' Donna insisted about 'The Hostage' from her *Lady Of The Night* debut (which features almost no disco). 'The last line was "his funeral was yesterday!" It was a great dance tune, I don't know why it didn't do better in the charts, I think it was because of the subject matter.' Yep, probably. (*Alamy stock photo*)

The 'First Lady of Love' enjoying the success of 'Love To Love You Baby' in early 1976. 'With "Love To Love You Baby" I came up with the image of Marilyn Monroe singing the song in that light and fluffy, but highly sensual, voice of hers,' Donna explained about her iconic muse for the 1975 single, which garnered her the 'First Lady Of Love' media title. 'Hers was the image I used when I laid down the first vocal track for the day.' Some like it hot! (*Alamy stock photo*)

Appearing on the aptly-titled West German music TV show *Disco* on 24 April 1976. 'After the *Love To Love You Baby* album we did *A Love Trilogy*,' Pete Bellotte said. 'I used to go into the English bookshop and bought Mervyn Peake's *Gormenghast* trilogy. The idea of a trilogy appealed to me. I came up with the idea of one side with three songs and the fourth track would be the three songs going into the fourth—our first concept album.' (*Alamy stock photo*)

Donna posing for the newspaper cameras during a promotional visit to London in 1976. Donna's second 1976 album was *Four Seasons Of Love*. 'I'd just read Lawrence Durrell's *Alexandria Quartet*,' Pete Bellotte explained, 'and thought it would be good to do one song for each season.' American photographer Mario Casilli snapped Donna in four different 'calendar' looks, including Donna as 'Black Marilyn' for the winter quarter/back cover. (*Alamy stock photo*)

By 1977 Donna had not only become a big star, but also a major touring attraction. 1977's 'I Remember Yesterday' was inspired by the shifting eras of Anthony Powell's 'Dance To The Music Of Time'. 'We started off with a dance band in "I Remember Yesterday" and "Love's Unkind",' Pete recalled. 'A take on The Shirelles' "Back In Love Again", a Supremes style funk thing "Black Lady"; disco with "Make Me" … and then I said we've got to have a futuristic song!' (*Alamy stock photo*)

Donna pictured with daughter, Mimi, her muse for 1977's *Once Upon A Time* album. 'Donna worked for ten years and suffered a very hard life with her daughter,' Giorgio told *NME* in 1977, 'and some of that has come out in *Once Upon A Time*'. That same year Donna told *Rolling Stone*, '*Once Upon A Time* is the first record I can really say is part of me'. She later clarified that she wrote this unique disco fairy tale 'for my daughter (Mimi)'. Aww. (*Alamy stock photo*)

A billboard on LA's Sunset Strip advertising Donna's *Live and More* album in 1978. 'Tonight is a very important night for me,' Donna proclaimed during her first live album performance before singing "Mimi's Song". 'My little girl is here tonight and I don't think you understand what it's like being the daughter of someone who's always gone. It's kind of scary, it's kind of lonely and I guess sometimes you'd think to yourself, "Is mommy ever coming home?"' (*Alamy stock photo*)

Donna in *Thank God It's Friday,* winner of an Oscar in 1979 for its song 'Last Dance'. While 'Last Dance', credited to Paula Jabara, won for Best Original Song, Giorgio Moroder also won that year for Best Original Score for the movie *Midnight Express*. Donna got to sing 'Last Dance' on the night, which beat out Olivia Newton-John's 'Hopelessly Devoted To You' from *Grease*, plus songs from *Same Time Next Year, Foul Play* and *The Magic of Lassie*! (*Alamy stock photo*)

Donna during a cover photoshoot for *On The Radio: Greatest Hits Vol. 1 & II* in 1979. In November 2024 The Donna Summer Estate's label Driven By The Music re-released this album as *On The Radio: Greatest Hits* (*Expanded*), boasting forty Donna singles from 1975–2008. The original 1979 album included extended versions of 'On The Radio' and 'No More Tears (Enough Is Enough)', plus 'Our Love' and 'Sunset People', which went missing in 2024. (*Alamy stock photo*)

On TV for her 1980 show, *The Donna Summer Special*, in January 1980. On the show Donna sang a medley of 'Bridge Over Troubled Water' and 'The Way We Were' with Robert Guillaume. She also sang a live take of 'Starting Over Again', which she co-wrote with husband Bruce. Released as a single by Dolly Parton in February 1980, it hit #1 on the country charts, making Donna the first black co-writer ever to feature on a #1 country song. (*Alamy stock photo*)

Above: Donna married her second husband, Bruce Sudano from Brooklyn Dreams, in 1980. 'Donna always considered herself to be a wanderer,' Bruce said in 2020 for the deluxe fortieth anniversary edition of 1980's *The Wanderer* album. 'From the time she was a kid they would say she would wander. She was able to pull something from her youth, conceptually, and at the same time pull a musical style from her youth in terms of emulating Elvis.' (*Alamy stock photo*)

Below: Quincy Jones spotted with Donna in NYC in 1983, after producing her 1982 album. 'At that I time I was pregnant, feeling very insecure, very non-musical, very unproductive,' Donna said in 1982 about her album, 'and all you want to create are baby clothes. You want to paint the room and don't really want to get into music. Quincy was a disciplinarian at a time when he really needed to be for me and that really helped me to get through the album.' (*Alamy stock photo*)

She works hard for the ... cake? Celebrating 1983's 'comeback' hit with husband Bruce. Donna also released the *A Hot Summer Night* video/laserdisc in 1983, filmed for HBO in front of 18,000 fans. In 2020 a remastered live CD/DVD (DBTMSNCD83) was issued by Driven By The Music. In 1983 *Attitude* picked then unreleased 'Forgive Me' as the stand-out cut, stating, 'had there been a roof on that California venue she'd surely have blown it off'. (*Alamy stock photo*)

Giving big skirt twirls on French TV show *Lahaye d'honneur* on 30 October 1987. In July 1987 Casablanca issued the fab *The Dance Collection: A Compilation of 12" Singles* featuring: 'I Feel Love' (12-inch 8:14), 'With Your Love' (promo 12-inch 7:32), 'Last Dance' (promo 12-inch 8:11), 'MacArthur Park Suite' (17:47), 'Hot Stuff' (12-inch 6:46), 'Bad Girls' (4:55), 'Walk Away' (promo 12-inch 7:15), 'Dim All The Lights' (promo 12-inch 7:10) and 'No More Tears (Enough Is Enough)' (11:46). (*Alamy stock photo*)

Performing 'This Time I Know It's For Real' on the UK's *Top Of The Pops* in March 1989. For the cover of 1989's *Another Place and Time* album, Donna wore full Japanese-style kabuki make-up. 'I'm an artist and I paint and I like to do different things,' she explained in a TV interview that year. 'I've never been in a position to say, "Look, I'm doing this and I don't really care what anybody thinks about it. I'm gonna do what I want to do!", so I did it!' (*Alamy stock photo*)

Donna gives good face during *Another Place and Time* promo interviews in May 1989. During the same 1989 TV interview with Arsenio Hall, Donna revealed that husband Bruce Sudano had become her manager. 'He's just managing me temporarily,' she explained, 'because probably we'll be doing a TV show—about my life with my family—and he'll be acting in that.' That never transpired, but Bruce remained heavily involved in Donna's career. (*Alamy stock photo*)

Left: Donna revisiting her 'Black Marilyn' (her words!) look in 1991. Donna's penultimate studio album, *Mistaken Identity* (with blonde hair and blue eyes on the cover!) was produced by Keith Diamond, who died in 1997. Donna paid him tribute, writing, 'Keith the boy, Keith the man, Keith the friend, Keith the brother, Keith the song, can never be forgotten because he carved, with love, his name on the very flesh of our hearts'. (*Alamy stock photo*)

Below: Donna in front of one of her paintings at a gallery showing of her art in the late 1980s. She began painting seriously in the mid-1980s as an escape from the crazy music industry, describing her style as 'Neo-Primitive' or 'Abstract Impressionist'. 'I find it very therapeutic and very peaceful,' she said about her paintings, which fetched up to $150,000 each. 'For me it's like a quiet storm where I can just release everything on a piece of paper, or a canvas.' (*Alamy stock photo*)

Donna received her star on the Hollywood Walk of Fame on 18 March 1992. For the ceremony Donna was joined by Dick Clark and over 600 fans. Speaking about what a difficult year she had been through after losing her sister, Donna then dedicated new song 'Friends Unknown', from her 1991 album *Mistaken Identity*, to her fans, singing it live. There is decent footage of her speech and this hair-raising performance on YouTube. Watch it now! (*Alamy stock photo*)

Launching her autobiography *Ordinary Girl* and album *The Journey* in London in 2004. In her thanks on this 19-track single/27-track double CD Donna gave credit to photographer Harry Langdon. 'You always captured me in the right light,' she wrote, 'and put up with my creative craziness'. Donna also thanked Giorgio Moroder ('you're my big brother'), David Geffen ('honesty and generosity') and the late Neil Bogart ('a true visionary'). (*Alamy stock photo*)

Performing at Florida's Seminole Hard Rock Café and Casino on 18 August 2010. Ten years later, in 2020, Driven By The Music released *Encore*—a hefty box set of thirty-three (!!!) CDs containing all seventeen of Donna's studio albums, plus eight bonus discs of extras, as a limited edition of just 1,500 copies (DETMCDBOX02). The new centrepiece of the *Encore* album, however, was Junior Vasquez's masterful studio (re)mix of the unreleased 'My Life'. (*Alamy stock photo*)

Summer: The Donna Summer Musical on Broadway during its March–December run in 2018. Written by Oscar-nominee Colman Domino, Robert Cary and Des McAnuff, the musical received two Tony nominations: one for LaChanze as Best Actress in a Musical, and the other for Ariana DeBose for Best Featured Actress in a Musical. The show opened with 'The Queen is Back' from Donna's *Crayons* album and finished with—what else?—*TGIF*'s 'Last Dance'. (*Alamy stock photo*)

Donna performing at Universal Studios' Mardi Gras celebration in Orlando in 2004. She developed her vocal skills as a child through doing breathing exercises while listening to gospel legend Mahalia Jackson records in her parents' bedroom. 'I believe every good singer is an actress, or an actor,' said Donna, who got her start in church, then musical theatre. 'The ability to project an image of what they are singing is part of what the creativity is about.' (*Alamy stock photo*)

Donna's star on the Hollywood Walk of Fame on the day she died, 17 May 2012. 'Michelle and I were saddened to hear about the passing of Donna Summer,' then President Barack Obama said in a statement. 'A five-time Grammy Award winner, Donna truly was the "Queen of Disco". Her voice was unforgettable and the music industry has lost a legend far too soon. Our thoughts and prayers go out to Donna's family and her dedicated fans.' (*Alamy stock photo*)

The legendary Giorgio Moroder (and his legendary disco moustache) in the 1970s. Giorgio came full circle in 2013, remixing (with Chris Cox) 'Love To Love You Baby' on 2013's patchy posthumous *Love To Love You Donna* remix album. 'That song really made Donna and myself,' Giorgio informed Djhistory.com in 2024. 'First it started in the discotheques in America … but the BBC blocking it, that was a lot of promotion for the song.' (*Alamy stock photo*)

Above: Pete Bellotte (left) pictured with Giorgio and German singer Andrea in the early 1970s. On 1993's *The Donna Summer Anthology* Donna thanked Giorgio and (the elusive) Pete Bellotte, among other luminaries like Neil and Joyce Bogart and Paul Jabara and her manager Susan Munao. 'Through the good, the bad, the happy and the sad, you're always a part of me,' she wrote. 'You were with me from the beginning and remain in my heart eternally'. (*Alamy stock photo*)

Below: Summertime: (L-R) Brooklyn Sudano, Bruce Sudano, Mimi Dohler and Amanda Sudano. Donna's family pictured at the 2024 Grammy Awards when she was posthumously awarded the Grammy Lifetime Achievement Award. As The Donna Summer Estate they oversee reissues by the Driven By The Music label, the use of her name/image as in *Summer: The Donna Summer Musical*, auctions like Christie's and the *Love To Love You Donna Summer* doco. (*Alamy stock photo*)

LaDonna Adrian Gaines, aka Donna Summer (31 December 1948–17 May 2012). The legend of the Queen of Disco lives on, especially through extensive back catalogue reissues like 2026's *Summer Time: The Singles Collection 1974-2010* (DBTMCDBOX03), with a colossal forty CDs. A seven-CD boxset with no extras, *Donna Summer—The Casablanca Studio Albums* (DBTMLPBOX04), also from Driven By The Music, was due to be released in October 2026. (*Alamy stock photo*)

Donna—the Queen of Disco … and so much more. 'I didn't mind being called the Queen of Disco at first, because it was a title the public gave me, but titles can be very limiting. I'm a singer and always been a singer. I didn't start out singing disco, I started out singing in church. I've always tried to push the boundaries and do different things, whether rock, gospel, or country. I never wanted to be stuck in one box.' (*Author's personal Donna Summer collection*)

'Eyes'

Warner Bros. Records: U 9103. Single release: May 1985 (UK)
Writers: Donna Summer, Michael Omartian
Producer: Michael Omartian

At times, listening to the *Cats Without Claws* album it's as if Donna, Bruce and Michael had made a list of their favourite pop hits of the year then tried to emulate them. Play Rockwell's 'Somebody's Watching Me', a #2 hit from early 1984, with chorus vocals by a certain Michael Jackson, side by side with Donna's 'Eyes' and there can be little doubt about it. Donna even takes on a spooky voice in the verses like Rockwell's Halloween perennial. The chorus of 'there's always someone watching/Eyes' hammers home the comparison. Omartian couldn't help himself and tossed in another unlovely squealing guitar sound (and a solo at one point), which doesn't add anything to Donna's 'Eyes'. The album's lyric sheet includes three additional lines to the song, which must have been cut at some stage: 'TV's on somebody's watching/They're getting in through your eyes/ Don't let them poison your mind.' Sadly, Donna's 'Eyes' reached just #97 in the UK charts, which was still two places higher than 'There Goes My Baby' at #99. ('Supernatural Love' missed the top 100 altogether.) With no hint of a music video to give 'Eyes' some additional support, it too was like a cat without claws.

Remix fix!

Although Madonna had moved on from John 'Jellybean' Benitez, both personally and professionally, he was still very in-demand for his remix services. Geffen hooked him up with Donna's third *Cats Without Claws* single for the UK market, 'Eyes'. Not only was Benitez a remixer/producer—who brought 'Holiday' to Madonna's attention and produced it for her debut album—but he had also become a pop star in his own right. His 1984 single 'Sidewalk Talk' (written by Madonna) went top twenty in the US. Around the time his 'Eyes' hit the market—edited in length from the original and remixed—the ballad Jellybean produced for Madonna, 'Crazy for You', was reaching #1 in the US and #2 in the UK. Jellybean's original 6:58 extended mix of 'Eyes' also appears on the *Cats Without Claws (40th Anniversary)* release.

'I'm Free'

Warner Bros. Records: U9103T. Single release: May 1985 (UK)
Writers: Donna Summer, Bruce Sudano, Michael Omartian
Producer: Michael Omartian

Donna liked to call 'I'm Free' 'a song my husband wrote', but it's pretty obvious husband Bruce Sudano freely wrote this inspired by his faith in Jesus Christ.

'When Donna and I would write together to test the song we were writing, we would slow it down and do it as a ballad,' Bruce was at pains to explain. 'We always felt that if the song held up as a ballad both lyrically and melodically it could almost always translate to tempo.' With lyrics such as 'the only thing that matters is that you've worked a miracle in me' and 'you saved me right in time', it's pretty clear 'I'm Free' is veiled contemporary Christian pop/dance music. With its calypso feel and grabby vocoder snatches, a throwback to 'Love is in Control (Finger on the Trigger)', 'I'm Free' still thrives as jaunty, joyful noise. It would also sound great on a dancefloor and now seems like the obvious hit from the *Cats Without Claws* album. Donna performed it on the 1984 Christmas special of *American Bandstand* as well as on the iconic *Soul Train* show. That suggests it was planned as the third American single in early 1985, but Geffen execs likely got cold feet after the poor reception of the *Cats Without Claws* album.

Remix fix!

A 6:18 remix of 'I'm Free' by John 'Jellybean' Benitez, which plays like a time capsule of dance music circa 1985, also appeared on the B-side of the UK 12-inch single 'Eyes'. Two versions of 7th Heaven's remix of 'I'm Free' (a radio edit of 3:51 and a club mix of 5:49) were included on the *Cats Without Claws (40th Anniversary)* edition, which hit in that free magical space somewhere between Giorgio Moroder and Stock Aitken Waterman.

'Forgive Me'

Writers: Dony McGuire, Reba Rambo
Producer: Michael Omartian

It does seem rather pointed that Donna included a song—a Gospel spiritual, no less—on this album called 'Forgive Me', at a time when her gay audience was outraged over her remarks about AIDS. There were protests, record burnings and lots of harsh words spoken at the time as the gay community dealt with a killer pandemic. Worse still, was there was no governmental support amid a right-wing fundamentalist Christian agenda, which didn't care about them or that they were dying in huge numbers. Donna, seen as part of the conservative Christian alliance—she cheerily performed at President Ronald Reagan's inauguration in early 1985—just seemed to add further provocation. Yet the story behind 'Forgive Me' is proof indeed of true Christian absolution.

Reba Rambo was one of the biggest stars of 'Jesus music,' or Christian rock, who fell in love, got divorced, then married her labelmate Dony McGuire, causing a major scandal not just in the faith music market, but also the wider Christian world. 'Forgive Me' is taken from their concept album *The Lord's Prayer* in 1980 (winner of 1981's Best Gospel Performance, Contemporary Grammy). The opening lyrics of 'Forgive Me'—'Every day I give you reason to cry'—sure seem selected to send a soothing message not only to Donna's gay audience, but also to herself, perhaps for not fully grasping the ongoing AIDS health crisis. While Omartian's overblown production threatens to overwhelm one of Donna's most heartfelt vocals, you can truly feel her absolution on 'Forgive Me'. For the second year in a row, Donna took home the Grammy for Best Inspirational Performance in 1985, this time for 'Forgive Me'. Performed by Donna in concert on her *Hard for the Money* tour, a live version had already been heard on the *A Hot Summer Night* concert release in late 1983/early 1984. During an extended intro, Donna informed the audience that she was not ashamed of being a born-again Christian. 'I love Jesus so much I've got to talk about him,' she tells the audience before pointedly adding, 'For those of you who hold grudges let them go!' Amen to that.

Remix fix!

Kylie Minogue's main music man and former Brothers in Rhythm member Steve Anderson served up a 4:40 remix and glittering 7:52 Extended Disco Mix of 'Forgive Me' on 2024's *Cats Without Claws (40th Anniversary)* edition. Steve's Disco Mix might just be the most heavenly slice of Donna music since the 1980s, showcasing what happens when you get a star remixer on board. His *Forgive Me* is a true shimmering blessing and musical revelation!

'Face the Music'

Geffen: 9 29142-7. Single release: October 1984 (B-side to 'Supernatural Love')
Writers: Donna Summer, Bruce Sudano, Michael Omartian
Producer: Michael Omartian

It's fairly easy to see why 'Face the Music' fell off the original *Cats Without Claws* album. Unoriginal, plodding and even in 1984 showcasing a rather dated early-eighties post-disco musical setting, it's only real saving grace is—of course!—Donna's fervent vocals. The biggest irony here is Donna singing 'face the music and dance' when this is a pretty hard song to dance to. It's also quite obvious that the inspiration for 'Face the Music' was Shannon's taste-making 1983 freestyle dance single 'Let the Music Play', which went top ten in the US in early 1984. It's the sort of song and style many fans wished Donna had tackled head on! As it was, 'Face the Music' became the spare Donna B-side, used twice.

While Europe had heard the 4:14 minute 'Face the Music' as an extra track on the 12-inch European release of *There Goes My Baby*, it showed up in the US and elsewhere a few months later as the B-side to the 'Supernatural Love' single. For Demon Music Group's 13th anniversary of the album in 2014, 'Face the Music' was finally added to the *Cats Without Claws* track listing, alongside extended mixes of 'Supernatural Love', 'Eyes' and 'I'm Free', plus Jellybean's 7-inch Remix Edit of 'Eyes'. It was also included on Driven by the Music's *Cats Without Claws (40th Anniversary)* reissue, along with eight brand new mixes of other songs from the original album.

16

All Systems Go (1987)

All Systems Go
Geffen: GHS 24102
Originally released: September 1987

Side One		Side Two	
'All Systems Go'	4:10	'Dinner with Gershwin'	4:38
'Bad Reputation'	4:13	'Fascination'	4:28
'Love Shock'	4:16	'Voices Cryin' Out'	5:18
'Jeremy'	4:37	'Thinkin' Bout My Baby'	6:17
'Only the Fool Survives'	4:35		

'Dinner with Gershwin'

Geffen: 7-28418. Single release: August 1987
Writer: Brenda Russell
Producer: Richard Perry Associate Producer: Brenda Russell

After a three-year break from the music business, Donna returned with the kooky but cool 'Dinner with Gershwin', the lead single from her thirteenth studio album, *All Systems Go*. It was recorded after producer Harold Faltermeyer had finished her album, or so he thought, and headed back to his movie soundtrack obligations. As Geffen execs searched hard for a song they thought would relaunch Donna's career, a tape of Brenda Russell's 'Dinner with Gershwin' landed at the label. Russell, who had sung on Donna's 'State of Independence' five years earlier, was planning to record 'Dinner with Gershwin' herself, but when David Geffen heard and loved it for Donna, he made a deal with Russell, giving her a co-producing credit on Donna's version. With Faltermeyer unavailable, one of the world's premier producers, Richard Perry, was brought in. 'It's about having dinner with Gershwin and the finer things in life,' Donna explained at the time of the album's release. 'It's sort of a commemoration of him. Stylistically, it's very modern pop. It doesn't sound like me at all. It's kind of synthetic. The lyrics are great.'

Getting this song the way everyone wanted it was an even bigger deal. Recording took almost a month, just for one song. Donna noted it was, 'the longest it's ever taken for me to do a record, but it was worth it. It's a really unique song, real clever lyrically—something special.' 'Dinner with Gershwin' did well in the UK, peaking at #13, where Donna giddily lip-synced on the popular weekly music show *Top of the Pops*. Alas it disappointed in the US, only reaching #48. An instrumental version of 'Dinner with Gershwin' appeared on the B-side of the single, while the original opened side two of the *All Systems Go* album. The six famous people mentioned in the song are: (composer) George Gershwin; (painter) Rembrandt; (physicist/chemist) Marie Curie; (painter) Pablo Picasso; (aviator) Amelia Earhart; and (gospel singer) Mahalia Jackson. Russell also played synths and contributed background vocals to Donna's version of 'Dinner with Gershwin'. The following year, in 1988, Russell scored her biggest solo success with 'Piano in the Dark', a US #6 hit, featuring Donna's old pal Joe Esposito. In 1990, Brenda released her own jazzed-up version of 'Dinner with Gershwin' on her *Kiss Me with the Wind* album. She later called Donna, 'amazing. She just had power ... I just thought she was unbelievable. She could sing her ass off.'

Vid bit!

Director: Brian Grant

There were two videos for 'Dinner with Gershwin'. The first—Donna in various historical settings—was scrapped and remains in the vaults. Are they saving this for 2027's 40th anniversary perhaps? Stay tuned, viewers! The 'Dinner with Gershwin' video that was issued is one of Donna's better efforts. Donna swishes about as photos of her superimposed next to all the luminaries mentioned in the song appear. It's a cute touch.

Remix fix!

The 12-inch single of 'Dinner with Gershwin' contained not just an extended version at 7:43, but also a new track, 'Tearin' Down the Walls', cut from the *All Systems Go* album... or was it?

'Tearin' Down the Walls'

Warner Bros Records: U 8237 (T). 12-inch release: September 1987 (UK only)
Writers: Siedah Garrett, Tony Maiden
Producer: Michael Omartian

And here is that 3:59 minute track that initially only appeared as a bonus track on the UK 12-inch of 'Dinner with Gershwin'. With Donna taking a festive, almost Gloria Estefan approach to 'Tearin' Down the Walls', Michael Omartian was back in the producer's chair for a brief one-off reappearance. Speculation has it Donna and Omartian were planning, and even recorded, tracks for another album together before Geffen pulled the plug. One song credited to Bruce Sudano and Michael Omartian, Italo-disco hymn 'Lovin' You', was released in 1988 by Italian music icon Raffaella Carrà on her *Raffaella* album. Donna even sang it as a duet with her on Italian television.

Just a month prior to the release of Donna's 'Dinner with Gershwin' single, Michael Jackson released the first single from his *Bad* album, a gooey ballad called 'I Just Can't Stop Loving You', which not only reached #1 in the US and UK, but was a duet with 'Tearin' Down the Walls' songwriter Siedah Garrett. The other co-writer of 'Tearin' Down the Walls' was guitarist Tony Maiden, a member of the band Rufus (Chaka Khan's former group), who co-wrote their US top five hit 'Sweet Thing' with Chaka. In 2015, Garrett posted a picture of herself on social media with the caption 'revisiting studio where I wrote a song and recorded background vocals for the incomparable Donna Summer in 1984'. With Garrett posing next to its recognisably pink album cover, this implied 'Tearin' Down the Walls' was originally part of the *Cats Without Claws* album.

Remix fix!

In 2014, the *All Systems Go* album was rereleased as a deluxe edition featuring 'Tearin' Down the Walls', edits of 'Dinner with Gershwin', 'All Systems Go' and 'Only the Fool Survives', extended versions of 'All Systems Go' (the remix) and 'Dinner with Gershwin' plus an instrumental of 'Dinner with Gershwin'.

'All Systems Go'

Warner Bros. Records: U 8122 (T). Single release: January 1988 (UK only)
Writers: Donna Summer, Harold Faltermeyer
Producer: Harold Faltermeyer

Anthemic album opener 'All Systems Go' is Donna all ready to go somewhere between dance and rock—yep, she's a proper pop star. This fired-up track takes its cues from the biggest white female names of that era (Madonna, Cyndi Lauper and Belinda Carlisle) rather than the major Black female artists (Whitney Houston, Janet Jackson and Tina Turner). To ensure Donna was not living behind the times, the lyrics are suitably programmed: 'Is your mind in computer mode/And all your senses in overload.' In fact, Donna boasts she has 200,000 watts of love and is starting to glow, then later is 'headin' out for planet Mars'. Perhaps the solar system is what she's really talking about. Donna herself called the 'All Systems Go' song 'something subtle', adding 'it really moves, so you want to be in the car when you hear it or on the dance floor'. Released as a single only in the UK, 'All Systems Go' peaked at #54. The *All Systems Go* album, meanwhile, really did try hard to be exactly what it said on the (cassette) box or record sleeve—all things to all people—and unequivocally demonstrate Donna's versatility. It was recorded in what was then West Germany by a man who was still West German: Harold Faltermeyer. The former protégé of Giorgio Moroder had been brought in as producer at Donna's urging after he'd finished the scores for the movies *Fletch* and 1986's *Top Gun*, which would win an Oscar for Giorgio's synth-pop classic 'Take My Breath Away' by Berlin. In 1987, besides producing most of Donna's *All Systems Go* album, plus the *Heart Over Mind* album for Jennifer Rush, Faltermeyer composed three movie scores: *Fatal Beauty, Beverly Hills Cop II* and *The Running Man*, in addition to producing a track for *Starlight Express*. In 2017, British gay magazine *Attitude* called *All Systems Go* 'a forgotten gem if ever there was one'.

Vid bit!

Director: Philippe Gautier

If you assumed 1984's music video for 'Supernatural Love' was Donna's low point, then you haven't seen this mess of Donna unsteadily lip-syncing in front of some bargain basement computer graphics. Some sites attribute this system breakdown to Russell Mulcahy (they wish!), but it's little surprise that this was Donna's final release on Geffen Records. The best response to this video is a comment left on the official page of the 'All Systems Go' video: 'I love Donna Summer and I love the song but this video is so horrendous to the point it makes me cringe. What the hell were they thinking?!' Everything's clearly not under control.

Remix fix!

The UK-only 12-inch of 'All Systems Go' was an 8:03 Extended Remix courtesy of American DJ/producer Bruce Forest, who also re-swizzled Elton John, Boy George and Whitney Houston.

'Bad Reputation'

Writers: Donna Summer, Joe Erickson, Peter Bunetta
Producers: Peter Bunetta, Rick Chudacoff

Radio-friendly 'Bad Reputation' was, according to Donna, 'where a mother is telling her daughter to be cool about sex. The tone of my voice is very authoritative. I don't bust my chops trying to sound like Donna Summer. I am an actress.' Donna worked on 'Bad Reputation' with Rick Chudacoff and Peter

Bunetta, who had just produced a top-ten US hit, 'Just to See Her', for Motown legend Smokey Robinson, which also won him a Grammy for Best Male R&B Vocal Performance the following year. 'I have been working with a lot of people trying to get this album right,' Donna confided. 'I did a song with David Foster for the Statue of Liberty restoration celebration. I was hoping the record would be released about the time of the ceremony, but it was not.' Donna did perform 'Silver Lady' at some of her mostly casino concert dates in 1986, around the time of the Liberty weekend that July, but it never made it on to the *All Systems Go* album and likely was never actually recorded.

'Bad Reputation', according to Faltermeyer, was actually a late addition to the *All Systems Go* album after he had departed to complete other movie projects. He also indicated later that there were a number of other songs completed for the *All Systems Go* album, which didn't make the final cut. One he mentioned was 'Money Talks', 'which I was surprised they passed on,' he stated, 'and there are a couple others that would have completed our original version for the album before "Dinner with Gershwin" and "Bad Reputation" became substitutes. The decision was made afterward by executives who were looking for a radio hit for 1987 and not something that would perhaps last beyond then.' Sadly, none of those extra tracks have since surfaced or been released. Perhaps the 40th anniversary issue due in 2027 will reveal all!

'Love Shock'

Geffen: 9 28165-7. Single release: November 1987 (B-side of 'Only The Fool Survives')
Writers: Donna Summer, Bruce Sudano, Harold Faltermeyer
Producer: Harold Faltermeyer

While 'All Systems Go' got all the computer references, 'Love Shock', which has aged shockingly badly in the production department, deals with 'radioactive love'. 'You've been infected by a non-stop electronic girl/Say it's love shock'. Singing about a highly contagious virus ('they've got no cure'!) could be considered in extremely poor taste, given that Donna was still under attack from the gay community over her alleged AIDS statements, and the epidemic continued to rage unabated. In May 1987 President Ronald Reagan, at the urging of Elizabeth Taylor, gave his first speech about AIDS, just a few months before Donna released the *All Systems Go* album. AIDS activist group ACT UP, meanwhile, formed in early 1987. It was to them Donna wrote a letter in July 1989 after ACT UP activists protested at her music being played at a Boston Gay Pride event.

Donna wrote about how in 1983 she was 'unknowingly protected by those around me from the bad press and hate letters I was receiving regarding this matter. During that time, I was pregnant (twice in eighteen months), was engulfed in a major lawsuit and several of my family members passed away. My manager, at that time, felt my life and emotional health was at stake so there was no response.' She added there had been a terrible misunderstanding, she had love for everyone regardless of sexual orientation and quoted a passage from the Bible about love and forgiveness. ACT UP soon after discontinued their protests at Donna's music being played, but the letter wasn't made public until after her death in 2012. 'Love Shock' was also the B-side of the 'Only the Fool Survives' single.

'Jeremy'

Writers: Donna Summer, Andreas Slavic, Hannes Treiber, Harold Faltermeyer, Pit Floss
Producer: Harold Faltermeyer

On this soft rock, FM-friendly ballad, Donna gives it her all, but ultimately 'Jeremy' doesn't rank even close to being one of her finest balladeering moments. Slushy, schmaltzy and smothered in clichés, even Donna (and the power of love) can't save 'Jeremy'. There's also a good reason why there's never been a song called 'Jeremy' before! However, it was clearly a track Donna loved, as she sang it a number of times on European television promotional appearances in 1987. Also receiving songwriting credits on 'Jeremy' were Slavic and Treiber, both Austrian musicians, and German engineer/producer Floss, who died in 2023. In 1989, 'Jeremy' reappeared as an extra track on the UK 12-inch of 'Love's About to Change My Heart'. In the charts, the *All Systems Go* album peaked at a miserable #122 in the US and failed to chart in the UK. It did best in Italy, where it reached #17. Yet *People* magazine's Ralph Novak championed it, and 'Jeremy', in his review, awarding it an 'A' grade. 'On ballads such as "Jeremy" or "Voices Cryin' Out" or downtempo duet with Starship's Mickey Thomas on "Only the Fool Survives", Summer gets to flex her considerable vocal power,' he wrote, but added thoughtfully, 'Summer is the victim of her own talent in a way—a performer as good as she is generates high, perhaps unfairly high, expectations. Who ever said showbusiness was supposed to be fair?'

'Only the Fool Survives' (Duet with Mickey Thomas)

Geffen: 9 28165-7. Single release: November 1987
Writers: Donna Summer, Bruce Sudano, Harold Faltermeyer, John Bettis, Michael Omartian, Virgil Weber
Producer: Harold Faltermeyer

Sometimes voices just don't mesh well for a duet, and that is the case on 'Only the Fool Survives'. While the song itself is, unfortunately, forgettable B-grade material done better elsewhere by all six co-writers credited, Donna and Mickey are also too similar in vocal tones. Oh, if it had only been Joe Esposito's deep, sexy, manly tone instead! Mickey Thomas was lead singer of Jefferson Starship and then, from 1984, the revitalised Starship. By the time he joined Donna on a duet of 'Only the Fool Survives', Mickey had sung on three US #1 singles for Starship: 1985's 'We Built This City' and 'Sara', and 1987's 'Nothing's Gonna Stop Us Now', so on paper at least he was the perfect, radio-friendly voice for Donna to team up with. Yet the fact it took six people to write 'Only the Fool Survives' indicates that the song went through a variety of incarnations before the recorded version.

Quite why there was no music video made for 'Only the Fool Survives' (when 'All Systems Go' got an unspeakably bad one) is perhaps due to the sense of 'end of contract' here. A minor hit only in Canada, 'Only the Fool Survives' was a resounding flop. Speaking of survival, we should also at this point discuss how Donna had effectively been cancelled from the charts, if not the music business, due to the ongoing simmering resentment in the gay world about her reported/ rumoured 1983 statements. Donna would have just one more surprise US top-ten hit, two years later in 1989, but after that she was banished from the top 40, with only three more entries at the bottom end of the top 100. Was Donna Summer the first victim of cancel culture, long before there was such a thing, let alone a term for it? The good news is that her family, via The Donna Summer Estate, have worked hard to repair the damage and restore her legacy since her death in 2012. They've achieved this through thoughtful releases (those bundles of 40th anniversary dance remix joy certainly help!), 2023's *Love to Love You, Donna Summer* documentary, and being open about Donna's flaws and blind spots, especially the continuing antagonism between her and the gay community. 'To have this asterisk on your legacy was devastating,' daughter Brooklyn Sudano told the *Guardian* in 2023. 'That was very difficult for her to get over because she loved people and particularly that community. Again, it's about healing. It's acknowledging this was a terrible thing that was super-hurtful.'

'Fascination'

Geffen: 7-27939 (7-inch Promo).
Writers: Dave Tyson, Eddie Schwartz
Producer: Harold Faltermeyer

A definite highlight of the *All Systems Go* album, 'Fascination' is a dreamy, swoony, synth-pop ballad ('Fantasy's fact you see in my life') that Harold

Faltermeyer believed should have been up for single consideration. Geffen even pressed promo 7-inch copies for it in 1987, fading the track to a 4:11 length (the B-side being a 4:31 remix of 'All Systems Go'), so there must have been a plan to do so at some stage, presumably revoked when the album tanked on the charts and sales-wise. 'Fascination' co-writer Schwartz was a Canadian musician who had some success as a solo artist in the US and his native Canada, but his biggest chart success was penning Pat Benatar's signature song, and US top-ten hit, 'Hit Me with Your Best Shot', in 1980. The other co-writer, Tyson, was also a Canadian songwriter/producer, who in 1990 co-wrote the #1 US single 'Black Velvet' for Alannah Myles. 'Fascination', which bears an uncanny resemblance to Sting's 'Fragile' (also from 1987), was covered a year later in 1988 by soul/R&B singer Leata Galloway on her *The Naked Truth* album. Galloway had previously featured on Paul Jabara's album, *Paul Jabara and Friends*, in 1983. (Donna did not appear on this, though a young Whitney Houston did).

It's noteworthy that Donna's original take on 'Fascination' is a precursor of sorts to the acclaimed work Faltermeyer would do producing Pet Shop Boys' 1990 must-hear album *Behaviour*, which essentially mapped gay life during the AIDS epidemic. Ultimately, and perhaps sadly too, Faltermeyer didn't pick up with Donna where he left off with his dancetastic work producing E. G. Daily's 1985 club hit 'Love in the Shadows'. Taken from her *Wild Child* album, it also featured a rockier cover version of Faltermeyer's 'Sunset People', originally on Donna's 1979's *Bad Girls* album. There is also fascinating speculation among fans that Giorgio Moroder was originally meant to reteam with Donna on her thirteenth album. That didn't happen because (take your pick): (a) Donna didn't like the songs he offered her and/or; (b) she found the material too un-Christian. Holy ****!

'Voices Cryin' Out'

Writers: Donna Summer, Harold Faltermeyer
Producer: Harold Faltermeyer

What the *All Systems Go* album is literally crying out for is a big dancefloor number. Would the mid-tempo 'Voices Cryin' Out' have worked better if it had been that danceable centrepiece? Evoking Cyndi Lauper's 1984 'Time After Time' ballad stylistically, Donna certainly uses her voice to carry this song further than the clunky production. '"Voices Cryin' Out" is my socially critical song on the album,' Donna told *Cashbox* magazine at the time.

> I started out writing it about people who are hungry and then it ended up also being about kids my daughter's age. She's 14 now and so she's almost as old as I

> am in her mind and all these things that are yet to come in her life are screaming at her 'come on and try me, come on', so she's feeling all this stuff going on inside her and yet she can't do it. So, there are these voices crying out to her and those lyrics are the best on the album, Musically, it's not a commercial song, but the message of the song is what it's about.

In other press interviews at the time of the album's release, Donna mentioned 'Voices Cryin' Out' being about young men going off to war, which is presumably what the line 'voices from some foreign shore' is a reference to. As part of Christie's 2023 'The Collection of Donna Summer' exhibition/auction, Donna's handwritten lyrics for 'Voices Cryin' Out' sold for $1,386 under its original title 'Voices Crying Out'.

'Thinkin' Bout My Baby'

Writers: Donna Summer, Jeff Lams, Keith D. Nelson
Producers: Donna Summer, Jeff Lams, Keith D. Nelson

Donna's favourite track on the *All Systems Go* album—which she co-wrote and co-produced with two members of her band—also marked only the second time Donna received a producer's credit. The first was 1979's 'My Baby Understands' on the *Bad Girls* album. Originally, this languid, Sade-esque chill-out tune was around the 10-minute mark, but hacked back to just over six minutes for the finished version. 'We cut it down to eight,' Donna insisted, 'and I had a real struggle with the company just for eight! They said it was too long, but I said, "You don't understand something. This is a song people are going to wait to hear".'

'Thinkin' Bout My Baby' was, Donna said,

> a song about a girl who's walking down the street. She's thinking about her boyfriend because she just had a fight with him and she's looking for him. It's a nice song, a real mellow song. It's sort of like 'Love to Love You Baby' in that you can put it out in a room and it doesn't invade you, but at the same time it seduces you. It's simple with nice vocals and a great saxophone solo [by her tour saxophonist Warren Ham]. Very musical.

The lyrics for the song include extra lines deleted from the album version: 'I was wanting just another chance/To make you feel my fine romance/Didn't know, want to go'. 'Thinkin' Bout My Baby' would be the last song on the last album Donna would release for Geffen.

'As it turned out, my move to Geffen Records was not that successful,' Donna mused.

> It looked like a great marriage on paper but turned out to be not so great in real life. When it became clear we were unable to recreate the kind of magic I'd had with Neil, David Geffen and I both agreed it would be in our best interests if I left the label while we were still friends. I apologised to David that it didn't work out and left Geffen Records. Our parting was amicable and David was very gracious.

However, there is another side, if not another place and time, to this story.

17

Another Place and Time (1989)

Another Place and Time
Atlantic: A2 81 987
Originally released: March 1989

Side One		Side Two	
'I Don't Wanna Get Hurt'	3:26	'Sentimental'	3:10
'When Love Takes Over You'	4:12	'Whatever Your Heart Desires'	3:52
'This Time I Know It's for Real'	3:36	'Breakaway'	4:01
'The Only One'	3:54	'If It Makes You Feel Good'	3:45
'In Another Place and Time'	3:21	'Love's About to Change My Heart'	4:00

'This Time I Know It's for Real'

WEA/Warners: U 7780. Single release: February 1989 (UK)
Writers: Donna Summer, Mike Stock, Matt Aitken, Pete Waterman
Producers: Stock Aitken Waterman

Shout it out with a megaphone: this time, Donna the Redeemer has returned for real! Eighteen months after *All Systems Go* went nowhere, Donna was back! Back! BACK! with a total triumph of a pop release. With nary a dud among its ten tracks, her fourteenth studio album, *Another Place and Time*, was preceded a month earlier by its lead single, the stunning return-to-form 'This Time I Know It's for Real'. After Donna's husband Bruce Sudano bent her ears to Rick Astley's 1987 single 'Never Gonna Give You Up' (a UK/US #1), Donna knew she had found the right team to work on her next album. 'I didn't really know their work, but Bruce felt we should work together,' she told *Billboard* in July 1989.

'After I heard their production on Rick Astley, I thought they'd done a good job so we met up in London. I realised they're straight-ahead guys who are passionately in love with music.'

Pete told *Record Collector* this single had a troubled genesis initially. 'The song hadn't come together and there were pieces of paper all over the floor with notes and ideas,' he remarked. 'Donna really pulled that together with her vocal. It shows what working with a truly great singer can achieve. What she did with that track was incredible.' The infernally catchy 'This Time I Know It's for Real' raced to #3 in the UK, Donna's first top-ten hit there in a decade, and soon after to #7 in the US, her first top ten there in six years. It even won SAW (Stock Aitken Waterman), a coveted Ivor Novello award for International Hit of the Year. 'Whenever you were with her, she made you feel so special,' Waterman said in 2012:

> She had all the talent but she gave you all the credit. She was not a diva in any shape or form. She was in the wilderness when we had the biggest record of our careers together. They warned us against working with her because the whole anti-gay thing had happened, but what a voice she had. She used to warm up in the ladies' toilet and everyone in our building would come to a standstill to hear her warm-up.

Mike Stock told *Billboard* in 2021, 'Donna Summer was just a joy. She took my song, "This Time I Know It's for Real", and transmuted it into pure gold. It's the fans' favourite over here.' Indeed it is. In a 2022 poll on the stockaitkenwaterman.co.uk site, fans voted in their thousands for the best SAW song of all time. The winner? Donna's 'This Time I Know It's for Real', besting Kylie Minogue's 'Better the Devil You Know' at #2 and Lonnie Gordon's 'Happenin' All Over Again' at #3. Best SAW album of all time went to Donna's *Another Place and Time*, ahead of Bananarama's *Wow!* at #2 and Kylie Minogue's *Rhythm of Love* at #3. A year later, the *Financial Times* ranked SAW's twenty greatest songs with 'This Time I Know It's for Real' at #8, calling it 'gleaming dance-pop with a nailed-on euphoric chorus'. 'This Time I Know It's for Real' was also one of the songs featured in 2023's SAW musical, *I Should Be So Lucky*. That made up for the fact it was omitted from *Summer: The Donna Summer Musical*, which premiered in 2017 and was co-written by Oscar nominee Colman Domingo.

In 2004, former N-Trance singer Kelly Llorenna scored a pumped up #14 UK hit with her cover version. Australian girl group Young Divas recorded a terrific take of 'This Time I Know It's for Real' in 2006, taking it to #2 there (Donna's original managed just #40 Down Under). Donna's 'time' had truly come again, for real!

Vid bit!

Director: Dieter Trattmann

While not considered among the finest music videos ever, at the very least on this occasion Donna looks like she's having a really good time.

There's over-enthusiastic dancers, big hair, boot scooting and hoop earrings, but then it was 1989. Mapping where Donna has to go to find her true love before she explodes, we finish in London where Donna and company (including her two youngest daughters Amanda and Brooklyn) dance off in front of the kabuki-style cover of the *Another Place and Time* album. Swiss-born director Trattmann was the London-based director tapped to handle the visuals and make them appealing for Donna's 'This Time I Know It's for Real' video. After directing music videos for the likes of Cliff Richard, Thompson Twins and Placido Domingo, he left for the US to work on television shows like *CSI* before moving into real estate investment. He also directed the video for Donna's 'Love's About to Change My Heart' under the name of Dee Trattmann.

Remix fix!

While it was a hard ask to better the original 3:36 masterpiece, Pete Hammond's extended version of 7:20 managed to make a good thing even better. A 'Euphoric Club Mix' of 7:11 on the 30th-anniversary edition of *Another Place and Time* proved to be barely different.

'Whatever Your Heart Desires'

WEA/Warners: U 7780. Single release: February 1989 (UK) (B-side of 'This Time I Know It's for Real')
Writers: Donna Summer, Mike Stock, Matt Aitken, Pete Waterman
Producers: Stock Aitken Waterman

Now we've got the good news story of Donna's comeback via 'This Time I Know It's for Real' out of the way, here's the real skinny on the Machiavellian music biz machinations that transpired before that. In 1988, Donna was still signed to Geffen Records when she made her new record with Stock Aitken Waterman (SAW). When Geffen heard the album, he hated it so much he sold Donna's contract to Atlantic Records. It's worth noting that Donna's two most successful albums of the decade while she was with Geffen—*She Works Hard for the Money* and *Another Place and Time*—were the only two not released through Geffen Records. As it turned out, Geffen selling off Donna was the best thing that could have happened to her.

After its UK success, her new record was a no-brainer for a US release and an album that would endlessly please her hardcore fans too. 'A great portion of this album is dance-oriented because I wanted to build back that base,' Donna pointedly told *Billboard* that year. To that end, 'Whatever Your Heart Desires', the B-side to 'This Time I Know It's for Real', was SAW's conveyor-belt hit-making at its uplifting pop/dance best and could even have been a (hit) single in its own right. 'Whatever Your Heart Desires' was also one of the three songs on the then forthcoming *Another Place and Time* album with Donna listed as co-writer.

'I Don't Wanna Get Hurt'

Warner Bros Records: U7567 Single release: May 1989 (UK)
Writers: Mike Stock, Matt Aitken, Pete Waterman
Producers: Stock Aitken Waterman

An effervescent fizzy pop track, perhaps better suited to SAW's then teen queen Kylie Minogue, Donna recorded puberty angst pop bop 'I Don't Wanna Get Hurt' against her better judgement. The album's second single in the UK reached a healing #7 and was also a significant hit in the rest of Europe. Remixed for the 'I Don't Wanna Get Hurt' 7-inch single by SAW's in-house remixer Pete Hammond (adding superfluous studio-tweaked vocals), Donna detested this mix so much she refused to appear in the video.

At Donna's insistence, Atlantic Records opted instead to release 'Love's About to Change My Heart' as the second single from *Another Place and Time* in the US. 'I Don't Wanna Get Hurt' did finally get a US release of sorts when a 12-inch version appeared on the 12-inch of Donna's 'Breakaway' single. Yet despite Donna's indifference (at best), 'I Don't Wanna Get Hurt' opened the *Another Place and Time* album and became her last new single to reach the UK top ten. In 2017, British gay magazine *Attitude* reassessed the appeal of the single, which caused Donna so much angst. 'The song is nothing short of a sensation,' they insisted, 'a powerful hi-NRG bullet that thwacks you right between the ears. Joyous!'

Vid bit!

Director: Pete Cornish
Uh-oh, it's a Donna video, but where is she? Well, if Donna wasn't particularly keen on this track (or on it being a single), because she thought 'I Don't Wanna Get Hurt' too juvenile for her, then she most certainly wasn't going to be in the video either (which thankfully uses the album version not the single mix). Instead, there's a bunch of hellishly attractive young people sporting way too much ripped denim. More like a clothes ad than a music video, the best thing you can say about this clip is at least nobody got hurt during the making of it. Hopefully. Better instead to seek out Donna's lip-sync-with-big-hat appearance on the British *Top of the Pops* television show as penance.

Remix fix!

Of all of Donna's studio albums, *Another Place and Time* stands as (ahem!) 'the only one' literally swimming in a plethora of original mixes/remixes, thanks to the 30th-anniversary edition of the album released in 2019. Not only did this massive compilation contain remixes of all ten album tracks, it added in six previously unreleased mixes. As if that wasn't enough—SAW fans alert!—the 'Deluxe Edition' added in a 30th-anniversary 'minimax' (6:16) and 'megamix' (12:15).

'When Love Takes Over You'

WEA: U7361. Single release: November 1989 (UK)
Writers: Mike Stock, Matt Aitken, Pete Waterman
Producers: Stock Aitken Waterman

Track #2 on the *Another Place and Time* album also became its fifth and final single and wasn't too dissimilar to much of the other material SAW produced in 1989—Kylie Minogue's 'Hand On Your Heart' (UK #1), Cliff Richard's 'I Just Don't Have the Heart' (#3), Jason Donovan's 'Every Day (I Love You More)' (UK #2) and Sonia's 'Can't Forget You' (#17). 'When Love Takes Over You', ever-so-slightly remixed for its 7-inch single release by SAW's in-house mixer 'Mixmaster' Dave Ford, petered out in the UK chart at #72 and failed to chart elsewhere. When there were so many other stronger tracks on Donna's *Another Place and Time* album, it seems Mike Stock might have been correct in his assessment it made for a weak single choice.

Legend has it British girl group Bananarama (whose SAW-produced cover of 'Venus' reached #1 in the US in 1986) were offered 'When Love Takes Over You' in 1988 but rejected it. Whether that's true or not, the song is definitely a better fit for Donna, as someone who has been through the trials of love and experienced enough to give a younger girl some 'good advice'. While Donna's attitude towards Geffen Records and David Geffen softened over the years, back in 1989 she wasn't so thrilled with his wheelings and dealings. 'When you're used to having #1 records in a row, it's tough when it stops happening,' Donna said at the time of the release of the *Another Place and Time* album.

> It was not a match made in heaven. I noticed that aside from their work in the hard rock category, they didn't really have much success in other areas. I felt betrayed about the whole situation, especially since I wanted to leave several years ago and they made me wait out my contract. It seemed no matter what I did musically, they couldn't get behind what I was doing.

Shifting to Atlantic Records (in the US), run by Ahmet Ertegun, she instantly 'felt it was like being with a record company in the old sense, plus Ahmet has been a music man all his life, worked with greats like Aretha Franklin and Bette Midler and established careers'. For a number of years, former Destiny's Child singer Kelly Rowland has been attached to a Donna Summer biopic and in 2009 had a UK #1 with her storming dance anthem 'When Love Takes Over' with French DJ David Guetta. Just imagine a version mixing those two diva tracks together!

Vid bit!

Director: Donna Summer
Tired of not having her vision captured by the directors of her music videos, Donna took on the role herself for 'When Love Takes Over You'. Husband Bruce

Sudano later explained that, by 1989, Donna had grown increasingly weary of trying to explain her creative vision to outside directors who did not fully grasp her artistic sensibilities. With very little budget left for a fifth video from the *Another Place and Time* album, Donna stepped up. In this goofy, but sweet, clip there's masses of hats, cows, a jukebox that doesn't seem to be plugged in and Donna singing in the mirror with the heaviest pink earrings you ever saw. If nothing more, the 'When Love Takes Over You' video finally shows us what happens when Donna's comedic side takes over (she must have been great fun at kids' parties!).

Remix fix!
SAW worked through PWL—Pete Waterman's parent company—as did their team of remixers. For 'When Love Takes Over You', two remixers get to flaunt their wares. Pete Hammond's Original 12-inch Mix (7:02) deconstructs the original, pumping up the bass and giving it an elegant sheen. Dave Ford's mixes include his busier Extended Remix (6:13), edited into the 3:38 7-inch single mix.

'The Only One'

Writers: Mike Stock, Matt Aitken, Pete Waterman
Producers: Stock Aitken Waterman

Here's one of those maddening songs where the verses are actually catchier than the chorus. That's presumably why 'The Only One' was never in contention as a single from the *Another Place and Time* album. While still a great track, the thin backing vocals (from SAW regulars Dee Lewis, Mae McKenna and Mike Stock himself) don't do the song any favours and are arguably one of the few things on Donna's SAW album that could have been bettered.

Reviews of the album varied wildly. *Billboard* glowingly declared 'every song sounds like a hit' deeming it 'one of Summer's most satisfying and consistent albums in a very long time'. *Rolling Stone*, meanwhile, gave it two-and-a-half stars, sniffily calling the album 'Stock Aitken Waterman's machine-tooled dance fluff'. *The Village Voice*'s Robert Christgau rated it as 'B+', but said Donna 'lights into these retooled tunes with a phoney enthusiasm that must have scared the shit out of Bananarama'.

Donna was aware of the criticism of the SAW trio, which viewed them as a pop music sausage-making machine. 'Maybe they're formularised in terms of what works in the marketplace,' Donna responded, 'but I feel everyone has a formula and they're geared towards the commercial arena. People's comments about their success may simply be plain, unadulterated jealousy. I've never seen producers who work harder than these three guys—I'm the first artist of any real statue that they've worked with and I found them to be very cordial, very gentlemanly.' In 2025, after years of being dismissed by critics, the SAW trio were honoured with a blue plaque at their former music studios in Borough, South London.

'In Another Place and Time'

Writers: Mike Stock, Matt Aitken, Pete Waterman
Producers: Stock Aitken Waterman

Side one's only ballad, and this album's title song, is a wistful, if not heartfelt, tune about how two lovers were just not in the right place at the same time. It showed the depth of the SAW team's lyrical maturity, yet there would be little of that on display in their later work as a trio until they went their separate ways in 1991. Perhaps that had to do with their slew of mostly young, often teen, artists, for whom songs like 'In Another Place and Time' seemed too mature and, ultimately, too adult. Donna decided to call her album *Another Place and Time* 'because it was recorded in another place known as London. We had a song by that name on the album and it just fit with the idea of the album.'

As it transpired, Donna and Pete Waterman actually had history in another place and time. In 1974, Pete met Donna while he was working as an A&R man for Magnet Records. Donna was a session singer at the time and lore has it that she passed on Pete's invitation to become a vocalist for a new disco outfit called Silver Convention, choosing instead to work with Giorgio Moroder. Whatever the place and time, Donna was one smart cookie! Here's yet another time and place coincidence. In 1994, Mike Stock and Matt Aitken (now legally emancipated from Pete Waterman) co-produced a remake of Donna and Barbra Streisand's 'No More Tears (Enough Is Enough)'. Featuring the vocal powerhouse duo of Kym Mazelle and Jocelyn Brown, the record crossed over from the clubs to the pop charts, reaching #13 in the UK charts. Mike said at the time he was determined to use 'real singers' on this remake. Just like he did in another place and time, hmm?

'Sentimental'

Writers: Donna Summer, Mike Stock, Matt Aitken, Pete Waterman
Producers: Stock Aitken Waterman

Not only was the giddy 'Sentimental' one of three songs Donna cowrote with SAW, the unashamedly Euro-dance ditty proved to be the unsteady starting point for the album they intended to make together. 'The first song we did was "Sentimental" and she wasn't sure of it, but I talked to her and we got it done,' Mike Stock told *Retro Pop* magazine in 2022.

> Then I thought, 'I've got to convince her it's worth doing the rest of the album with us!' I went home that night and started rattling around in my head what

> would become '*This Time I Know It's for Real*'. The next morning, I got up and finished it off in the bath and during the car journey to the studio so, by 11 o'clock I've got the whole thing. When I got into the studio I laid the drums down, got a chord sequence. Donna came in around lunchtime and put it down. I know that was the clincher for her to devote the next month to finishing off the album because she was unsure of 'Sentimental' but '*This Time I Know It's for Real*', when we heard it back, we got very excited.

Stock also said of SAW's working relationship with Donna that, 'there are a few artists that you go, "Hang on a minute, this is just a dream." Donna Summer came in and it was a breeze and a fantastic thrill.' Ah, almost makes you get sentimental now, don't it?!

'Breakaway'

Atlantic: 7-88792. Single release: October 1989 (US)
Writers: Mike Stock, Matt Aitken, Pete Waterman
Producers: Stock Aitken Waterman

In all, *Another Place and Time* spawned an impressive five singles—half of its tracks. In retrospect the appealing mid-tempo charmer, and gentle female empowerment anthem, 'Breakaway' might have made a better second single in both the US and elsewhere than being relegated to fourth single. 'I thought "Breakaway" was a great song,' Donna told *Dance Music Report* a year later in 1990. 'I loved the song, but Atlantic wanted a different track and maybe that made a difference.' As the fourth single from the album, 'Breakaway' was remixed for the 7-inch single—'gimme a break!'—by SAW's Harding/Curnow B-team, robbing the song of some of its original misty charm.

'Breakaway' peaked at #49 in the UK but missed the US charts altogether. It became a major hit in Latin America, however, charting in Peru and Argentina and becoming Donna's seventh #1 in Brazil and one of her most recognisable songs in those territories. At the time of the release of the *Another Place and Time* album, *Smash Hits* reviewer Ian Cranna awarded it 8/10, calling the record, 'the most sensible thing she's done for years'. He also pointed out 'there'll no doubt be endless hit singles from this LP (the last song "Love's About to Change My Heart"—a bit of a surging 'epic'—will be massive), but best of the lot is a gentle nursery rhyme-type affair called "Breakaway"'.

Vid bit!

Director: Dieter Trattmann
Donna wasn't available for filming at the time of the US release, so a video was curated using footage from previous UK videos (and no new footage), including 'This Time I Know It's for Real' and 'Love's About to Change My Heart'.

Remix fix!

The 1989 'power' mixes of 'Breakaway' (a radio mix, edit and extended mix of 6:09) by house music legend Tony Humphries showed up on the US 12-inch. Unfortunately, they collectively manage to take a terrific tune and squash its specialness and subtle sadness. Harding/Curnow's UK mixes (Full version of 6:44 and Remix Edit of 3:34), which 'take a walk on the wild side', released at the end of 1990, are something of an improvement, but really nothing can better SAW's original album version.

'If It Makes You Feel Good'

Writers: Mike Stock, Matt Aitken, Pete Waterman
Producers: Stock Aitken Waterman

The closest thing to disco on the *Another Place and Time* album, the irrepressible 'If It Makes You Feel Good' sure sounds like a classic forgotten gem begging to be covered. With an infectious chorus, Donna hitting all the right notes and a positive lyrical tale reminding us all 'you're not alone in the world', it's not surprising Donna's was actually the third rendition of the song SAW had recorded since writing it. 'If It Makes You Feel Good' was first released in 1986 in a much less interesting version by SAW's British soul singer Princess on her self-titled debut album.

In 1988, a version closer to Donna's was recorded by teen model/SAW protégé Mandy Smith (who the following year married Rolling Stones' bassist Bill Wyman when she was 18 and he was 52) for her only album, *Mandy*. During sessions for the *Another Place and Time* album, which Donna called 'easy, no pressure', she said they had some discussions about what she wanted prior to the recording. 'I have to have input and I got that from these guys,' she marvelled. Decades later with the *Another Place and Time* album considered a high point in Donna's back catalogue, Pete Waterman stated, 'ultimately *Another Place and Time* stands as one of the most enjoyable albums we ever recorded and part of our hi-NRG history, thanks to Donna's astounding ability to make any song she sang her own'. It sure does make us feel good.

'Love's About to Change My Heart'

Atlantic: 7-88840. Single release: August 1989
Writers: Mike Stock, Matt Aitken, Pete Waterman
Producers: Stock Aitken Waterman

The second US single, and the third in the UK, 'Love's About to Change My Heart' demonstrated SAW's canny ability to draw the best out of their artists. Donna is given a big glistening 30-second opening moment to let her vocals soar and then—what do you know?—it kicks off into an upbeat thumping tempo change reminiscent of 'Last Dance', 'Dim All the Lights', 'On the Radio' and 'No More Tears (Enough is Enough)'. Oh, and then there's another big breakdown and dance restart in the last 30 seconds, just for good measure. *Billboard*, in their review, highlighted that 'Love's About to Change My Heart' 'recalls Summer's hits of the past—pulsating dance rhythm, inspiring lyric and a vocal that radiates.' Reaching #20 in the UK, unfortunately the *Another Place and Time* album closer could only muster #85 in the US, although it went top three in the Netherlands.

After SAW's career-saving work on Donna's *Another Place and Time* album, it would have seemed like the most obvious thing to reassemble the same team for another record. That never happened, sadly. Material SAW wrote, which could have helped shift Donna into a pop/house direction, was handed instead to singer Lonnie Gordon. Her stupendous 1990 UK #4 hit, 'Happenin' All Over Again', would have been perfect for Donna. That's especially disheartening since the last minute of Donna's album's last track, 'Love's About to Change My Heart', features a notable house music piano riff as if this is where Donna should be heading next.

Donna did come to Pete Waterman's door again in 1993, but by then SAW had disintegrated, becoming a hostile legal nightmare. 'I was excited to work with Donna Summer simply because of her superb vocal ability. I really regret we never made a second album with her,' Mike Stock told the *Guardian* in 2017. 'She had a magic to her few artists have. I'd sing her my song, she'd learn it, then she'd sing it back with whistles and bells and all sorts of things going on. She had that skill and feel for music.' In 1994, Mónica Naranjo recorded a Spanish-language version, 'Fuego de pasión' (Fire of Passion) on her self-titled debut album (a million seller in Mexico).

Vid bit!

Director: Dieter Trattmann

During her lifetime, Donna never really seemed to acknowledge, or even understand, how important a good music video was. Aside perhaps from 'She Works Hard for the Money', there's very little else of any quality in her music video back catalogue. Donna, as we all know, shone brightest when live on stage, on the dancefloor, or on record. Here's yet another example of 'great song, lousy video'. Definitely the best of the *Another Place and Time* videos, Donna is a true trouper, giving it her big-haired best amid some serious skirt flouncing, while the hired help dance in giant clocks, shadowy figures play violins on fake leafy sets and moody male models stare blankly. Set to PWL's 7-inch mix of 'Love's About to Change My Heart', it's easy to forgive the cheesy visuals because this is, frankly, such an ecstatic song.

Remix fix!

While the PWL 7-inch mix of 'Love's About to Change My Heart', courtesy of Phil Harding, added a touch of extra pizzazz to the album version, DJs Robert Clivillés and David Cole were brought in for a remake aimed at the US market. The duo's smoother house music inspired mixes, edited by Luie Rivera, were such dancefloor dynamite at the time Donna's song reached #3 on the US dance chart.

18

Mistaken Identity (1991)

Mistaken Identity
Atlantic: 7 82285-2
Originally released: August 1991

'Get Ethnic'	5:21	'Friends Unknown'	3:44
'Body Talk'	4:58	'Fred Astaire'	4:40
'Work That Magic'	4:59	'Say a Little Prayer'	4:07
'When Love Cries'	5:15	'Mistaken Identity'	4:08
'Heaven's Just a Whisper Away'	4:06	'What Is It You Want'	4:40
'Cry of a Waking Heart'	4:36	'Let There Be Peace'	3:59

'When Love Cries'

Warner Bros. Records: 9031-75433-2. Single release: August 1991
Writers: Donna Summer, Keith Diamond, Paul Chiten, Larry Henley, Eve Nelson
Producer: Keith Diamond

Before the *Mistaken Identity* album was released, some two-and-a-half years after *Another Place and Time*, a lot of major events had happened in Donna's life. Her daughter Mimi was in college in Connecticut, so the rest of the family moved to nearby Westport. Tragically, Donna's younger sister Amy was dying of lung cancer some two hours' drive away in Boston. 'Amy lasted about eight months,' Donna recalled in her memoir, 'and her passing was very hard for me to deal with. I'd never known how painful the loss of a sibling could be and how it puts you in touch with your own mortality. It took me a long time to come to terms with her passing.' This tumultuous moment in Donna's life occurred just as 'When Love Cries', her penultimate album's debut single, was being released. That meant Donna was not available to make a music video or for promotion.

The origin of the song leans heavily on Soul II Soul's trademark smooth groove, so much so that it even 'borrows' a clutch of the British soul collective's recognisable string bursts. Songwriter/producer Eve Nelson, according to Donna, 'came in and had written this groove. I started singing to the groove in the car and we taped the words, so we captured the song's feel immediately. We wanted to keep it very simple and very emotional and make it the cry of a woman who's alone and away from the man she loves'. Released in the US as the first single, minus a video, 'When Love Cries' reached #77 in the charts, which did not bode well for the *Mistaken Identity* album. Released a fortnight later, the album failed to chart in either the US or the UK. It would ominously end up as Donna's penultimate studio album (excluding 1994's Christmas album). She would record only one more album in her lifetime and that would be some seventeen years later.

'What Is It You Want'

Warner Bros. Records: 9031-75433-2. Single release: August 1991 (B-side of 'When Love Cries')
Writers: Donna Summer, Keith Diamond, Donna Wyant, Anthony Smith, Vince Lawrence, Dave Resnik
Producer: Keith Diamond

The B-side to the 'When Love Cries' single suffered the same issue affecting much of *Mistaken Identity*: Donna's recognisable voice just wasn't very recognisable. The closest thing to a dance track on the *Mistaken Identity* album (where it was track #11 of 12), Donna called 'What Is It You Want', 'our comedy track. Everybody's made up of a lot of different colours and I wanted this album to express different sides of my character through the songs—my gentleness, my weakness, my strength, my humour and what I'm driven by are all there. I originally wanted to call this song "The Laugh Track".' Many fans thought this might have made a better A-side than 'When Love Cries', especially as it taps into the exploding house music scene with Madonna's 'Vogue' being the biggest selling US single the previous year. The other big miss with the *Mistaken Identity* album is there was nothing else danceable included. Donna and producer Keith Diamond attempted instead to clone a Janet Jackson, Paula Abdul and Mariah Carey style of pop/R&B. *Mistaken Identity* was thus truly a missed opportunity. That last incredible 'nothing' at the end of 'What Is It You Want', however, could almost make you forgive everything else which didn't work here. Alas, Donna's *Mistaken Identity* album is hard to like and even harder to love.

'Get Ethnic'

Writers: Donna Summer, Keith Diamond, Paul Chiten, Anthony Smith, Larry Henley
Producer: Keith Diamond

In the year preceding the release of *Mistaken Identity*, the US singles chart had seen singles by Janet Jackson, Mariah Carey, Paula Abdul and Madonna all hit #1. Not wishing to emulate Madonna's sexually charged records ('Justify My Love' was #1 in early 1991), the benchmark for Donna's album was up-tempo tracks closer to Janet Jackson and Paula Abdul. Here's a good example via beat/ vibe producer Keith Diamond, who cleverly merged Janet Jackson's Jimmy Jam and Terry Lewis produced 'Rhythm Nation' (down to its 'do your rhythm thing' lyrics) and guitar-driven 'Black Cat' (a US #1 in October 1990) with elements of Paula Abdul's 'Straight Up' (a 1989 US #1).

On paper it was a smart move, but putting them all together when the material was a pale imitation of better songs is what ultimately let the side down. 'Get Ethnic' is also unfortunately titled, if not terribly naïve and anachronistic these days, especially since the advent of 'cultural appropriation'. '"Get Ethnic" is about having pride in what you are,' Donna explained in 1991 for the album's release. 'In the US, there is a tendency to de-emphasise your background, but at some point, people should be free to be who they are. Be yourself because that is what makes this country interesting.' If only 'Get Ethnic' was as interesting as Donna's quote.

'Body Talk'

Writers: Donna Summer, Keith Diamond, Paul Chiten, Anthony Smith, Larry Henley
Producer: Keith Diamond

Caribbean-born producer Keith Diamond was heavily involved in the church. That's presumably why Donna was keen to team up with him, with his previous work including Aretha Franklin, Billy Ocean (with whom he wrote 1984's US #1 'Caribbean Queen'), Al Green and Dionne Warwick. Diamond brought a street-smart sensibility to Donna's *Mistaken Identity* album—something she had never really had before—and you can really hear that influence here on 'Body Talk'.

'When you watch all of these new dances, you can see people really talking with their bodies,' Donna said in the press kit for her album. 'When guys go out, they don't need to say, "Hey baby, I love you!", when they're saying so much with their body language. That is what the essence of the song is all about—I can hear your body talk.' While Donna's musical risk-taking was admirable, you can't help but feel that 'Body Talk' is watered-down Janet Jackson. Much like the blonde hair, blue-eyed leather-queen look Donna sported on the album's record cover, 'Body Talk' ultimately isn't convincing or feel truly authentic.

'Work That Magic'

Warner Bros. Records: U5937CD. Single release: November 1991
Writers: Donna Summer, Keith Diamond, Eve Nelson, Anthony Smith, Larry Henley
Producer: Keith Diamond

The starting point for writing 'Work That Magic' was Keith Diamond having just fallen in love prior to working on what would be Donna's *Mistaken Identity* album. 'We were writing from a frame of reference of real intensity and passion,' Donna noted. 'It's a feeling you can't hide—a fidgetiness in your soul where you wait breathlessly for the next time you are going to hear from the person you love and the man and the woman meet, fall in love and it's magic.' Now there's a statement that surely wouldn't have endeared Donna to any of her remaining gay fans, especially considering the opening line of 'Work That Magic' is 'and the man and the woman fell in love'. It was remixed for the UK market by producer (and background Tears for Fears member) Ian Stanley. He gave it a more contemporary house music soundscape, but the single only reached #74.

'Work That Magic' co-writer Nelson was brought to Donna's album project by Keith Diamond to programme drum machines and synths and write with Donna. 'She was an idol of mine. I was totally overwhelmed,' Nelson said years later:

> Donna has, in my opinion, one of the most unique-sounding voices to date I've ever heard. Whitney kind of followed in her footsteps a little. Donna had this amazing way of being totally soulful, hot and hip. Her Black roots were definitely in her voice, but then there was this incredible tone and the way she would hold a note for twenty seconds. Of course, you can't deny how charismatic she is. When Donna would approach a vocal, the minute she'd open her mouth, it was freaking gorgeous. She closed her eyes and *went* there. She is very concerned about great melodies and honest lyrics. She really wants to say something. She doesn't want bullshit. She is the most unbelievable artist.

Vid bit!

Director: Studio-commissioned

You want a goofy, silly, doesn't-make-much-sense-but-who cares Donna video? Work your eyeballs on this magic little number. A brave attempt to force Donna to join the exploding house music scene, there are plenty of outfit changes, men dressed as mime artists, Donna hamming it up as an opera diva, three male dancers with their chests out and legs with bows on them and even floating plastic dolls. If nothing else, the visuals are never static and work well with the music, borrowing their look from any of the C+C Music Factory videos airing at the time. Though why Donna is covered in snow at the beginning and end remains magically unclear (and possibly why no one has claimed credit for it!).

Remix fix!

The original album version of 'Work That Magic' is a fairly uninspired production, aping current house music sounds without adding anything special. The Ian Stanley remixes gift the song a heftier bass feel and house groove to make it truly work on the dancefloor. 2014's Driven by the Music re-release of *Mistaken Identity* included three remixes—the full-length ISA remix (6:18), single mix (4:12) and George Karras' Vocal Club Dub/Summertime Remix) (7:36), which is less a dub and more an extended version of the original. It left off Stanley's less interesting Capricorn ISA Mix (4:32) from the B-side of the original UK 12-inch.

'Heaven's Just a Whisper Away'

Writers: Keith Diamond, Larry Henley, Anthony Smith
Producer: Keith Diamond

With Mariah Carey and Whitney Houston ruling radio and the charts in 1991 with their power-ballads, Donna wasn't about to be left out, especially given her impressive pipes, which had inspired both divas. Mariah and Donna would finally perform on stage together almost a decade later for VH1's *Divas 2000: A Tribute to Diana Ross* concert/TV special (see Appendix). 'Keith played "Heaven's Just a Whisper Away" for me the first day in the studio,' Donna explained. 'I thought it was a really romantic, beautiful, emotional song. I fell in love with it and we recorded it.' There's a heavenly clip online of Donna in 1991 performing 'Heaven's Just a Whisper Away' from *Showtime at the Apollo* (the legendary Apollo Theatre in New York's Harlem), which only offers further proof that this should have been a single, if not the first single, from the *Mistaken Identity* album. A 1992 clip of Donna performing it live on television in Chile adds additional evidence to a case for 'Heaven's Just a Whisper Away' being a long-lost great Donna Summer ballad. Legend has it there was plenty of additional material recorded for this album, which remains locked in the Atlantic vaults. Will it take until its 40th anniversary (in 2031!) for fans to finally hear what Donna stashed away? Watch this space, Donna collectors.

'Cry of a Waking Heart'

Writers: Betsy Cook, Bruce Woolley
Producer: Keith Diamond

Grammy-nominated American singer/songwriter Betsy Cook worked with George Michael and Marc Almond, while her Grammy-nominated song 'Telling Me Lies' was recorded by Linda Ronstadt, Dolly Parton and Emmylou Harris for 1987's *Trio* album. Bruce Woolley wrote hits for The Buggles ('Video Killed the Radio Star'), Grace Jones ('Slave to the Rhythm') and John Farnham ('Two Strong Hearts'). The pair worked on Cook's 1992 album, *The Girl Who Ate Herself*, with production from Ian Stanley, remixer of Donna's 'Work That Magic' single for the UK market. When Donna first heard 'Cry of a Waking Heart', she didn't think she could sing it.

> My husband said, 'Listen to the song again!' I put it on and he sang it to me and said, 'This is you!' There's this incredible line that goes 'behind the familiar the view is strange' and that just blew me away. 'Cry of a Waking Heart' is definitely a love song, but about two people who realise if they're going to continue, they have to set each other free.

Donna's ethereal falsetto vocal antics here are truly something to behold and admire. *Billboard* singled out the track as one of the *Mistaken Identity* stand-outs. 'The singer cuts loose here, consistently testing and expanding the boundaries of her range,' the trade paper wrote. 'This is most evident on the stirring ballad 'Friends Unknown' and her tribal, single-worthy "Cry of a Waking Heart".'

'Friends Unknown'

Writers: Donna Summer, Keith Diamond, Anthony Smith, Vanessa Smith
Producer: Keith Diamond

Although Donna said she loved all the songs on *Mistaken Identity*, her personal favourite was 'Friends Unknown'. 'This is the first time I had a chance to thank my audience directly and say it in a song,' she admitted.

> When you're on stage you go, 'Thank you so much', but it always sounds so trite. My best asset is my voice, so when I sing something, I know my fans will

> get the message. I'm more than thankful for every time that they were there. When I shed a tear, when I need a prayer, or when I just need an uplift, a little note comes that says, 'I love you' or 'Thank you for your music'. That really means a lot to me and this was a nice chance to say, 'thank you' back.

Donna magically performed this at her 1992 Hollywood Walk of Fame induction ceremony, telling the crowd, 'This year has been a very difficult year. I wrote this to say thank you to all the fans and people who have been so kind to me over the years. I just want you to know how much I appreciate you. I really truly do. If I never see you again, you're always in my heart.' Is the amazingly gracious and grateful 'Friends Unknown' another attempt by Donna to patch up things with her gay fans? Quite possibly. In 1991, she sued *New York Magazine* for reprinting the 'AIDS is God's retribution against gays' statement and won the case. Donna's husband Bruce believes 'Friends Unknown' is the true hidden gem ('or knockout number') in his wife's back catalogue. To that end, it was included as the showstopper in 2017's *Summer: The Donna Summer Musical* for what Bruce calls a 'tear-the-roof-down moment in the show'.

'Fred Astaire'

Writers: Donna Summer, Keith Diamond, Anthony Smith, Donna Wyant
Producer: Keith Diamond

Song writer Anthony Smith was originally from Alabama, but moved to Nashville, the city Donna would move to in 1994 with her family. Smith had songwriting credits for a number of country artists including Reba McEntire, Vince Gill and Kenny Rogers. He later appeared as a 'mentor songwriter' on reality television show *Gone Country* alongside Jermaine Jackson and George Clinton. Smith scored a huge ten songwriting credits on Donna's *Mistaken Identity* album, so clearly he and Donna clicked musically. 'Fred Astaire', which namechecks the legendary Hollywood 'hoofer', was, according to Donna, 'a hang out with the gang and party kind of song. Everybody's out there dancing and looking for the right person, the one who's going to dance best with them.' Mr Astaire (who died in 1987, the year Donna released her *All Systems Go* album) was enjoying a major renaissance in popular culture at the time, getting a namecheck in Madonna's 'Vogue' single in 1990. Donna's 'Fred Astaire' and Madonna's 'Vogue' share the phrase 'dance on air', which came from his famous anti-gravity scene in the 1951 *Royal Wedding* movie. Donna's 'Fred Astaire' might have been more footloose and fancy-free, however, if 'Vogue' producer Shep Pettibone had worked his magic here instead.

'Say a Little Prayer'

Writers: Donna Summer, Keith Diamond, Anthony Smith, Donna Wyant
Producer: Keith Diamond

Not to be confused with the Bacharach/David classic, 'I Say a Little Prayer', a hit for both Aretha Franklin and Dionne Warwick, Donna's 'Say a Little Prayer' is 'about a girl getting dressed up to go out and land Mr. Right,' according to Donna. 'She's dressed to kill, hoping it will help her get the guy. We wrote it at the beginning phases of the recording and I loved the idea of the song.' With more than just a nod to Paula Abdul's hits of the era, 'Say a Little Prayer' has not aged well, sounding laboured and tinny. Co-writer Donna (McLaughlin) Wyant, who nabbed four credits on the *Mistaken Identity* album in total, was a close friend of Donna's. The pair met while performing in *Hair* in the 1960s (alongside British singer Maxine Nightingale (who had the #2 US disco hit 'Right Back Where We Started From' in 1976).

'On *Mistaken Identity*, I've tried to make sure there is something for the dance and high energy crowd, something for the pop and rock music fans, something for the urban/R&B listeners—a little something for everybody,' Donna was at pains to point out. 'I feel this album best represents me because I've always liked exploring many different types of music.' Amen to that.

'Mistaken Identity'

Writers: Donna Summer, Keith Diamond, Anthony Smith, Donna Wyant
Producer: Keith Diamond

In the midst of the writing and recording sessions for Donna's *Mistaken Identity* album, African-American Rodney King was brutally beaten by LA policeman in March 1991 after a high-speed car chase on the freeway. A bystander filmed the beating, with four policeman later tried for using excessive force. Three were acquitted while the jury couldn't reach a verdict on the fourth, kicking off the LA riots in April and May 1992. The 'new jill swing' title song of *Mistaken Identity* was, Donna explained,

> a socially critical song. I got the idea when I heard about that assault on a man in Los Angeles where he was beaten by several police officers while others stood by and watched. To the best of my knowledge, it wasn't the first time this sort of thing had happened. I just felt I had to comment about it, so I distanced the song from the actual events by putting myself in Rodney King's place. In the song, I am arrested by the police, but I didn't commit the crime.

There's also a secondary reading of Donna's lyrics here—'No one cared to listen/Someone had to take the heat/Sometimes there's no justice/When you're a victim of the street'—which could be viewed as referencing Donna's ongoing battle against anti-gay statements she claimed she never made. Two months after *Mistaken Identity* was released, Donna filed a $25m libel suit against *New York Magazine* over them attributing anti-gay remarks to her. 'The article hurts me deeply,' Donna said in a statement. 'I would never say the things attributed to me in this article.' Published in its 5 August 1991 issue, exactly a week before Donna released 'When Love Cries' as the lead single from *Mistaken Identity*, the magazine quoted an 'industry source' claiming Donna had refused to include a song written as an apology to the gay community for saying homosexuals were 'sinners and that AIDS was a divine ruling' on the album. 'That is completely false,' Donna retorted. 'I did not say it. I do not believe it.' Donna insisted the song, 'We Are Gonna Win', written by Paul Jabara (see Appendix), was from 1984 and was not released because its writer did not uphold a distribution agreement she had made with him. Donna also added that she believed the article 'came out a week before the album as a stumbling block. This is not an anti-gay rumour, it is a personal attack on me.' After death threats against her and her three children, the matter was settled out of court. Jabara tragically died of AIDS in September 1992 at the age of 44.

'Let There Be Peace'

Warner Bros. Records: U5937CD. Single release: November 1991 (B-side to 'Work That Magic')
Writers: Donna Summer, Keith Diamond
Producer: Keith Diamond

The B-side to the 'Work That Magic' single was also the *Mistaken Identity* album's big gospel closer. Written during the time of the Gulf War (August 1990– February 1991) by Donna and Keith Diamond, she was inspired to write it when she was sitting in her kitchen listening to the news. 'Suddenly, I felt goosebumps all over my body,' she said. 'Thinking about all those people going over there, my heart was filled with tears. I found myself wishing I had so much authority that I could proclaim peace.' Bruce Sudano has selected 'Let There Be Peace' as a lost classic in Donna's catalogue. 'There are so many hidden gems,' he added.

> There is 'Voice Crying Out', there is 'All Systems Go', there is her singing 'Lush Life' on the Quincy Jones record. There is 'Fascination', another cool song. Donna is always recognised for the dance hits, but she made a point of including on every album ballads and different kinds of songs because she never wanted to be pigeonholed. It's really her hardcore fans that truly appreciate that.

In their three-star review of Donna's *Mistaken Identity* album, *Rolling Stone* wrote 'in-between the misguided opener ("Get Ethnic") and the strained closer ("Let There Be Peace") lies striking evidence of Summer's enduring talent. Something about her voice hits home, whether she's aiming for the heart ("Work That Magic"), the soul ("Say a Little Prayer"), or the feet ("Fred Astaire").' *The LA Times*, in its two-star review, pointed out that

> at fortysomething, Summer sounds as if she's still in search of her own musical identity. There are dance tracks here that are virtually indistinguishable from records Summer was making more than a decade ago when she was the queen of disco. While a few of those dance numbers get by, the only song that actually seems to mean something to the singer is 'Friends Unknown', an intense, heartfelt ballad.

However, one of Donna's oldest friends, and most successful collaborators, was just about ready to carry on where they had both left off.

'Carry On' (Donna Summer and Giorgio Moroder)

Virgin: 115 502. Single release: September 1992
Writers: Giorgio Moroder, Marietta Waters
Producer: Giorgio Moroder

Carrying on as if they had never left off, after more than a decade, Donna and Giorgio were finally reunited on a record. In March 1992, Giorgio released a solo album, *Forever Dancing*, with the very first track being the ebullient 'Carry On'. Donna sang its verses with Giorgio singing background vocals on the chorus, just like Donna's bad 1980s dream had never happened. The song's co-writer Marietta Waters had appeared on the *Top Gun* and *Fire & Ice* soundtracks as Marietta and her 1986 solo single, 'Born to Dance', was produced and written by Harold Faltermeyer. Donna's daughters Brooklyn and Amanda also sing backing vocals here along with Waters and Giorgio (and Larry Lee). Reaction to the Donna/Giorgio reteaming was so strong in Germany that a single of 'Carry On' was issued, featuring an illustration of Donna on the cover (with pink and orange hair!). It hit #65 in the German charts and would be Donna's last new release for another two years, although in 1993 it reappeared as the closing song on the grandiose *The Donna Summer Anthology* compilation.

That wasn't the last of 'Carry On' though, which lived up to its name. In 1997, two years after anti-retroviral medication suddenly stopped AIDS in its tracks, the Donna/Giorgio collab was remixed and released. Not only did it reach #65 in the UK, but the following year it also won the inaugural Grammy for Best Dance

Recording (besting Daft Punk and Pet Shop Boys among others), thanks in part to her executive assistant Brian Edwards. Of the 1997 release, *The Advocate*'s Barry Walters astutely wrote,

> As a personality, Summer remains a ditz, but as a voice of the dance floor she remains the ultimate artist and this soaring survival anthem reminds us why. The words may deal with perseverance, a theme we know all too well, but the melody and her performance is all about transcendence. It's been decades since Summer has sounded as if she's singing about us, for us, with us.

If only Donna and Giorgio had carried on even further!

Vid bit!
Sadly, no video was commissioned for this historic piece of music. Instead, check out a lip-sync Donna and Giorgio did for German television in 1992, currently floating around the internet, with both Donna and Giorgio looking impeccable.

Remix fix!
For the 1997 remix pack of 'Carry On' (on Interhit Records in the US) remixes came courtesy of Outta Control, Chris Cox of Thunderpuss fame and Eric Kupper (whose version has aged the best of the bunch). In addition, a Hot Tracks Mix was included, mixed by J. Mark Andrus. *Billboard* called them 'all quite nice, though it's hard to move away from the original Moroder production, which is as bright as a sunny Sunday afternoon tea dance'. The Almighty Records UK edition offered handbag house Almighty/7th Heaven remixes by Jon Dixon and Martyn Norris, plus a techno-lite 'Euro Mix' by Gemini & Maureen. In 2001, a re-produced, if not much improved, version of 'Carry On' by Eric Kupper entitled the Hysteria Radio Mix appeared on the *Gay Happening Vol. 7* compilation (Dance Street: DST 70770-2).

'La Vie En Rose' (from *Tribute to Edith Piaf* album)

Amherst Records: AMH 5500-2. Album release: January 1993
Writers: Edith Piaf, Louis 'Louiguy' Guglielmi (English lyrics: Mack David)
Producer: Jacques Arnoul

'Every day, words seem to turn into love songs!' The opening song on a Canadian thirteen-track *Edith Piaf Tribute* album, or *Tribute to Edith Piaf* as it was called in France, was Donna's version of Edith Piaf's signature tune 'La Vie En Rose'. A million-seller for Piaf when it was released in 1947, Grace Jones recorded a bossa nova version thirty years later in 1977, finally becoming a #12 UK hit in

1985. Donna's contemporary/easy listening version of 'La Vie En Rose' is only in English, apart from the four words of the title. *Billboard* called Donna's rendition of this classic tune a "charming take". The other artists who contributed to the collection were Corey Hart, Ann Wilson, Jason Scheff, Pat Benatar, Willy DeVille, Juice Newton, Ivan Lins, Emmylou Harris, Leon Russell, K.T. Oslin and Chris Spedding.

Remix fix!

In 1994, a four track 12-inch/single of 'La Vie En Rose' appeared (AB Disques—AB 0366 1) boasting three mixes by Carl Ward and Colin Peter (Techno Mix, Extended Soul Mix and Full Bass Mix), plus Humberto Gatica's US Radio Mix. A promo CD single also appeared on Amherst Records (CD DJ19) with the Radio Edit and an Album Version (5:06) mixed by Humberto Gatica. Other mixes called Stringapella Mix and Remodelled Mix have also appeared on French editions.

19

Christmas Spirit/Endless Summer... and more (1994–1996)

Christmas Spirit
Mercury: 314 522 694-2
Originally released: October 1994

'White Christmas'	2:55
'The Christmas Song'	4:20
'O Come All Ye Faithful'	4:40
'Christmas is Here'	3:22
'Christmas Medley'	5:20
'I'll Be Home for Christmas'	3:30
'Christmas Spirit'	4:53
'Breath of Heaven'	6:04
'O Holy Night'	4:12
'Lamb Of God'	7:24

'White Christmas'

Writer: Irving Berlin
Producer: Michael Omartian

Two years after 'Carry On', her kinda final collab with Giorgio Moroder, Donna returned in 1994 with around half an album's worth of new material, even if the bulk of it was Christmas related. Before you even ask, no, it's not a disco Christmas record, not even slightly. A month before *Christmas Spirit* hit stores (and two months before the *Endless Summer* compilation) *Billboard* published a special '20th Anniversary Celebration' of Donna's career. 'I have longed to make a Christmas album,' she told the magazine.

> Every year I start off planning to do one, then February and March roll around and it doesn't happen—my life takes off and I never get a chance to do it ... Michael Omartian did a wonderful job producing and I absolutely adored playing with the Nashville Symphony Orchestra. When they first started playing 'White Christmas' tears just welled up in my eyes and I had to leave the room because it sounded so beautiful and it had taken so long to finally start this project. It was just a wonderful feeling and that comes across on the record.

Originally written by Irving Berlin in 1942 for the Bing Crosby movie *Holiday Inn*, 'White Christmas' won an Oscar. It returned in the 1954 musical, *White Christmas*, also starring Crosby and since been covered by artists such as Darlene Love, Barbra Streisand and Frank Sinatra. Donna's stirring version is a strong opening, setting the festive tone for what's to come on the rest of *Christmas Spirit.*

'The Christmas Song'

Writers: Mel Tormé, Bob Wells
Producer: Michael Omartian

Donna recorded her Christmas album in Nashville, so it was only natural she called on the Nashville Symphony Orchestra for musical assistance. The album was recorded much earlier in 1994, around Easter, which was, to quote Donna, 'pretty peculiar'. Written in 1945 at the end of the Second World War, 'The Christmas Song' is also known as 'Chestnuts Roasting on an Open Fire' and was first recorded by the Nat King Cole Trio in 1946. Other notable versions include those by Doris Day, The Jackson 5 and Ella Fitzgerald. The opening trifecta on the *Christmas Spirit* album of 'White Christmas' 'The Christmas Song' and 'Oh Come All Ye Faithful' might make you think this was going to be an entire faith music album and, in many ways, it is a true affirmation of Donna's born-again Christianity. 'I've chosen to stay in the world's eye, to give a positive image,' Donna explained once. 'It's a very spiritual and helpful place to be. I love it.' Praise be! Donna also performed 'The Christmas Song' on *Good Morning America* and was seen recording it on *Entertainment Tonight* (both online).

'O Come All Ye Faithful'

Writers: Frederick Oakeley, John Francis Wade
Producer: Michael Omartian

This might be the highpoint of *Christmas Spirit*: Donna's vocal and Omartian's production create a heavenly rendition of a classic. A traditional Christmas carol from the eighteenth century, 'O Come All Ye Faithful' is also known by its Latin title of 'Adeste Fideles'. Lyricist Oakeley was an English Catholic priest who lived from 1802–80 and translated 'Adeste Fideles' into English. For Donna's rendition, let her teleport you to a cathedral on high, complete with celestial choir. Oh, come let us adore Donna and her angelic final note! It's also worth noting that Omartian was now one of the hottest producers in the world again. He had just come off producing the 1991 album *Heart in Motion* for Christian crossover singer Amy Grant, selling over five million copies in the US alone. It's quite possible that he introduced Donna to Amy's version of 'Breath in Heaven', which appears later on the *Christmas Spirit* album. Donna had also duetted on television with Marilyn McCoo on 'O Come All Ye Faithful' on 1982's *A Solid Gold Christmas*.

'Christmas is Here'

Writers: Donna Summer, Bruce Sudano, Michael Omartian
Producer: Michael Omartian

The first of three Donna originals on the *Christmas Spirit* album, 'Christmas is Here' is a song about 'a wonderful time of the year' and 'feasting and fun' which evokes a goofy, innocent charm obviously aimed at delighting small children. It wouldn't be long before Donna would once again hear the pitter patter of little feet around her own house. In 1997, her oldest daughter Mimi gave birth to her first daughter, Vienna Dohler, which made Donna a grandmother at the age of just 49. Interestingly, one of lines in 'Christmas is Here' is 'grandma is making sugar cookies and baking'. Wonder if it took her so long to bake it that she'll never have that recipe again? Anyways ... there is a recipe for a 'MacArthur Park' cake in honour of Donna after her 2012 passing at spectacularlydelicious com.

'Christmas Medley'

Writers: William Chatterton Dix, George Frideric Handel, Isaac Watts, Gloria Shayne, Noël Regney
Producer: Michael Omartian

Rather than recording three additional songs for her *Christmas Spirit* album, Donna ingeniously found a way to weave three songs into one 'Christmas Medley'. It opens dramatically with 'What Child Is This?', a Christmas carol from 1865 written by Dix to the tune of the English folk song 'Greensleeves'. After 'What Child is This?' comes 'Do You Hear What I Hear?', written in 1962 by married couple Shayne and Regney about the Cuban missile crisis. Bing Crosby's version became a hit in 1963 and has since been covered by numerous artists including Mahalia Jackson, Diahann Carroll and Whitney Houston, on 1987's *A Very Special Christmas* charity album. The medley closes with the world's most popular hymn, 'Joy to the World', written in 1719 by English minister Isaac Watts and sung to Handel's *Antioch*. It was also recorded by Mariah Carey in 1994 and by Whitney Houston two years later on her *The Preacher's Wife* soundtrack. Donna in full gospel mode towards the end of the track is a true joy.

'I'll Be Home for Christmas'

Writers: Buck Ram, Kim Gannon, Walter Kent
Producer: Michael Omartian

Someone found a letter Donna wrote, not on the radio this time, but on Christmas Eve where the lovelight beams. This sweet sentimental ditty has long been a Christmas staple for those who want to be home on 25 December, but can only be there in their dreams. It was made famous by crooner Bing Crosby, truly the master of Christmas songs, who turned this into a standard. Written in 1943 during the Second World War about American soldiers who were far from home, other big names who have covered 'I'll Be Home for Christmas' include Elvis Presley, Johnny Mathis and, two years before Donna's rendition, Amy Grant on her Christmas album, *Home for Christmas*. Hollywood legend Crosby died at the age of 75 in 1977, the same year Donna released 'I Feel Love'.

'Christmas Spirit'

Writers: Donna Summer, Bruce Sudano, Michael Omartian
Producer: Michael Omartian

The second of the Summer/Sudano/Omartian originals, here is a churchy Christmas affair about Donna's favourite season as a child, building into an evangelical sermon ('he came to earth to bring us everything'). *The New York Times* review of the album stated:

> earnestness reigns on Donna Summer's Christmas album, which concentrates on the religious side of the holiday. Backed by orchestras and small pop-jazz groups she shows off the creamy voice that her disco hits never revealed. But she works so hard to instil songs with devotion and fervour that any hint of joy is lost. Her Christmas sounds like overtime, not a holiday.

In 2024, bookseller Barnes & Nobles summed up her record thus: 'Donna Summer's contribution to the Christmas album market sounds good, courtesy of producer, Michael Omartian, but it's about what you'd expect.' 'Christmas Spirit' was repackaged—complete with new cover and on vinyl for the first time—by Universal Music a decade after its original release. The unwieldy title—*20th Century Masters: The Best of Donna Summer: The Christmas Collection*—finally entered *Billboard*'s Top Holiday Albums chart in 2007.

'Breath of Heaven'

Writers: Chris Eaton, Amy Grant
Producer: Michael Omartian

This song was originally released in 1995 by its writer, Christian singer/songwriter Chris Eaton, on his *Wonderful World* album. He also notably penned Cliff Richard's 1990 UK Christmas #1 'Saviour's Day'. In 1992, Christian music star and crossover pop star Amy Grant asked to record 'Breath of Heaven' and Eaton gave permission for her to rewrite some of the lyrics from the perspective of Mary, Jesus's mother. Grant's restrained version was the lead single from her 1992 *Home for Christmas* album, known as 'Breath of Heaven (Mary's Song)', topping the US Christmas Adult Contemporary Chart. Donna's version, which follows Amy's, is like a cinematic rendition of the nativity story. It's also a song with great meaning to Donna ('help me be strong') as it got Donna through the death of her sister Amy. 'It would be another Amy who helped me through my grief,' Donna wrote in her memoir. 'Amy Grant's song "Breath of Heaven" helped to soothe the pain whenever I felt like I couldn't take it another minute. It's amazing how notes and words can comfort you. Her song gave me such peace after a long time of grieving. It was the help I needed.'

'O Holy Night'

Writers: Adolphe Adam, John Sullivan Dwight
Producer: Michael Omartian

Donna has a long history with 'O Holy Night'. Some twelve years before she recorded it for her *Christmas Spirit* album, she performed it live on 1982's *Solid Gold Xmas Special*. In one of her most spectacular wigs, she delivered a powerhouse take on 'O Holy Night' with an incredible big finish. That's a very different version to the one she recorded for this album. 'That song starts off fairly conservatively,' Donna pointed out, 'then it goes into a fairly funky gospel choral in the end.' While not quite the disco Christmas we might have been expecting, or hoping for, it is most certainly a very gospel, evangelical and African-American church take on 'O Holy Night'. Originally called 'Cantique de Noël', 'O Holy Night' is a sacred song now a Christmas standard, originally written in 1843. The same year as Donna's *Christmas Spirit* album, Mariah Carey released her version on her *Merry Christmas* album. Others who have covered 'O Holy Night' include Ella Fitzgerald, Michael Crawford and later Celine Dion, Josh Groban and the cast of the *Glee* television show.

'Lamb of God'

Writers: Donna Summer, Michael Omartian
Producer: Michael Omartian

Donna's final *Christmas Spirit* songwriting offering, 'Lamb of God', was also a promotional single used to plug the album, which in many ways was overlooked, both commercially and critically, by the release of the *Endless Summer* compilation just a month or so later. The concept of 'the lamb of God' is how Jesus' death was a means of redemption for humanity and the ultimate sacrifice to atone for the sins of all people. Donna's lyrics stick firmly to that notion: 'Behold the lamb of God/The mighty King of God/The chosen one of God'. Donna's own conversion to Christianity happened in October 1979. 'My baby sister had met a man who had spoken to her,' she related. 'I told my husband I wanted to meet this man and know what God wants from me because I hear him calling me. I felt the holy spirit and I spoke in tongues and felt the weight of a ton of bricks lift off my shoulders—the guilt, the lies, all of the perversion—go off of my shoulders.' Hallelujah!

'Melody of Love (Wanna Be Loved)'

Casablanca: 856 367-2/Mercury: 856 367-2. Single release: October 1994
Writers: Donna Summer, David Cole, Robert Clivillés, Joe Carrano
Producers: Donna Summer, Welcome Productions

Once Donna had recovered from the death of her sister Amy, she realigned herself spiritually so that 'everything else came into focus, in better perspective, beginning with a renewed desire to return to performing. I was ready to get back into the music'. To that end, Donna signed with PolyGram (the label which had bought out Casablanca) and began writing material for the *Endless Summer* compilation. One of the new tunes was the return-to-form dance tune 'Melody of Love'. Giving 'Melody of Love' extra cool cred, house music icon Lil' Louis, whose orgasmic 'French Kiss' was a UK #2 hit in 1989, was responsible for programming it. Prior to the single/album release, Donna informed *Billboard* she was doing 'two cuts to start' with Clivillés and Cole. 'We've had a few writing sessions. Right now, their album's just out, next we are going to finalise the cut.' Sadly, just three months after the release of this single, David Cole died of AIDS in January 1995. The Mariah Carey/Boyz II Men song 'One Sweet Day', released in November that year, was a tribute to him, spending sixteen weeks at #1 in the US. Carey's sister Alison was diagnosed as HIV+ in 1988, dying on the same day in August 2024 as their mother, Patricia Carey.

Vid bit!
Director: Ralph Ziman
South African music video director Ziman was brought in to give Donna a sexy elegance on 'Melody of Love' and it was mission accomplished. Sitting at a windswept piano, standing on a balcony with statement earrings, or just literally 'walking on air', this wasn't a video that aspired to be anything more than a showcase for Donna's voice, beauty and screen presence.

Remix fix!
Housemaster David Morales' Classic Club Mix lived up to its name as a true Donna club classic. Other mixes came courtesy of Eddie Gordon, AJ & Humpty, Mijangos and West End (used in the alternative dance music video with slightly tweaked footage). NB: The 'I Feel Love '95' single also contained the Junior Vasquez remix of 'Melody of Love'.

'Any Way at All'

Mercury: 856 803-4. Single release: April 1995
Writers: Donna Summer, Bruce Sudano, Eric Silver
Producer: Michael Omartian

Over a decade after their triumph with *She Works Hard for the Money* (and lesser returns for *Cats Without Claws*), 1994 saw Donna and Michael Omartian collab not just for a spot of Christmas cheer, but also a slew of new tunes. One of the fruits of their latest working relationship, 'Any Way at All' could easily have appeared on the *Christmas Spirit* album. It's a languid, if slightly treacly, power-ballad, with Donna pulling out all the vocal stops, showing Mariah, Whitney and Celine how it should be done. The lyrics could either be about a great love, or a higher love, with devotionals like pray and faith liberally sprinkled throughout. 'Any Way at All' made for a nice new bookend to 'Melody of Love' on *Endless Summer*, which also contained 16 Donna classics. 'Any Way at All' co-writer Bruce Silver was a Nashville staple who had worked with The Dixie Chicks, Shania Twain and Cyndi Lauper.

The B-side on this 'Any Way at All' single, which failed to chart anywhere, was a medley of 'Dim All The Lights', 'Hot Stuff', 'Bad Girls' and 'Last Dance' (all done in 3:43!), and Masters At Work's 'I Feel Love (86th Street Radio Edit)' (4:35) on the cassette. The latter wouldn't get a proper release until the September 1995 *I Feel Love '95* remake, alongside the primary and blissful Rollo & Sister Bliss mixes. There's a praise-raising 1994 live rendition of Donna performing 'Any Way at All' on *The Jay Leno Show* worth investigating too.

'I Feel Love (1995 Remixes)'

Manifesto (UK): FESCD 1. Single release: August 1995
Writers: Donna Summer, Giorgio Moroder, Pete Bellotte
Producers: Rollo and Sister Bliss

By 1995 Casablanca had been folded into the larger PolyGram family (later consolidated as the Universal Music Group) with its new sub-label Manifesto keen to reignite Donna's back catalogue. Brought on board for what was not so much a remix as a remake were Rollo and Sister Bliss, enjoying huge success as part of the Faithless dance outfit at the time. Donna agreed to record new vocals—displaying a noticeably deeper, if not even sexier purr—since the original masters were reportedly lost in a fire. The Rollo/Sister Bliss remix transformed 'I Feel Love' into a pulsating nineties club banger, building and edging until Donna finally boiled over into steamy, throbbing, diva house bacchanalia. DJ/ production outfit Masters At Work also concocted a subdued, more minimalist remix, 86Th St', featuring additional vocals and lyrics from Donna, alongside a barely-different-from-the-original 'Summer '77 Re-EG '95' mix by original engineer Jürgen Koppers. The remix package reached #8 in the UK, but failed to make an impact in the US. Somewhat ironically, and tragically, Donna's mother Mary Ellen Gaines died from pancreatic cancer, aged 65, the same month these 'I Feel Love' mixes were released. Donna's 2003 memoir, *Ordinary Girl*, is dedicated to her.

Vid bit!

Director: Tim Fox (some sources list it as Manifesto label boss Eddie Gordon, who actually was credited as 'director' of Donna's 1995 single remix)
For this 1995 remake a stylish Bruce Weber-esque B&W clip was shot, minus Donna. A CCTV operator/voyeur gets steamed up ogling some of her building's sexy occupants and subsequently can't control her urges and joins in. It could have been corny, kitschy and given off the wrong feels, but it is certifiably softcore music video porn at its best. Wonder how Donna was feeling about that?

'Ordinary Miracle' (from 'Let It Be Me')

Rysher Entertainment: no home video. Movie release: November 1995
Writers: Tina Shafer, Peter Zizzo, Dina Calitti
Producer: Narada Michael Warren

Jennifer Beals and Donna Summer already had some serious history, via 1983's box office blockbuster *Flashdance*. Over a decade later they were again interconnected—Jennifer acting in a dance movie and Donna singing a dance song over the end credits. Alas, that's about as good as the news gets about 'Let It Be Me' (which later had a title change to 'Love Dance'). A planned theatrical release in 1995 was nixed due to financial issues with the distributor, Savoy Pictures. It aired instead on HBO, but was never released on home video. A soundtrack, featuring one new song sung by Donna, 'Ordinary Miracle', was also never released. A clear attempt to recapture the magic of *Flashdance,* Donna's extraordinary vocal, with her usual flashes of brilliance, saves this from being simple and ordinary and the miracle of the internet has now let this be.

'State of Independence (1996 Remixes)'

Manifesto (UK): FESCD 7. Single release: March 1996
Writers: Jon Anderson, Vangelis
Producer: Quincy Jones

Since its original release in September 1982, the divine 'State of Independence' has been released twice. In Europe it was re-released in 1990 to accompany *The Best of Donna Summer* compilation, with remixes by London producers The Boilerhouse Boys (Andy Dean and Ben Wolfe). Their 'No Drum' mix, which does exactly as the title suggests, is a stately creation you need to hear now! After the success of the 1995 'I Feel Love' remixes, Manifesto aimed to repeat that with 'State of Independence' in early 1996. A perky collection of mixes by Phil Ramacon, Sold Out, DJ Dero and Jules & Skin, and most notably those by Murk including a jazzy dub, reached #13 on the UK charts. Yet can anything match the original Q version, as overblown and overproduced as it may be? When that all-star choir kicks in towards the end there is true musical, if not spiritual, magic happening. Try not to get goosebumps. 1990's 12-inch Millennium Mix, adding inspiration grabs from a Martin Luther King speech, finally got a proper, albeit digital, release in 2024 by the Driven By The Music label. In 1992 this version was reworked as 'Spiritual High' by British act Moodswings. Featuring vocals by Pretenders' Chrissie Hynde, it peaked at #47 in the UK and came in two parts, 'Spiritual High (State of Independence)', on their debut album.

'Does He Love You?' (duet with Liza Minnelli)

Angel Records: DPRO 7087 6 100-29-2 8 (promo single). Album release: March 1996
Writers: Billy Stritch, Sandy Knox
Producer: Brooks Arthur

Seven years after Hollywood legend-with-legendary-mom Liza Minnelli released her last pop album (the stunning *Results* produced by Pet Shop Boys) she returned with *Gently* (Angel Records: CDQ 7243 8 35470 2 9). This time around, however, her material was romantic standards and classic chestnuts. Donna joined Liza as her duet/sparring partner on 'Does He Love You?', a 1993 hit country ballad originally by Reba McEntire and Linda Davis. There are not many performers who can match Liza, or Barbra Streisand for that matter, in a duet, but Donna did! 'Singing with Donna Summer was amazing,' Liza said in a US television interview, 'because she is such a wonderful singer. She's swell, but, boy, the power in her voice. I thought I would just go and sing along and this woman *sang* and I thought, "Oh my God, I've got to do something good here and really live up to it!". It was thrilling.' A rare Liza/Donna promo single serviced a 4:36 radio edit to US radio of the album version. 'Does He Love You?' has since been recorded by Patti LaBelle in 1997 as a solo number and as a duet by Dolly Parton and Reba McEntire in 2021.

'From a Distance' (from 'One Voice: Olympic Album' album)

MCA Records: MCAD-11403. Album release: April 1996
Writer: Julie Gold
Producer: Michael Omartian

This collection of folk, world and country tunes in aid of the summer Olympics in Atlanta, Georgia, was produced almost entirely by Michael Omartian. Alongside Amy Grant, Trisha Yearwood and Willie Nelson, Omartian was also credited with instrumental album-opener 'Atlanta Reel '96' featuring a barrel of country musicians. Donna got to be part of a trio with Nanci Griffith and Raul Malo on a rendition of Julie Gold's now standard 'From a Distance'. Originally released in 1981 by Griffith, this spiritual hymn became a US/UK top-ten hit for Bette Midler in 1990/1991 during the Gulf War. Gold even won the Grammy for Song of the Year. Attempting to capture the spirit of the Olympics on their trio rendition of 'From a Distance', Griffith sings in English/Spanish, Malo (leader of country act The Mavericks) sings in Spanish and—zipping up her boots and going back to her roots!—Donna warbles in German (then in English). An idea which perhaps looked great on paper, it just makes you wish Donna had recorded 'From a Distance' in English… and by herself. Griffith sadly passed away in 2021 aged 68.

'Someday' (from 'Mouse House: Disney Dance Mixes' album)

Walt Disney Records: 60914-7. Album release: September 1996
Writers: Alan Menken, Stephen Schwartz
Producers: Michael Becker, Marco Marinangeli

Cashing in on the nineties house music sound was none other than Mickey Mouse himself. This compilation featured artists (Donna by far the most well- known) remaking Disney movie hits. 'Someday' featured in the Disney animated feature film *The Hunchback Of Notre Dame,* originally released in June 1996. A US version was released by R&B male vocal group All-4-One (#30 US) and a UK version by R&B female vocal group Eternal (#4 UK). Although 'Someday' failed to receive an Oscar nomination, Donna's swirling nu-disco rendition spins it to a discotheque dancefloor far from the Notre Dame cathedral. It's a shame this was aimed at kids, because presumably most of Donna's fans never really knew of one of Donna's earliest forays into house music. There is a two-track Mexican CD-pro of 'Someday' (with another of the tracks from *Mouse House*), while reputed Almighty Mixes of 'Someday' online appear to be by someone else, namely Joey Gardner.

'Whenever There is Love' (duet with Bruce Roberts)

Universal: UDS-56034. Single release: November 1996
Writers: Bruce Roberts, Sam Roman
Producers: David Foster, Bruce Roberts

Taken from the box office disaster hit *Daylight*, starring Sylvester Stallone, this had the potential to be a powerhouse movie theme duet with Donna and long-time pal Bruce's voices blending perfectly together. It's such a shame then that 'Whenever There Is Love' is such an overwrought, overblown bomb. Ladies and gentlemen of the Academy, this was no Oscar winner, nominee, or even minor chart hit. Perhaps the best thing that could be said about 'Whenever There Is Love' is at least now you don't have to sit through the movie to hear Donna/ Bruce's duet. Sam Roman was credited as co-writer on the release of 'Whenever There Is Love', a pseudonym for Edgar Bronfman Jr, the boss of Universal Pictures, who had produced and released the film. There's a live version of Donna and Bruce performing 'Whenever There Is Love' on US television at the time of its release, which is a lot more captivating than the recorded version. Also of note is

Donna's 1981 *I'm a Rainbow* album finally getting a release two months before this single in August 1996 (see Chapter 12). Speaking of whenever there is love, sometime in 1996 Donna's father Andrew Gaines married his second wife, (Dr) Mary Ellen Strong. In her 2003 memoir Donna thanked her evangelist stepmom for "emotional support and prayers". She died just six months after Donna in 2012 aged 91.

Vid bit!

Director: Randee St Nicholas

Amid moody, blue-coloured scenes of Donna and Bruce singing their duet are sequences from the *Daylight* movie. With the lighting on 'Whenever There Is Love' Donna almost appears white-skinned, which might have been because the record company at the time assumed the audience wouldn't accept a love song sung by an interracial pairing. At the very least Donna's hair looks expensive and glossy. Then in her late forties, Donna had never looked better. Director St Nicholas was one of the most prolific music video directors of the 1990s.

Remix fix!

The 12-inch contained four club-ripe remixes by Junior Vasquez (Club Mix—9:47, Club Dub—7:49, Riff Dub—4:56 and Tribal Beats—4:01) alongside an instrumental and 7-inch version of 'Whenever There Is Love', injecting a welcome kick of nightlife into the *Daylight* theme. A French version by Donna, 'Tant Qu'il Y Aura L'Amour', with lyrics co-written by Lara Fabian, was also released in some territories, while a Spanish version, *El Amor Verdadero*, made the movie's DVD in Spanish-speaking regions and was the European B-side.

20

Live & More Encore!... and more (1999)

Live & More Encore!
Epic: EK 69910
Originally released: June 1999

'MacArthur Park'	6:38	'Bad Girls'	3:06
'This Time I Know It's for Real'	3:12	'Hot Stuff'	4:19
'I Feel Love'	3:50	'My Life'	5:58
'On the Radio'	4:29	'Last Dance'	7:08
'No More Tears (Enough Is Enough)'	4:21	'Love Is The Healer'	3:23
'Dim All the Lights'	6:03	'I Will Go With You (Con Te Partiró)'	4:10
'She Works Hard for the Money'	4:31		

'My Prayer For You'

Brentwood Kids Company: 83061-04445-2. Album release: April 1999
Writers: Donna Summer, Nathan DiGesare
Producer: Nathan DiGesare

Now both a mother and grandmother, children were a central part of Donna's life. For the *Sing Me To Sleep, Mommy—A Collection Of Original Ballads & Lullabies* album she co-wrote and sang 'My Prayer For You'. Her bedtime tale about how God will protect a child is sung initially, and perhaps unnecessarily, in a child's voice until—thank God!—she turns on that glorious Donna voice. Other names on this album, targeted at the Christian children's market, included Debby Boone, Sandi Patti and Kathy Troccoli. On the same album Donna co-wrote the dramatic 'Star Against The Night' for contemporary gospel singer Veronica Petrucci.

'I Will Go With You (Con te partiró)'

Epic: 49K 79202. Single release: June 1999
Writers: Francesco Sartori, Lucio Quarantotto, (English lyrics) Donna Summer
Producer: Hex Hector

Mamma mia, it's Italian Mama Summer! 'VH-1 called and wanted me to do a Divas concert and decided in the long run they should just do me alone,' Donna told Rosie O'Donnell. Recorded live at New York's Manhattan Center, on 4 February 1999, the *Live and More Encore!* show/concert/album/video was her new label Epic's attempt to reclaim Donna's status as a major music legend. Her first live album since 1978, and first television concert since 1983, *Live & More Encore!* was a total triumph. Besides ten of her classic tracks, including a duet with Aussie singer Tina Arena on 'No More Tears (Enough Is Enough)', there were three new songs on the CD, plus four more on the DVD. 'I Will Go With You' was released as the first new track and if it sounded vaguely familiar that's because it was originally a major European hit in 1995 for Andrea Bocelli called 'Con te partirò'. A second version, partially sung in English with Sarah Brightman and renamed 'Time To Say Goodbye', was released a year later and became a huge global hit, apart from in the US. So three years later the decision was made to get Donna to compose some English language lyrics and release a dance version, now entitled 'I Will Go With You'. This not only hit #1 on the US dance charts, but edged up to #79 on the main chart and #44 in the UK and Germany. It was also a top-ten hit in Spain and Belgium. 'It's a beautiful song I'm very proud of and love to sing,' Donna said of the tune her husband Bruce convinced her to go with. 'In essence it musically reflects where I've been, where I am and where I'm going… since no official English lyrics exist, I decided to reinterpret it.'

Vid bit!

Director: Rocky Schenck
It's odd that a song so clearly targeted at 'the pink dollar' wound up with such a relentlessly straight video, but then it was the 1990s! Donna sports a very Whitney Houston 'I Will Always Love You'-era wig and does a lot of sitting, like Whitney did in that video. There are interpretative male dancers, a happy hetero couple, then halfway through a brief wig switch for Donna. 'I Will Go With You' is not big budget, but at the very least has a big finish (thanks to Donna's spectacular high note) and would be her final proper music video. The DVD of *Live & More Encore!* featured the original video, plus a remix video of 'I Will Go With You'. View the live version on *The Rosie O'Donnell Show* that year (same wig though!), where she and Rosie also comically duet on 'No More Tears (Enough Is Enough)'.

Remix fix!

Donna's new label Epic (part of Sony Music) was gung-ho on reconnecting with the pink dollar and wider dance community via house, progressive house and tribal house mixes. The maxi-single of 'I Will Go With You' contained remix contributions from the late Peter Rauhofer, Ralphi Rosari, Joe Carrano, Warren Rigg, Skillmasters and the song's producer Hex Hector himself. Rosabel, Messy Boys and Trouser Enthusiasts also added remixes.

'Love On & On'

Epic: 49K 79202. Single release: June 1999 (extra track on 'I Will Go With You')
Writers: Denise Rich, George Lyter, Michael O'Hara
Producer: Richie Jones Remix: Hex Hector

Originally recorded by the UK's Lorraine Cato in 1997 (remixed by David Morales), who had some success in the British charts that decade, 'Love On & On' comes on like the perfect Donna Summer song she never wrote herself. According to fan reports, before the *Love & More Encore!* concert was recorded, the original version of 'Love On & On' leaked to radio in NYC. Because of its popularity with listeners the track presumably finally found its way, in remixed form, to the B-side of 'I Will Go With You'. There were also later reports that Donna's version was intended for the soundtrack of the 1998 movie *54*, set in New York's infamous disco hotspot Studio 54. Now to be found on YouTube in all its glory, it sure does sound like the lost Donna disco classic you wanna let go on and on. It did seem odd the *54* soundtrack featured the biggest artists of the disco era, like Sylvester, Chic and Diana Ross, yet Donna was noticeably missing from the line-up. One suspects Donna vetoed her music being used in the movie/ soundtrack due to the sex and drugs in the script. It wouldn't be the first time either. In 1987 Donna chose not to record '(I've Had) The Time Of My Life' for the movie *Dirty Dancing* because she objected to the movie's title.

'My Life'

Writers: Paul Barry, Gary Miller, Donna Summer, Pete Waterman
Producers: Bruce Sudano, Donna Summer, Wayne Isaak, Bruce Gilmer, Lee Chestnut

'This is my life this is my song/Standing right here out on the stage is where I belong'! When Donna reunited with SAW's Pete Waterman a decade after their triumphant *Another Place and Time* teaming, he brought two British co-writers on board for 'My Life', a new song but a live recording, on *Live & More Encore!*. That same year Paul Barry co-wrote one of the biggest hits of the 1990s, Cher's *Believe*, while Gary Miller appears to be one of the original producers of Donna's 'I Will Go With You' before it was re-produced by Hex Hector. Quincy

Jones-founded *Vibe* magazine called 'My Life' a 'tingly "Last Dance"-esque anthem' from Donna's then-planned stage musical called *Ordinary Girl.* As the title suggests, the lyrics were a retelling of Donna's own life story. 'The "My Life" project is a "conthearto",' Donna quipped to *New York Amsterdam News* in 1999. 'That's the name I coined describing a combination of a concert and a theatrical music piece.' Why this lost Donna classic, which Donna performed often in concerts in the 1990s, was never afforded a proper release, we will never know. *Billboard* at the time noted that 'My Life' came from the tragically never- produced *Ordinary Girl* musical, but Donna also performed another song, 'No Ordinary Love Song', in concerts. Sadly, 'My Life' co-writer Miller lost his own life in 2022 at the age of 62.

Remix fix!

On 2024's mammoth *Encore* boxset, released by Driven By The Music, a 6:16 'long edit' of Junior Vasquez's passable Private Collection Mix of 'My Life' was included.

'Love Is The Healer'

Epic: 668308 2. Single release: January 2000
Writers: Donna Summer, Nathan DiGesare
Producers: Nathan DiGesare, Thunderpuss (Chris Cox and Barry Harris)

Donna's first release of the new decade, the new century and new millennium was truly of epic proportions (not to mention her second and final single on the Epic label). The other new recording on the *Live and More Encore!* album, 'Love Is The Healer' was Donna living her best life, not as the Queen of Disco, but as the Queen of House. A US dance #1 (and top-ten hit in Spain), for some unfathomable reason this was not released as a commercial single in the US. There was also no music video for 'Love Is The Healer'—it was almost as if Epic gave up on Donna after just one single and one live album. There is, however, a stunning live performance of Donna belting out 'Love Is The Healer' on *The Queen Latifah Show* available online, plus she sang it on VH1's *Divas 2000.*

Remix fix!

Eric Kupper's blissed out loved-up 'I Feel Healed' 7-inch (3:56) and 12-inch mix (8:13) cheekily interpolated 'I Feel Love'. If you've ever been near a dancefloor when this mix drops you already know what a rush of pure healing dancefloor pleasure it emits. Thunderpuss (who dropped the 2000 from their name for obvious reasons) couldn't compete at all with their throbbing, but fairly regulation, 8:58 Club Mix. Hear Kupper's healing mix now!

'If There Is Music There'

Writers: Donna Summer, Michael Omartian
Producers: Bruce Sudano, Donna Summer, Mike Hanna

Originally only included on 1999's long-form *Live & More Encore* video/ DVD were four new live songs: 'If There Is Music There', 'Riding Through The Storm', 'Don't Wanna Work' and 'Nobody'. This awesome foursome finally got a proper release in May 2013, a year after Donna passed away, on the compilation *Playlist: The Very Best of Donna Summer* (Epic/Legacy—88883710842). 'I got together with Michael Omartian, with whom I'd written several songs and albums including *She Works Hard for the Money* and asked him if he would help me write my musical,' Donna wrote in her memoir. 'There was one song that was living inside of me I had to get out—"If There Is Music There". We sat down and started writing and in the first two days had three songs we both felt were better than anything we had ever done before.' Donna then brought husband Bruce and Al Kasha on to her planned musical, which had become 'one of my major projects'. *Billboard* wrote in their review of the *Live & More Encore!* show that when Donna effortlessly sang heartfelt ballad 'If There Is Music There', 'there wasn't a dry eye in the house, including hers'. This powerful yet tender Broadway-ready showstopper re-emerged in 2023's *Love To Love You, Donna Summer* doco.

'Riding Through The Storm'

Writers: V. Michael McKay
Producers: Bruce Sudano, Donna Summer, Mike Hanna

It's gospel time as Jesus holds Donna in his arms while she brings it back to church. A barely serviceable live production does at the very least allow Donna to ride/rise above with her storming vocals. 'Riding Through The Storm' was written by V. Michael McKay, a member of the gospel group Michael McKay And The Redeemed Family Ensemble. In 2000 he was inducted into the Gospel Hall of Fame. Originally recorded in 1991 by gospel singer Yolanda Adams, it was listed as 'Through The Storm' on her album of the same name. Coincidentally, or perhaps not, Mervyn Warren, who would co-write Donna's 'The Power Of One' the following year, was also a producer on Adams's album.

'Don't Wanna Work'

Writers: Donna Summer, R. Mitchell
Producers: Bruce Sudano, Donna Summer, Mike Hanna

Switching genres, Donna next tackled country on the *Live & More Encore!* concert with 'Don't Wanna Work'. It's not actually a song about working hard for the money 9–5, but about Donna not wanting to work that hard at love if it makes her cry. Complete with sturdy singalong chorus, it's a surprise no country artist has picked this up to cover it since. Yet Donna had a long history with country music. In 1980 Dolly Parton recorded Donna's song 'Starting Over Again', making it a country #1. 'The song was written about my parents' impending divorce,' Bruce Sudano, who co-wrote it with Donna, recalled.

> I was in my late twenties and learned my parents were getting divorced. Even though I was an adult it still shook me up emotionally. There I was in the back bedroom of our house working this song out and Donna opened the door, stuck her head in and said I should write something in the song about all the king's horses and all the king's men. I said OK. I finished the song, and as it would be with Donna and her creative writing ability, the line of the song almost everybody remembers is, 'All the king's horses and all the king's men couldn't put mommy and daddy back together again'. Donna was scheduled to go on *The Tonight Show* to perform her new single that was coming out. She said to me that day, 'I'm going to sing "Starting Over Again" on the show tonight.' I said, 'That would be great, but you really shouldn't do that. You'll be on the show to promote your new single and you need to do that.' She said, 'Maybe if I sing this song, your parents will reconsider and stay together.' I said that it was a sweet thought, but I didn't think it was within the realm of possibility. She said, 'You never know. I'm going to do it'. So, she went on to Johnny Carson's show and sang 'Starting Over Again', and the next day Dolly Parton's people call up and request the song and Dolly recorded it. Then fifteen years later Reba McEntire also recorded it and made it the title of her album.

'Nobody'

Writers: Donna Summer, Mike Hanna
Producers: Bruce Sudano, Donna Summer, Mike Hanna

Now 50 years old, Donna was determined the comeback opportunity of her VH-1 concert would not only showcase her back catalogue of hits, but also her new music and projects. 'Nobody' was yet another song from Donna's musical that would have to wait some years until it would be released outside the *Live & More Encore!* VHS/DVD. Debuting the smooth R&B-flavoured 'Nobody' for the audience, it was such a new song Donna had never sung it live before. Her band had also barely had any time to rehearse it before showtime. 'I sang that for you!' Donna told the audience when she finished. The line 'nobody can love you like I do' seemed like yet another poignant tribute to her diehard fans. Long-time Donna Summer band member Bob Conti made a telling observation some years after the release of *Live & More Encore!*, saying, 'There was something in that original band with Mike Warren, Virgil Weber, Richard Adelman and Doug Livingston that was more energetic and lively,' he insisted. 'You can hear the difference on Donna's *Live and More* album from 1978, versus her *Live & More Encore!* album from 1999. It's a totally different listening experience.'

'When I Look Up' (duet with Darwin Hobbs)

EMI Gospel: EGD 0252. Album released: April 2000
Writers: Cedric Caldwell, Victor Caldwell, Hallerin Hill
Producers: Cedric Caldwell, Victor Caldwell

With a silky drawl often drawing comparisons with Luther Vandross, gospel great and 'Worship pastor' Darwin Hobbs released his second album, *Vertical*, in 2000. Besides a duet with Michael McDonald, it featured another pairing, 'When I Look Up', with Donna. If you've ever wanted to hear Donna duetting with Luther Vandross then this might be about as close as you're ever likely to get. The song itself is adroit R&B soul, focusing on a love for Jesus in place of romantic love. It's a shame that for most of the song Darwin and Donna sing separately. Only towards the end do they join together in perfect Christian harmony. Fun fact: another track on this album, 'So Amazing', is a gospel rendition of Luther Vandross's 1996 hit, later recorded as a Grammy-winning duet in 2005 by Beyoncé and Stevie Wonder. In the UK Darwin's *Vertical* album was retitled *Everyday,* complete with a slightly different track listing.

'Dreamcatcher' (from *Naturally Native: Original Soundtrack Recording*)

Silver Wave Records: SD 924. Album release: May 2000
Writers: Donna Summer, Mike Hanna
Producer: James Marienthal

Naturally Native was an American film drama written and directed by Native American woman Valerie Red-Horse. Funded by a Native American tribe from Connecticut, the movie failed to get a distributor when completed in 1998, going straight to video. Donna was by far the biggest name involved in this soundtrack, but who were the others here (Walela! Murielle Hamilton! Mystic River Singers!)? 'Dreamcatcher', which is almost six minutes long, is best described as a languid country and western ballad in which Donna sings about 'lights dancing on your pillow'. If you've never heard this track, or never even heard of it before, there's a good reason for that. A dreamcatcher, in case you've never come across one, is a handmade Native American hoop usually hung above a bed as spiritual protection.

'The Power Of One'

Atlantic: 85021-2. Single release: July 2000
Writers: Mervyn Warren, Mark Chait,
Producer: David Foster

The *Pokémon 2000* soundtrack included contributions from The B-52's, Westlife, Laura Pausini and Weird Al Yankovic. The English-language version of this Japanese movie was released in July 2000 and on a budget of $30m *Pokémon* made almost $133m. 'A friend of mine called me and said, "You've got to hear this song, it's perfect for you!",' Donna explained at release time. 'I like singing positive songs, I like singing songs that make people happy and I like singing songs that encourage people to do great things.' Co-writer Mervyn Warren, a former member of *a cappella* group Take 6, was a multiple Grammy winner involved in film/TV and gospel/Christian music, while Mark Chait was a film composer and concert pianist. Strangely, no music video was made for the song, which might explain why it failed to chart. In 2011, however, Donna's *The Power Of One* gained new and unexpected attention. Black Republican candidate Herman Cain quoted its lyrics ('Life can be a challenge/Life can seem impossible/But it's never easy when there's so much on the line') as part of his presidential campaign, failing to acknowledge the correct source until much later, then bowing out of the presidential race. A staunch anti-vaxxer, he died in 2020 of Covid-19.

Remix fix!

Dance mixes of 'The Power Of One', ranging from Tommy Musto's ear-pleasing Main Vocal Mix to Jonathan Peters' almost unlistenable Sound Factory Club Mix, were released some months later in October 2000, reaching #2 on *Billboard*'s Dance Club Songs chart.

21

Child of the Promise (2000)/ *The Journey: The Very Best Of Donna Summer* (2003)

Child Of The Promise—A Musical Celebrating The Birth Of Christ

Sparrow Records: SPD 1702. Album release: September 2000
Writers: Michael Omartian, Stormie Omartian
Producer: Michael Omartian

As its title suggests (in case you missed it!) *Child Of The Promise—A Musical Celebrating The Birth Of Christ*—is very much a Christian musical. Donna isn't the only big-name Christian artist involved. Written by Michael Omartian and wife Stormie, this ambitious project also features Michael Crawford, Richard Marx, Amy Grant and Vince Gill. Of the thirty songs comprising this mammoth effort, Donna's vocals appear on four. She is solo on 'Elizabeth Recitative' (1:22) and 'When The Dream Never Dies' (3:23), then duets with Crystal Lewis on 'Mary And Elizabeth Recitative' (0:48) and 'I Cannot Be Silent' (4:12). Using scripture put to contemporary Christian rock music, it's definitely something for those who: (a) love musicals; (b) love a good Christian story; (c) love Christian musicals and (d) all of the above. Donna takes the role of the elderly Elizabeth, related to Mary, mother of Jesus, who miraculously became pregnant with John the Baptist. Without the catchy pop punch of *Jesus Christ Superstar*, however, *Child Of The Promise* can be hard going to listen to, especially Donna and Crystal's strident duet of 'I Cannot Be Silent'. Donna's big solo number, 'When The Dream Never Dies', while no 'I Don't Know How To Love Him', does allow Donna a chance to utilise all of her own childhood promise and then some.

'Rosie Christmas' (from *Another Rosie Christmas* album)

Columbia: CK 85102. Album release: October 2000
Writers: Donna Summer, Denise Rich, Garianno Lorenzo
Producer: Ric Wake

'A Rosie Christmas is a Christmas full of love'! Who knew? The sequel to 1999's *A Rosie Christmas* album, the cleverly-titled *Another Rosie Christmas* featured a new Donna song, 'Rosie Christmas'. Yup, it was all about television talk show host Rosie O'Donnell. The album reached #45 in the US charts, selling over half a million copies, with other big names involved including Destiny's Child, Ricky Martin and Barry Manilow. House music legend Eric Kupper played keyboards on the fluffy, almost SAW-esque 'Rosie Christmas', which may be why it's almost the disco Christmas record we always prayed for from Donna.

'Take Heart' (from *The Mercy Project* album)

Word Entertainment: DOP 01931. Album release: November 2000
Writers: Donna Summer, Bruce Sudano, Nathan DiGesare
Producer: Nathan DiGesare, Bruce Sudano

This compilation album was inspired by the Mercy Ministries of America organisation, a notoriously anti-gay and pro-life Christian charity. All artists on this record were female Christian singers including Amy Grant, Darlene Zschech and Michelle Tumes. Donna's contribution was the inspirational ballad 'Take Heart'. Perhaps the best that can be said about it is that Donna's voice soars high above the schlocky production (a children's choir also appear momentarily) and her lyrics meant well. Due to bad press the organisation rebranded as Mercy Multiplies in 2015. Lord, have mercy!

'Someone To Watch Over Me' (from *Keeping The Dream Alive* album)

Epic: EK 61402. Album release: December 2001
Writers: George Gershwin, Ira Gershwin, Howard Dietz
Producers: Bruce Sudano, Donna Summer, Mike Hanna

In 2001 the charity compilation album *VH-1 Music First: Race To Erase MS— Keeping the Dream Alive* was issued, featuring Donna's live rendition of the standard 'Someone to Watch Over Me'. Unceremoniously cut from the *Live & More Encore!* CD, it was kept in the television show and on the video/ DVD.

Here, at last, was Donna finally not just having dinner with Gershwin, but singing Gershwin! Originally written in 1926 for the musical *Oh Kay!*, the song evolved from an up-tempo jazzy number into the definitive slow torch song, with Frank Sinatra, Barbra Streisand and Linda Ronstadt also recording versions. Spending time in her Manhattan apartment in September that year close to the Twin Towers, Donna later privately claimed her lung cancer diagnosis was a result of toxic dust inhalation from the 9/11 terrorist attacks. The tragic event also sent Donna into a spiral of depression, which took two years to overcome.

'You're So Beautiful'

UTV Records: UTVFO5121-2. Promo released: February 2003
Writers: Donna Summer, Tony Moran, Nathan DiGesare
Producer: Tony Moran

Less than a decade after her last compilation, *The Journey: The Very Best of Donna Summer* was issued, essentially replacing two songs on 2003's *Endless Summer* with three newer ones. Yet some six months earlier 'buzz' track 'You're So Beautiful' was promoted to club DJs with mixes by producer Tony Moran, and Glenn Friscia, to gauge interest. Donna was back in business! It wasn't until September that *Billboard* reported how 'You're So Beautiful' was 'being championed by numerous circuit and big-room DJs', but without a label home. Literally no sooner had they spoken than it appeared as one of three new tracks on *The Journey*, released just two weeks before Donna's memoir, *Ordinary Girl: The Journey*. In a stroke of PR synergy Donna's husband Bruce Sudano released his second solo album, *Rainy Day Soul*, on the same day as Donna's album. While *The Journey* sold well and charted high (#6 both in the UK and on the US Catalogue Album charts), the tribal house 'You're So Beautiful' got sent to DJs as a 12-inch promo called 'The New Mixes' (UTVFO5126-1 ST01) by Tony Moran/Mac Quayle and Frank Lamboy. The 12-inch DJ promo reached #5 on the US Dance Club Songs chart, while the Ultimate Club Mix appeared on the limited edition of *The Journey*. In 2005 a revised edition of *The Donna Summer Anthology* was issued with new cover art and a tweaked track listing, including a 4:05 Tony Moran edit of 'You're So Beautiful'.

The Journey: The Very Best Of Donna Summer (2003)

Mercury/UTV Records: B0001009-02
Originally released: September 2003

US edition

'Love to Love You Baby'	3:22
'Could It Be Magic'	3:54
'I Feel Love'	3:46
'I Love You'	3:18
'Last Dance'	3:19
'MacArthur Park'	3:54
'Heaven Knows'	3:39
'Hot Stuff'	3:50
'Bad Girls'	3:57
'Dim All the Lights'	3:58
'No More Tears (Enough Is Enough)'	4:48
'On the Radio'	4:05
'The Wanderer'	3:46
'Love is in Control (Finger on the Trigger)'	4:19
'State of Independence'	4:25
'She Works Hard for the Money'	4:10
'This Time I Know It's for Real'	3:36
'I Will Go with You (Con te partirò)'	4:08
'That's The Way'	3:45
'Dream-A-Lot's Theme (I Will Live for Love)'	4:54

US limited edition bonus disc

'I Feel Love' (12-inch Version)	8:15
'Hot Stuff' (12-inch Version)	6:46
'This Time I Know It's for Real' (12-inch Version)	7:24
'Dream-A-Lot's Theme (I Will Live for Love)' (12-inch Extended Version)	9:16
'You're So Beautiful' (Ultimate Club Mix)	10:50

'That's The Way'

Writers: Giorgio Moroder, Keith Forsey
Producer: Giorgio Moroder

Another decade after they last carried on with 'Carry On', Donna and Giorgio reunited again for the poppy, almost Britney-esque 'That's The Way'. Legend has it 'That's The Way' was originally intended for Gwen Stefani, but landed with Donna instead. A bunch of adequate remixes by Almighty were also commissioned. While it was great to see Donna and Giorgio back in business, the end result was one of their most underwhelming collabs. Quizzed in 2003 as to whether there was a full-length album in the works, Donna replied, 'well, as soon as I can get it finished. When I'm doing music I want to do music. I'm not one of those who can just hop in and do one song, so hopefully I'll be able to get this album done by next spring.' As it transpired the journey there was half a decade away.

'Dream-A-Lot's Theme (I Will Live For Love)'

UTV Records: UTVFO5128-1. 12-inch Promo released: March 2004
Writers: Donna Summer, Nathan DiGesare
Producer: Giorgio Moroder

The third of three new songs on *The Journey* was 'Dream-A-Lot's Theme (I Will Live For Love)', written for a planned children's musical called *The Legend Of Dreamway*. Produced again by Giorgio, he spun the song in a speedy, hi-NRG direction that must have blown the roofs off gay clubs with its anthemic chorus. Released as a 12-inch promo single to DJs, it reached #20 on the US Hot Dance Club Play chart. In 2003 Donna spoke to *Windy City Times* about her new material.

> I've written several stories and actually I have songs that emerge from these. One of the songs I recorded, 'Dream-A-Lot's Theme', is from a children's story concept about a prince and takes place in the dream-way when people are asleep, when people close their eyes. It's what happens to us when we dream. The prince of dreams, he's the prince of that realm, and he guards your dreams for your life. His whole objective is to guard your childish dreams from the time you're born. I have so much material, if people don't cut me loose from the disco it'll never be heard in my lifetime probably. I'm hoping that won't be the case, because I've become a much better and more sophisticated writer over the years.

A spellbinding ballad version of *Dream-A-Lot's Theme* is also available online, while titles 'Dreamway' and 'Dreamway Express' appear to be from this unreleased children's musical.

'Power Of Love' (from *So Amazing: An All-Star Tribute To Luther Vandross* album)

J Records: 82876-62472-2. Album release: September 2005
Writers: Luther Vandross, Marcus Miller
Producer: Hani, The Underdogs

Released just a few months after his death in July 2005, this collection of Luther Vandross classics recorded by superstar artists reached #4 in the US charts and #25 in the UK. Truly living up to its title, *So Amazing: An All-Star Tribute To Luther Vandross* was bursting with big-name talent including Aretha Franklin, Mary J Blige, Beyoncé, Stevie Wonder, Celine Dion, Elton John and Patti Labelle. Luther Vandross's biggest pop hit was 1991's *Power Of Love*, reaching #4 in the US charts (and #46 in the UK), and assigned to

Donna for this album. Luther's pop/R&B classic got a burbling dance coating via producer Hani Adnan Al-Bader, who had previously worked his magic on Michael Jackson, Justin Timberlake and Christina Aguilera. He shared duty on Donna's cover with R&B songwriting/production duo Damon Thomas and Harvey Mason Jr, aka The Underdogs. Donna and Luther had some serious history. In 1979 he sang background vocals/vocal arrangements on Donna's duet with Barbra Streisand, 'No More Tears (Enough Is Enough)', credited as Luther Waters, and he was credited for background vocals on 1977's 'I Love You'. Donna's 'Power Of Love' release came just a few months after her father, Andrew Gaines, died aged 80 on 14 December 2004. At his funeral Donna and her siblings sang, 'our favourite family song "We Come This Far By Faith"'. Donna was also compelled to write a song, 'Welcome To Heaven', in his honour.

Remix fix!

Hani also powered up a bunch of promo remixes (J Records: 82876 74077 1), while an RCA Music Group promo included club-powered remixes from both Offer Nissim and Peter Rauhofer. Lamentably it reached a lowly #43 in the US club charts.

'Are You Brave?' (from *Songs From The Neighborhood—The Music Of Mister Rogers*)

Memory Lane Syndication:CD711. Album release: October 2005
Writer:Fred Rogers
Producer:Dennis Scott

Songs From The Neighborhood—The Music Of Mister Rogers gathered together a cavalcade of American artists who had grown up with US kids' television fixture Fred 'Mister' Rogers to pay tribute to him. Not only did Rogers wear a signature red sweater, but he was also a Christian minister, which probably endeared him to Donna and family. His television show aired on PBS from 1968 until 2001. He died in 2003 at the age of 73. 'Are You Brave?', which Rogers wrote, was sung twice on his show—in 1986 and 1996—and included on his 1992 *You're Growing* CD/cassette. Producer Dennis Scott won a Grammy for his work on this album, while Rogers' story inspired the 2019 movie *A Beautiful Day In The Neighborhood*, starring Tom Hanks. 'What a pleasure to work with a legend,' Scott said in a 2005 interview also featuring footage of Donna recording 'Are You Brave?' in the studio. 'She's larger than life and a lot of fun. She wanted to do something new and fresh with this song and not necessarily something that harkened to her disco days. We came up with an arrangement we feel accomplished that.' Starting as a sweet ballad before breaking into a faster R&B groove, 'Are You Brave?' is a decent enough tune deserving a decent remix. Roberta Flack, Amy Grant and Crystal Gayle are among the other twelve artists featured on the album. A collective of all the artists sing the one new track on the album, 'Thank You For Being You', written by Scott, which is so sickly saccharine it could rot toddlers' teeth.

Vid bit!
A DVD was included with the *Songs From the Neighborhood* CD featuring interviews and studio footage, plus a 'Thank You For Being You' video with Donna (in her 'brave' sunnies).

'I Got Your Love'

Mercury: B0006043-32. Single release: December 2005
Writers: Donna Summer, Bruce Roberts
Producer: Peter Stengaard

The simple fact Bruce Roberts co-wrote 'No More Tears (Enough Is Enough)' will always endear him to Donna fans, but that he has also co-written some of her lamest material is worth considering. Here's another example of one of his compositions letting Team Donna down. Produced unimaginatively by Dane Peter Stengaard, 'I Got Your Love' was played during an episode of the television series *Sex and the City* in 2003. It took another two years before it was issued as a single, hitting #4 on the US Hot Dance Club Play chart, thanks to some on-trend mid-noughties remix work from Ralphi Rosario, L.E.X. and Eddie Baez. Stengaard would return some five years to produce Donna's final single.

'A Whole New World' (Dave Koz featuring Donna Summer) (from *Dave Koz—At The Movies* album)

Capitol Records: CDP 0946 3 11405 2 5. Album release: January 2007
Writers: Alan Menken, Tim Rice
Producers: Phil Ramone

In early 2007 saxophonist Dave Koz released a collection of stage and screen classics, *At The Movies*, his first album after coming out as gay in 2004. Drenched in his usual schmaltzy jazz style, Koz called upon an impressive line-up of guest vocalists including Anita Baker, Barry Manilow and Vanessa Williams. 'A Whole New World', from Disney's 1992 *Aladdin* movie, reaching #1 in the US sung by Peabo Bryson (who passed in 2026) and Regina Belle, was chosen for

Donna. Minus a singing partner, but with Koz blowing his worldly instrument to accompany her, their vocal/sax duet veers close to easy listening muzak. Fortuitously, it's rescued by Ramone's restrained production, that Oscar-winning melody and Donna's always superlative vocals.

22

Crayons (2008)

Crayons
Burgundy Records: 88697 22992 2
Originally released: May 2008

'Stamp Your Feet'	3:52	'Science Of Love'	3:48
'Mr. Music'	3:14	'Be Myself Again'	4:19
'Crayons'	3:21	'Bring Down The Reign'	4:33
'The Queen Is Back'	3:27	International Edition Bonus Track 'It's Only Love'	6:58
'Fame (The Game)'	4:03	i Tunes Bouns Track	
'Sand On My Feet'	3:51	'I'm A Fire (Matty Soulflower Club Mix)'	9:00
'Drivin' Down Brazil'	4:43		
'I'm A Fire'	7:11		
'Slide Over Backwards'	4:10		

'I'M A FIRE'

Sony BMG Music Entertainment/Burgundy: (no number). Single release: March 2008
Writers: Donna Summer, Al Kasha, Sebastian Arocha Morton
Producer: Sebastian Arocha Morton

Fast approaching 60, at the end of 2008 Donna released her seventeenth and final studio album, *Crayons*. Two singles were released ahead of the album's launch in May, with the first being 'I'm A Fire' in March. There were so many remixes– over thirty!—that it took two maxi CD singles to house them. Still, it did the trick because when 'I'm A Fire' went to #1 on *Billboard*'s Hot Dance Club

Songs chart it made Donna the only artist to have a #1 dance hit in every decade since the 1970s. Although a true dance burner, 'I'm A Fire' possessed, according to Donna, 'a mellow softness to it that makes it sound unlike a thumping typical dance tune'. Just to make sure it had some extra heat, 'I'm A Fire' even featured some lyrics in Spanish. Standout remixes came from Redtop, Baggi Begovic & Soul Conspiracy, Craig C and Solitaire's unmissable disco-house club mix. Producer Sebastian Arocha Morton would go on to work on Bruce Sudano's *Life And The Romantic* solo album in 2010. Legendary songwriter Alfred Kasha, who contributed to the 'I'm A Fire' track and whom Donna called 'a quiet man with thunder in your soul', died in 2020 at the age of 83.

'Stamp Your Feet'

Sony BMG Music Entertainment: (no number). Single release: April 2008
Writers: Donna Summer, Danielle Brisebois, Greg Kurstin
Producer: Greg Kurstin

'I've been around so many times before!' The first official *Crayons* lead single, 'Stamp Your Feet', released a mere few weeks after 'I'm A Fire' in April 2008, was Donna getting her game on and bringing it for this 'biggest' (or is it 'big ass'?) sound. It was originally titled 'The Player's Anthem' because, so Donna said, it talked about 'being a player in life, coupled with the idea of being a player on an actual field, the whole thing, dealing with the pain and doing things even though you are afraid'. *Billboard* mistakenly called the song 'Stomp Your Feet', then claimed 'it rocks a big room like a hipper Celine Dion anthem'. In its original form something of a stadium rock tune, 'Stamp Your Feet' was transformed into a club stomper by Jason Nevins, DJ Escape/Tony Coluccio, DiscoTech, Granite & Sugarman and a pumping mix by Ranny that might be the best of the bunch. Not surprisingly 'Stamp Your Feet'(space) also raced to #1 on *Billboard*'s Hot Dance Club Songs.

Vid bit!
Sony weren't prepared to spend any more money than they had to, hence the 'video' for 'Stamp Your Feet' was Donna pretending to sing it in a studio. Boo! Better is when Donna memorably performed 'Stamp Your Feet', together with 'Last Dance', live on *American Idol* in 2008 with the female contestants (and— *ooh chile!*—that high note she hits at the end).

'Mr. Music'

Writers: Donna Summer, Evan 'Kidd' Bogart, Jonathan Rotem, Meredith Wilson
Producer: Jonathan Rotem

Imagine a cross between Madonna's 2000 hit 'Music' and her 2003 duet with Britney Spears, 'Me Against The Music', and you might arrive somewhere close to 'Mr. Music'. Regrettably, the very first line, 'I got my iPod', hasn't aged well. '"Mr. Music", he's like any DJ, the guy on the radio station, the guy in the DJ booth, the guy that's changing your moods, the guy that keeps you going, the guy that's on the radio in the morning when you're driving,' Donna told the press at the time of the release of *Crayons*. 'He's everything you need him to be. Music fast forwards you from one place to another because it takes you away from where you are in a strange way and elevates your mood. When I play "Mr. Music" it's euphoric, it's very happy.' Part of the team involved in penning 'Mr. Music' was Evan Bogart, the son of her former boss, Neil Bogart, who died in 1982 when Evan was just four years old. Working with Bogart Jnr, who 'looks just like his dad' according to Donna, was 'interesting and very joyful'. 'She's still got it,' Bogart responded. 'Her voice is so powerful; she still has that Donna diva swagger.' 'Mr. Music' also, randomly, contains a portion of the song 'Belly Up To The Bar Boys' taken from the sixties musical *The Unsinkable Molly Brown*. There is an 'in-studio music video' for 'Mr. Music', which again looks like it cost around $5 ... with change!

'Crayons' (featuring Ziggy Marley)

Writers: Donna Summer, Danielle Brisebois, Greg Kurstin, Ziggy Marley
Producer: Greg Kurstin

Time to turn the beat around as Donna flips to a pop/reggae groove reminiscent of Rihanna's 'Pon De Replay' 2005 debut, even taking on a kind of Creole patois singing voice. If fellow *Crayons* vox Ziggy Marley sounds like he might be the son of reggae legend Bob Marley, then that's probably because he is. Donna described the background of *Crayons*, and the overall aesthetic of her album, as 'a menagerie of colours and styles, with hints of different ethnic traditions and sounds. My dream is when people hear the music it will remind them of their youth, their childhood and the joy and wonderment they felt exploring their first pack of crayons.' Fun fact: the same year Donna released *Crayons* was the 50th anniversary of Crayola's box of sixty-four crayons. Co-writer (and former child star) Danielle Brisebois said working with Donna was one of the biggest blessings in her life. 'Being in a room when she is singing,' she exclaimed, 'is the musical equivalent of the best massage you have ever had'.

'The Queen Is Back'

Writers: Donna Summer, Evan 'Kidd' Bogart, Jonathan Rotem
Producer: Jonathan Rotem

Not only was the queen (of disco) back, she was now your Fairy Godmother, according to the tongue-in-cheek lyrics of 'The Queen Is Back', which might just be the best on the album, taking aim at the cesspool of celebrity. 'I'm making fun of myself,' Donna insisted. 'There's irony. It's poking fun at the idea of being called a queen. That's the title that has followed me. We were sitting and writing and that title kept popping up in my mind and I'm thinking, "Am I supposed to write this? Is this too arrogant to write?"'. But people call me "the queen", so I guess it's okay to refer to myself as what everybody else refers to me as.' No doubt her gay audience also saw the double entendre in the song's title and took it to heart. As with 'Stamp Your Feet', Sony filmed Donna singing in a studio singing 'The Queen Is Back' for what they euphemistically call an 'in-studio music video'. We call it cheap and a missed opportunity.

'Fame (The Game)'

Sony BMG Music Entertainment: (no number) Single release: November 2008
Writers: Donna Summer, Toby Gad
Producer: Toby Gad

The final rock house single from *Crayons* came with some famously game, and infamously good, remixes by Ralphi Rosario. Wouldn't you know, it also hit #1 on the US Hot Dance Club Songs chart. 'Fame (The Game)' might also, remarkably, feature Donna's first proper attempt at rapping on a record! 'The song went fast,' co-writer and producer of 'Fame (The Game)', Toby Gad, explained.

> She had started the hook to a different track and I loved the idea, so I wrote the verses in two hours and recorded her on the day. Two weeks later the label called me from the mastering room and said, 'We can't use the track, can you write new music to it?' So I had half a day to produce a new track to it and send it straight to the mastering studio.

Gad, who wrote three of the twelve tracks on *Crayons*, added, 'it's such an honour for me to work with her. I was blown away by her voice. With Donna, her first take is usually the keeper.'

'Sand On My Feet'

Writers: Donna Summer, Toby Gad
Producer: Toby Gad

Listening to the love gush out of Donna as she sings this stripped-back, acoustic number, it's obvious 'Sand On My Feet' is all about the love of her life, husband

Bruce. She even gives a shout-out to Bruce in the album's liner notes, calling him, 'my husband and lover boy—all that I need is sand on my feet and you'. Awww. Donna wrote the song at her Florida beach cottage with Toby Gad, and said it was 'one of the few times I've written from my own point of view'. Gad remembers he spent four days at Donna's 'amazing' beach house.

> One day we were just looking out the window at the ocean. I jammed on the guitar and she sang whatever she saw and felt about the beach and about the love for her wonderful husband. Then she got hungry and went to the kitchen to cook. I followed her with the guitar in the kitchen and said, 'Donna, I know you're hungry, but we need to finish this song idea!' So we continued writing the song while she was cooking.

When Donna performed 'Sand On My Feet' live she would project a picture of the view of the ocean from her house.

'Drivin' Down Brazil'

Writers: Donna Summer, Danielle Brisebois, Greg Kurstin
Producer: Greg Kurstin

Although the title suggests the country of Brazil, Donna was actually inspired to write 'Drivin' Down Brazil' after seeing a man getting into a classic Bonneville car on Miami's Brazil Street. 'I just made up this story,' Donna revealed. 'He's on Brazil Street and he's headed straight down to the actual country from there. It's Friday night and he's going to go see his girlfriend. He's envisioning her and he's got this long drive ahead of him.' From that beginning 'Drivin' Down Brazil' took on a Brazilian bossa nova flavour, even including a little Portuguese. When Donna toured Brazil in 2009—fourteen years after her last visit—she made a point to include 'Drivin' Down Brazil' in the setlist. A Latin America flavour wasn't the only spice added to Donna's *Crayons* as she attempted to incorporate many different sounds to give a more global feel to the album. 'When you make music, obviously you have to find your market while you are working at the same time,' Donna explained. 'My idea, when I was in, was global.'

'Slide Over Backwards'

Writers: Donna Summer, Nathan DiGesare, Jakob Petren
Producer: Nathan DiGesare

Donna Summer, the storyteller, made a bold reappearance on 'Slide Over Backwards'. Creating a character with the name of Hattie Mae Blanche Dubois, she takes on the character's voice (a bluesy swamp queen) and even featured a picture she painted of her inside the album sleeve. 'Hattie Mae is a bartender in the south,' Donna clarified.

> She grew up in a very rough environment. Her parents died when she was young. She really had to fend for herself at a very early age. The streets were pretty much her home. She had some relatives that gave her handouts, but really was pretty much on her own. She wanted to sing, but her life was hard. Finally, she evolves to a place where she owns, by default, this little po' boy restaurant. It's like a little diner the local people love. It's actually becoming quite famous and on certain days of the week she gets a little piano player in there and she sings. This is her moment to shine.

Donna also told Australia's *The Age* newspaper that she had 'other songs that I've written for her, in the same voice'. While critics called 'Slide Over Backwards' Donna's attempt at Tina Turner's 1973 hit 'Nutbush City Limits', many missed that a major nineties popstar provided background vocals on the song: former Ace of Base singer Jenny Berggren. An alternate version of 'Slide Over Backwards', most likely the original demo, has also surfaced online.

'Science Of Love'

Writers: Donna Summer, Toby Gad
Producer: Toby Gad

Donna was inspired to write the very noughties pop-sounding 'Science of Love' while watching television's Science Channel. 'There was a show about attraction between men and woman and brain sex,' Donna explained. 'It was not about sex as such, but about attraction between people and how you look at people. I thought to myself that there is a real science to love even though we don't realise it.' Donna performed 'Science of Love' on Sirius Radio's 'Artist Confidential' segment, where she was interviewed about the *Crayons* album. 'Singing my old hits is wonderful,' she admitted, 'but at some point there's a thing in me going, "I need some new songs!". I can't keep doing this to my fans. They deserve some new songs. I figured if I'm not going to do something new then I might as well retire.'

'Be Myself Again'

Writers: Donna Summer, Wayne Hector, Lester Mendez
Producer: Lester Mendez

On the verge of turning 60, here's the haunting ballad ("Let me introduce myself/ I'm a woman that you've never seen") that allowed Donna to make a whole new album some seventeen years after her previous one, *Mistaken Identity*. 'When my record company came to me about two years ago they wanted me to do oldies, what Rod Stewart was doing. They said, "Well, we don't know what market you'd be in at this point and we don't know if we could get you into the mainstream market anymore!". That was a valid point, but I didn't feel it was necessarily the truth,' Donna said. She then played the Sony execs 'Be Myself Again', inspired by British balladeer James Blunt. 'I was thinking to myself, 'I would love to do a song like "You're Beautiful" where I don't sing very many lyrics, where there is just the simplicity of a broken heart, no frills. They never mentioned that oldies thing again. Not once.' The sole effort on the *Crayons* album by Cuban producer Lester Mendez, he was then known for his work with Shakira, Dido and Josh Groban. 'Be Myself Again' co-writer Wayne Hector coincidentally went on to work with James Blunt soon after Donna's record.

'Bring Down The Reign'

Writers: Donna Summer, Jamie Houston, Fred Kron
Producer: Jamie Houston

Album closer 'Bring Down The Reign' is Donna in socially conscious mode, praying for an end to the ongoing genocide in Sudan's Darfur region in northern Africa, featuring the Agape Children's Choir. To prove she was putting her money where her mouth was, Donna donated any royalties from 'Bring Down The Reign' to charities providing aid in Darfur. Reviews for the *Crayons* album were decidedly mixed. The *Guardian* gave it two out of five stars, stating, 'most of the cuts on *Crayons* are adequate, but there is a distinct lack of the unmoored, thrilling sensuality that Summer used to trade in so effortlessly'. Yet the BBC called *Crayons*, 'a fine encapsulation of her career to date—a pinch of dance, some frothy pop, a power ballad or two, all given a 2008 sheen'. *The Village Voice*, meanwhile, decreed '*Crayons*' second half is a victory lap with no Summer in sight—she's already past us', while *Billboard* summed it up as 'a surprisingly lively set'.

'It's Only Love'

Sony BMG Music Entertainment: (no number). Single release: June 2008
Writers: Donna Summer, Al Kasha, Sebastian Arocha Morton
Producer: Sebastian Arocha Morton

Just before you'd given up hope there might be a glitter bomb of old school disco Donna on *Crayons*, the international bonus track and US third single (available initially only on Circuit City editions) 'It's Only Love' landed.

Amid a Moroder-esque electro-disco setting Donna was in sexy whisper mode, informing us, 'I don't need nothing but you and music'. Released as a single in the summer of 2008, it failed to chart. There were no remixes and no video, with Amazon listing it as a separate single with its own cover. That did this terrific song a true disservice. Donna wrote about her co-writer and producer on 'It's Only Love', Sebastian Arocha Morton, on the *Crayons* liner notes: 'Your latin passion and attentiveness to my energy in the studio was so fuelling. I am a fire. You and I are a great match'. Indeed, based on this and his other *Crayons* contribution, 'I'm A Fire', they certainly were, and it's a shame they never got to work together again.

23

'To Paris with Love'/ *Love to Love You Donna...* and beyond (2010–25)

'To Paris With Love'

Driven By The Music/Chalkboard: (no number). Single release: August 2010
Writers: Donna Summer, Bruce Roberts
Producers: Peter Stengaard

This chic, understated single would ultimately be Donna's final solo single while still alive. Already it was obvious that the power in her voice was gradually being siphoned away by her cancer diagnosis. The first release of 'To Paris With Love' featured the original version and a radio edit, plus remixes from WAWA, Craig C and MENDy. A second batch of ten remixes from Eddie Amador, DJ DLG, Automatic Panic, Uner and David Herrero dropped a month later. Other mixes from Jandry and DJ Strobe appeared on a European promo maxi-single, not from Driven By The Music, suggesting these were fan edits. In 2024 dance label Peace Bisquit posted about 'To Paris With Love' on SoundCloud. 'Back in 2010 Peace Bisquit were fortunate and honoured to work with one of our absolute favourites,' they wrote. 'The song went to #1 on the *Billboard* dance charts for the week ending November 6, 2010. This marked five decades of Donna having #1s on the *Billboard* charts. We could not have been more humbled when Donna the icon began to use the WAWA mix for her live concert tour performances. Brooklyn Dreams come true!' 'To Paris With Love' was Donna's eighty-ninth single and her sixteenth #1 on *Billboard*'s US Dance Club Songs. It was also the final single in the exhaustive (but no new material!) forty- disc *Summer Time—The Singles Collection 1974-2010* boxset (Driven by the Music/Crimson DBTMCDBOX03), released in 2026.

'Un-Break My Heart/Crazy/On the Radio Medley' (with Seal) (from *Hit Man Returns: David Foster & Friends* album)

Reprise:526181-2. Album release: March 2011
Writers:Diane Warren, Seal, Guy Sigsworth, Donna Summer, Giorgio Moroder
Producer:David Foster

Just over a year before she died of lung cancer Donna was still belting out her hits (and those made famous by others) at her last big public appearance at this tribute to hitmaker and superstar producer David Foster. Some of the other big names who appeared that evening were Chaka Khan, Michael Bolton and Earth, Wind & Fire. Donna chose to sing Toni Braxton's 'Un-Break My Heart', written by Diane Warren, accompanied by David Foster on the piano, before Seal joined her to duet on this 1996 US #1. The pair then segued into Seal's US#7 1990 hit 'Crazy' before finishing with 'On the Radio'. Footage from the concert also appeared on the *Hit Man Returns: David Foster & Friends* DVD, which as a bonus has Donna, ominously, performing 'Last Dance' as the final song.

'Angel' (O'Mega Red featuring Donna Summer)

Stay Grindin' Inc/Big Shot Music Group. Download/stream release: April 2012
Writers:Omega Red, Donna Summer, Mackensie Dutton
Producer:Oliver Grey

'Angel', Donna's final recording, was truly a family affair. Rapper O'Mega Red was actually one of Donna's relatives, Robert Grant, born in 1978—the same year Donna scored her first US #1 single and album. 'Angel' was a tribute to his mother (Donna's cousin) and grandmother. This hip-hop track, recorded in 2011, features Donna on lead and background vocals singing, 'I'm your angel' and 'I'll be your halo'. 'Angel' was notably the only recording Donna worked on with a rap artist and her last recording before her death. 'Angel' later featured on O'Mega Red's album, *Red October*, eventually released in 2018. It is fitting that Donna's final recording, released on 19 April 2012, just before a month her death on 17 May at the age of just 63, is called 'Angel'. The internet also has a version of Donna's 2008 song 'Crayons' featuring a rapping O'Mega Red alongside guest Ziggy Marley.

Love To Love You Donna

Verve Records: B0019066-02
Originally released: October 2013

'Love to Love You Baby' (Giorgio Moroder Feat. Chris Cox Remix) 4:21
'Dim All the Lights' (Duke Dumont Remix) 6:01
'Hot Stuff' (Frankie Knuckles and Eric Kupper as Director's Cut) 5:59
'I Feel Love' (Afrojack Remix) 5:59
'Love is in Control (Finger on the Trigger)' (Chromeo & Oliver Remix) 4:01
'Sunset People' (Hot Chip Dub Edit) 7:38
'Working the Midnight Shift' (Holy Ghost! Remix) 5:29
'Bad Girls' (Gigamesh Remix) 5:22
'MacArthur Park' (Laidback Luke Remix) 5:40
'I Feel Love' (Benga Remix) 7:13
'On the Radio' (Jacques Greene Remix) 5:58
'Last Dance' (Masters At Work Remix Short Version) 6:30
'La Dolce Vita' 4:13
Bonus tracks (Deluxe Edition)
'Our Love' (Krystal Klear Remix) 5:04
'MacArthur Park' (Laidback Luke Remix Instrumental Version) 5:40
'Bad Girls' (Boys Noize Club Mix) 5:44
'Sunset People' (Hot Chip Re-Edit) 10:55

Not to be confused with 2023's *Love To Love You, Donna Summer* documentary, 18 months after Donna passed away this fascinating, if flawed, album of remixes and one new song was issued through the prestigious Verve Records label, part of the bigger Universal Music Group. Originally planned as a tribute album, the project came together at Verve because of the connection between its chairman, none other than David Foster, and Donna's family. Yet as with most such curated albums—fourteen different remixers—some feel the love and others are decidedly unlovely, baby. That said, this is a remix album worthy of your money, if only to get your hands on some truly lovely hot stuff! That Donna and Frankie Knuckles never met on record before this is a true crime. His standout mix (with Eric Kupper) of 'Hot Stuff' is a true melding of disco and house and everything else in between. Other highlights are Hot Chip's 'Sunset People', perfect for cruising down LA's Sunset Boulevard, Duke Dumont's 'Dim All The Lights', perfect for dancing your heart away in dimly-lit safe spaces, and Giorgio (and Chris Cox's) 'Love to Love You Baby', taking a more reconstructed then deconstructed route. Three of the remixes from the *Love to Love You Donna* album were issued as promo/DJ singles. Chromeo & Oliver's shimmering 'Love is in Control (Finger On The Trigger)', sprinkled with disco dust, arrived first in July 2014 with the identical 4:01 version from the album, plus a dub at the exact same running time (Verve Records: 00602537506613). There also appears to be an official video for it from Verve involving lots of stock footage of folks dancing, writing and intense colour blocking of Donna from the original 'Love is in Control' video. Laidback Luke's not-laidback-at-all 'MacArthur Park' came minus a video, yet still hit #1 on the

US dance charts, some 35 years after the Jimmy Webb disco-ised classic topped the charts in 1978. Sadly, less than six months after the release of this album in 2014, house music legend Frankie Knuckles died of diabetes at the age of 59.

Vid bit!
Director: Remo Camerota
Giorgio Moroder featuring Chris Cox's update of 'Love to Love You Baby' made a splash with a trippy lippy video busting out with girls who aren't Donna smearing themselves in paint and a mural of Donna that sings. It's garish, kitschy and so stupid we almost hate ourselves for liking it, baby.

'La Dolce Vita'

Writers: Donna Summer, Giorgio Moroder, Nathan DiGesare
Producers: Giorgio Moroder, Nathan DiGesare

Proving there was still plenty of new Donna Summer material left in the vaults, 'La Dolce Vita' was the one unreleased track included on the *Love To Love You Donna* album. It seems only fitting Donna that was singing a song in Italian (well, the title at least) co-produced by an Italian. 'The song was begun a few years ago in Nashville with Nathan DiGesare (also Donna's keyboard player) and then tweaked over time when we went back to Nashville to visit,' Bruce Sudano told *Spin* magazine. 'I wanted a new song on the CD, but couldn't get approval of the demo until Giorgio came on and reworked the track and added his touch. The vocal used is actually one from early on in the writing process.'

'Enough Is Enough 2017' (with Barbra Streisand)

Citrusonic Promotion: (no number). Single release: December 2016
Writers: Paul Jabara, Bruce Roberts
Producers: Gary Klein, Giorgio Moroder

An 'unofficial' release, but clearly official enough to be allowed by those who owned the rights to the original Donna/Babs duet, 'Enough Is Enough 2017' appeared right at the very end of 2016. A maxi CD contained twelve remixes: three from IDeaL & JBreak, two from Dirty Disco SCAR and (the hilariously named) Tweaka Turner, plus one each from C-Rod, Mindskap and Madonna's favourite remixer of the time, Offer Nissim. Quite why this release arrived at this time (a few years short of the 40th anniversary) is anyone's guess. Maybe Team Babs were upset the track didn't make it on to the *Love To Love You Donna* album! Complete with its original title, 'Enough Is Enough' did well enough to land at #3 in the US dance charts.

'Nether Lands' (from *A Tribute To Dan Fogelberg* album)

Full Moon: 538312682. Album release: November 2017
Writer: Dan Fogelberg
Producers: Norbert Putnam, Jean Fogelberg

Soft rock singer/songwriter Dan Fogelberg is best known for his 1980 US #2 hit 'Longer'. Donna, it transpired, was a big fan. Tragically, Fogelberg died in 2007 from prostate cancer aged 56, but in 2010 his widow, Jean, began work on a compilation of covers of his songs with Donna one of the first artists to sign on. She chose Fogelberg's ambitious 'Nether Lands', a single he released in 1977 from the album of the same name, and recorded in 2010. Donna told producer Norbert Putnam how during a very difficult time in her life she'd had some tough decisions to make and would start each day playing 'Nether Lands' to inspire herself. A powerhouse performance, it's incredible to think Donna was dying from lung cancer when she recorded her stirring version. Featuring Garth Brooks, Amy Grant, Eagles and more, *A Tribute To Dan Fogelberg* wasn't released until 2017, with proceeds going to prostate cancer research. Donna's daughter Amanda Sudano and husband Abner Ramirez, aka Johnnyswim, have since performed 'Nether Lands' in concert.

'Hot Stuff 2018'

Mercury Records: (no number). Promo release: April 2018
Writers: Harold Faltermeyer, Keith Forsey, Pete Bellotte
Producer: Giorgio Moroder, Pete Bellotte Remix: Ralphi Rosario and Erick Ibiza

Another year, another Donna compilation. Ho hum, except in this case ... wait just a minute! *Summer: The Original Hits* was sold as 'the classic hits that inspired the *Summer* musical' while *Summer: The Donna Summer Musical* was at the time midway through a run at Broadway's Lunt-Fontanne Theatre. The US/Japanese CD of *Summer: The Original Hits* (Casablanca: B0028247-02) bizarrely included 'White Boys' from the 1968 German cast version of *Haare*, plus Ralphi Rosario and Erik Ibiza's 2018 rework of 'Hot Stuff' (3:37) and Rosabel's Radio Mix of 'MacArthur Park' (also 3:37). 'Hot Stuff 2018', also featuring gay fave remixes by Dave Audé and DJ SPen & Michele Chiavarini, hit #1 on *Billboard*'s Dance Club Songs (making it Donna's seventeenth on that chart). As if that wasn't enough hot stuff baby tonight, a year later in 2019 Giorgio remade 'Hot Stuff' with an uncredited Donna soundalike. Taken from his 77-track *Club Remixes Selection* album it was available via Solaris Records on Bandcamp. In 2022 Giorgio told *NME* 'Hot Stuff' was 'the song that makes me want to dance'. But wait ... there's more hot stuff coming...

'Hot Stuff' (Kygo x Donna Summer)

RCA Records: (no number). Single release: September 2020
Writers: Harold Faltermeyer, Keith Forsey, Pete Bellotte
Producer: Kygo

Just two years later in 2020, 'Hot Stuff' was revitalised, reimagined and remixed by 'tropical house' Norwegian DJ/producer Kygo. The previous year he had reworked Whitney Houston's little-heard version of Steve Winwood's 1986 US #1 'Higher Love', transforming it into a huge global hit, taking it to #2 UK and #63 US. With Donna's original vocals the basis of their sorta collab, the gameplan clearly was to introduce 'Hot Stuff' to a whole new generation. 'Donna Summer is one of my favourite artists of all time,' Kygo said at the time. 'Her catalogue of music is brilliant and her vocals are unmatched. I am honoured and humbled to get to work on an iconic track like "Hot Stuff".' Although arguably a little underwhelming, the Kygo x Donna collab did reasonably well across Europe, hitting #1 in Belgium.

Vid bit!

Director: Bo Webb

While the original 1979 pre-MTV era 'Hot Stuff' missed getting a music video, Kygo's 2020 remake didn't (oh, and before you ask, there's no Donna here, just her voice). Initially stripping away the overtly sexual nature of the lyrics, around the two-minute mark out pop the disco sequins, boogie moves and some feverish hairography. This gorgeously filmed clip is a testament to the sizzling chemistry between the two leads, real-life acting couple at the time Madelyn Cline and Chase Stokes from the *Outer Banks* television series. The clip was directed by that show's cinematographer, Bo Webb.

'Run (Piano Diaries)' (Donna Summer and Toby Gad)

Kite: Digital file/streaming. Single release: June 2025
Writers: Donna Summer, Toby Gad
Producer: Toby Gad

After working with Donna in the late noughties Toby Gad turned into a true superstar songwriter/producer, penning 'If I Were A Boy' for Beyoncé, 'Living For Love' for Madonna and US #1 'All Of Me' for John Legend. Some seventeen years after he worked on Donna's *Crayons* album Gad finally released the reflective 'Run' as part of his *Piano Diaries* project, reimaging some of his back catalogue. 'I wrote four songs with Donna Summer, three of them were released on her last album, and this was the one song that was not released, but once again, the one song I liked the most,' Toby said about 'Run' (known in demo form as 'Run For

It'). 'Donna was not only an amazing singer who was totally in charge of her voice, much like Beyoncé when I worked with her, but also a great songwriter, intuitively finding words that are honest, authentic and have emotion.' The track also enjoyed a brief, but celebrated, stint on *Billboard*'s Adult Contemporary chart.

Vid bit!

Director: Sam King

The 'Run' music video featured teenage dancer London Payne as the embodiment of a young Donna. 'We were so emotional filming this,' Gad said. 'That is a song I wrote with Donna Summer before she died.'

Remix fix!

Alongside a bunch of so-so remixes, Mousse T ran off with a decent disco version.

APPENDIX

Enough Is (Not) Enough—The Extra Days of Summer

If what you've just read in this book wasn't enough to make you love to love Donna, baby, then here's more and more! Donna also performed numerous songs live which she did not receive a proper studio recording, with the most significant of those included here too.

1973

'Let's Get Together/In My Blue Balloon' (Family Tree)

A West German post-hippie collective who appeared on television's *Hits A Gogo* singing these two songs. It's definitely Donna visually, but not audio-wise.

1976

'The Family' (Roberta Kelly)

Oasis: OC 407.

One of Donna's besties, Roberta was another singer on Giorgio and Pete's roster. For Roberta's debut album Donna provided backing vocals on Italo-disco track 'The Family', also the B-side of Roberta's 'Trouble-Maker' single.

'Happiness In The World' (Tom Winter)

PROM: 6.22492 AS.

Donna provided backing vocals on this electro-reggae number from Winter's *Winterference* LP.

1977

'Medley: Shut Out/Heaven Is A Disco' (Paul Jabara)

Casablanca: CALP 5005.

Donna is credited as 'special guest' on the 9:30 minute opener of Jabara's *Shut Out* debut album. Featuring one of the greatest lyrics in music history—'To get off my bummer/I play Donna Summer'—'Shut Out' was also released as a single on its own. Pure disco camp!

'Old Fashioned Girl' (Brooklyn Dreams)

Millennium: MNLP 8002.

Donna featured on 'Old Fashioned Girl' from the budding trio's self-titled debut album, written by band member/Donna's future husband Bruce Sudano in 1974. 'Eddie sang lead on it with Donna singing an interlude in a beautiful high falsetto, which was the first time we worked together on a record,' Bruce remembered. 'We returned the favour, singing background on her song "I Remember Yesterday". All of this evolved into our collaboration with *Heaven Knows*.'

'Gospel Medley' and 'A Song For You' (from *The Mac Davis TV Special*)

For an NBC television special from country star Mac Davis this 'Gospel Medley' featured the unlikely teaming of Mac, Dolly Parton, Tom Jones and Donna. This seven-minute musical sermon ('Sounds Good to Me', 'Old Landmark', 'I'll Fly Away', 'Operator', 'I Hear Music in the Air' and 'Think About It') is sure to get you clapping and praising Jesus even if you're a non-believer. Donna also compellingly belted out Leon Russell's 'A Song For You', made famous by the Carpenters, on the show. Davis died in 2020.

'Swing Low Sweet Chariot' (with Lou Rawls)

Long before she was born again, Donna duetted divinely on this spiritual hymn for television's *The Midnight Special*. Like Donna, Rawls died of lung cancer, but six years earlier in 2006.

1978

'Burning Up With Fever' (Gene Simmons)

Casablanca: NBLP 7120.

For his solo album KISS member Gene Simmons requested labelmate Donna bring the heat and add vocals to hard rock track 'Burning Up With Fever'. Donna can also be heard (with later actress Katy Segal) on the rocktastic 'Tunnel Of Love'.

'Something's Missing' (Paul Jabara)

A track on Paul Jabara's second solo album, *Keeping Time*, a duet version of 'Something's Missing' with Donna was kept in the vaults until it was released in 1989 on *Paul Jabara's Greatest Hits ... And Misses* compilation. Donna's old Boston buddy Marcia Hines recorded a version in 1979 which went top ten in Australia and New Zealand. The *Keeping Time* album also included Jabara's solo, and brief, version of 'Last Dance'.

'With A Little Luck' (from *Paul Anka's Monte Carlo TV Special*)

Donna covers Wings' US #1 'With A Little Luck', does her best Shirley Bassey impersonation and is pure gold. During the same special Donna also sings 'Sisters' with Suzanne Somers. Around this period Donna also often covered Stephen Sondheim's theatrical showstopper 'Send In The Clowns' in her concerts, with audio available online.

1979

'He Is Your Brother', 'Put A Little Love In Your Heart' (A Gift Of Song)

At *The Music For UNICEF: A Gift Of Song* concert, held at NYC's United Nations, Donna sang 'Mimi's Song' live. She also briefly sang 'Fairy Tale High', then joined for a collective singalong to ABBA's 'He Is Your Brother' and Jackie DeShannon's 'Put A Little Love In Your Heart', plus a duet with Rita Coolidge on 'You've Got A Friend'. On the released album, however, 'Mimi's Song' was the *Live and More* version, with her other contributions omitted. They are online though. Yay!

'Foggy Day', 'Never Lose Your Sense Of Humour' (Paul Jabara)

Casablanca: (single) NB 1002 (album) NBLP 7163.

For his third album, comically titled *The Third Album*, Jabara lured Donna in again, in between composing 'Last Dance' and 'No More Tears (Enough Is Enough)' for her. The main part of this foggy duet, the theatrically disco 'Never Lose Your Sense Of Humour', which Donna co-wrote with Jabara and Greg Mathieson, got a release as a single but failed to chart. It does, however, feature the next best lyric in music history—'Instead of the plumber/I called Donna Summer'. More pure disco camp!

'Too Much For The Lady' (Brooklyn Dreams)

Casablanca: NBLP 7165.

On Brooklyn Dreams' second album, *Joy Ride*, Donna contributed vocals for her 'special appearance' on 'Too Much For The Lady', although she sounds more like a French hooker to be honest. 'Too Much For The Lady' also has some nowadays questionable lyrics ('let her roll your rock down'). Composers are Donna with Brooklyn Dreams and the producer was Jürgen Koppers. Donna also co-wrote 'Your Love's So Good To Me' and 'Diago' on the album. 'Jürgen was a good guy but he wasn't a producer,' Joe Esposito said years later.

> He was an engineer trying to be a producer. We did the album in two weeks. It was very quick. It was like driving on the autobahn—the car was very smooth, it was nice, but it was quick. We had a couple of good songs on there. It was more disco. Nothing ever happened with that, although I like the album cover.

'Watchin' Daddy Dance' (Sunshine)

This unreleased album recorded by Donna's sisters as Sunshine was nixed in the wake of Donna's lawsuit against Casablanca. Co-produced by Donna and Jürgen Koppers (with Bruce Sudano on 'Watchin' Daddy Dance') it featured the title track written by Donna and Brooklyn Dreams as a tribute to her father. Other songs that may have been part of this project include 'What Are You Saying?', 'Jealous Eyes', 'Sunshine', 'Let's Dance', 'Step Step Away', 'I'm The One' and 'Where I Should Be'. Another mooted song which Donna wrote for Sunshine, 'It's Over', she recorded on her 1984 *Cats Without Claws* album as 'Maybe It's Over' (see Chapter 15). Three minutes of footage of Sunshine recording the title track in the studio with Donna was captured by French television, airing in 1978, and available online.

'Heaven In My Eyes—Discotheque' (Twiggy)

Sepia Records: SEPIA 8002.

Recorded in 1979, but finally released in 2007, this disco album by British supermodel Twiggy was produced by Donna and Jürgen Koppers. A highlight is the slinky 'Sugar Daddy' written by Bruce Sudano ('I'm gonna find me a sugar daddy right away'). The original eight tracks were bolstered by four 2007 remixes from Australian DJ The OUTpsiDER. A true lost disco classic that deserves to be heard at a discotheque near you!

'Bridge Over Troubled Water' (with Robert Guillaume)

Taken from 1980's *The Donna Summer Special* (with some bonus insider humour!) these two old chums duet on a cover of Simon & Garfunkel's 'Bridge Over Troubled Water'. Donna also covers jazz standards 'The Man I Love', 'I Got It Bad (And That Ain't Good)' and 'Some of These Days', as heard on her

Live and More album (see Chapter 8), dolled up like a twenties flapper in a dragtastic red dress. Guillaume passed in 2017 aged 89.

1980
'I Will Survive' (The Grammy Awards)

Donna joins host Kenny Rogers to warble a medley of nominated songs: 'Reunited', 'I Will Survive', 'Honesty', 'Chuck E's In Love', 'Minute By Minute', 'After The Love Has Gone', 'She Believes In Me' and 'What A Fool Believes'. The best eight minutes on YouTube right now!

1981
'Fugitive Kind' (Bruce Sudano)

Millennium: BXL1-7760.
On husband Bruce's debut solo album Donna contributed backing vocals to the tracks 'Pretenders', 'A Girl Like You', 'Modern Age Love Affair', 'Talk To Me' and 'True Love' (which she also co-wrote). Donna and Bruce also wrote 'Starting Over Again', which she had performed on television and became a hit for Dolly Parton (see Chapter 9). Bruce's heartfelt take was released as a single (Millennium: JH-13104) with a stereo mix on the A-side and a mono mix on the B-side.

'Don't Wanna Lose You' (Madleen Kane)

Chalet Records: CH0702.
Swedish model/singer Madleen Kane released her *Don't Wanna Lose You* album in December 1981, including US dance #1 'You Can', written by Giorgio and Pete, and produced by Giorgio. Could this delightful, post-disco record have been the album Donna might have made if she hadn't become a born-again Christian? Start mass debating now!

1983
'Country Music Medley' (*The Eddie Rabbit Special*)

For this 1983 television special starring country music crossover star Eddie Rabbit, Donna (in pink cowgirl outfit!) appeared singing Tammy Wynette's 'Stand By Your Man', Don Gibson's 'I Can't Stop Loving You' and 'Oh, Lonesome Me', plus her own touching 'Starting Over Again'.

1984
'Papa Can You Hear Me?' (Live)

At that year's Academy Award ceremony Barbra Streisand chose not to sing her grand showstopping power-ballad 'Papa Can You Hear Me?' from *Yentl*, her directorial debut. Who better to step in to sing it then but old pal Donna, delivering a spellbinding rendition. The category was won, however, by Irene Cara's 'Flashdance ... What a Feeling', co-written and produced by Giorgio Moroder.

'She Works Hard for the Money' (Live)

Atlantic: (CD) 82754. A*Vision Entertainment: (VHS/Laserdisc) 50740-6.
Released on VHS, CD and laserdisc (remember that, kids?) was this compilation of live performances from the 1984 Grammy Awards called *Grammy's Greatest Moments Volume 1*. Donna's 'She Works Hard for the Money', complete with working women/dancers running through the crowd, Donna in waitress outfit and a female basketballer, was included. Quite the spectacle and well worth the money!

1986

'This Girl's Back In Town (Paul Jabara)

Warner Bros. Records: 9 25381-1.
In March 1986 Paul Jabara released his final solo album, *De La Noche: The True Story (A Poperetta)*. 'Donna Desmondes Divine' sings on 'This Girl's Back In Town', which obeys Jabara's beloved ballad-bursting-into-disco format. A vinyl 12-inch promo, remixed by Victor Flores, was also issued (Warner Bros. Records: PRO-A-2497) with a portion of the royalties going to AIDS org AmfAR. In 1988 Raquel Welch released a version (with OTT video), which was a minor US dance hit. There are also online versions of Donna singing lead on 'This Girl's Back In Town' (plus duet versions with co-writer Bob Esty), which appear to be fan/DJ crafted from guide demos made for Welch (and they are pretty good too)! Jabara's concept musical's final track, 'Finale (Montage) Mama's Fever', also lists Donna among the 'girls' as vocalists.

1987

'The Planet Is Alive'

Included in a Pope John Paul II doco DVD (Prelude Worldwide Ministries), this well-meaning song/video tries hard to be another 'State of Independence'. Available online, Sarah Vaughan previously sang this as 'Let It Live', based on JPII's poetry!

'Celebrate Me Home'

Sunfish: Streaming
This live 1987 inspirational cover of Kenny Loggins' Christmas staple, originally from 1977, was added to streaming services in 2025 from the (semi) unofficial *Find The Love (Live)* album.

1989
'Spirit Of The Forest' (Spirit Of The Forest)

Virgin: (UK 7-inch) VS 1191 (US 12-inch) 7 96551-0.
A rainforest-friendly recording conceived by a gaggle of famous music stars to promote ecological awareness. Besides Donna some of the others involved were Kate Bush, Debbie Harry, Olivia Newton-John, Joni Mitchell, Jon Anderson and Iggy Pop. A music video also featured Donna briefly. The song itself was not a hit ... and doesn't sound like one either! Songwriter Kenny Young, who wrote 'Spirit Of The Forest', passed away in 2020 aged 79.

1994
'Last Dance, Amazing Grace, Rejoice, She Works Hard for the Money' (on Family Matters)

Donna appeared as Aunt Oona on the *Family Matters* sitcom a number of times and was always brought on to sing, as you would expect/hope. If only she had recorded 'Amazing Grace' from the show: that truly would have been, well, amazing. Donna also often performed the song live, footage of which is available to enjoy online.

1996
The Three Divas (NYC concert)

For one night only Broadway's Lunt-Fontanne Theatre was taken over by 'The Three Divas', aka Donna, Gloria Estefan and Chaka Khan. The charity event also featured a tribute from host RuPaul. Donna, who had laryngitis, was unable to sing solo on the night, but joined Chaka and Gloria on stage for 'I'm Every Woman'. Prince also showed up for the finale of Gloria's cover of 1976 disco nugget 'Turn The Beat Around'. This gathering of gals would later inspire VH1's *Divas* series of concerts.

1999
'The Star-Spangled Banner'

A cappella Donna croons the USA's nation anthem at a Boston baseball game. Footage available online.

2000
VH1 Divas 2000: A Tribute To Diana Ross (TV show)

Filmed on 9 April 2000, at New York's Madison Square Garden, *VH1 Divas 2000: A Tribute To Diana Ross—An Honors Concert For the VH1 Save The Music Foundation* aired on 11 April on VH1. Bizarrely it was never released on

CD/DVD. Donna performed 'Bad Girls', 'Love Is A Healer' and a cover of the Diana Ross & The Supremes 1967 hit 'Reflections'. The headliners were Donna, Diana Ross (of course!), Mariah Carey and Faith Hill, with guest performances from Destiny's Child, RuPaul and two members of The Supremes: Lynda Laurence and Scherrie Payne.

2001
'Adonai'

On 17 May 2026, the 14th anniversary of Donna's death, songwriter Paul Rein uploaded a dynamic dance remix of 'Adonai' which he and Paul Barry wrote with her in 2001 for a planned Sony Music project called *Angel* which was nixed. Rein also posted that the trio wrote other songs included 'Dangerously Cool' and 'New York City Groove'—based on a sample from Crusaders' 'Street Life'—which remains unreleased, or not uploaded yet! The hope is a partnership the Donna Summer Estate cut in 2026 with Primary Wave will end that!

2003
'You Got Me Believing' (Joe 'Bean' Esposito and Brooklyn Dreams)

Animated movie *Foodfight!*, with the voices of Charlie Sheen and Hilary Duff, was originally slated for 2003, but a month after Donna's death in 2012 finally saw a direct-to-video release. 'You Got Me Believing', performed by Joe Esposito and Brooklyn Dreams, was written by Donna and husband Bruce Sudano. Joe and BD also perform a version of the Marvin Gaye classic 'I Heard It Through The Grapevine' on the soundtrack.

2004
'No More Tears (Enough Is Enough)' (duet with Westlife)

Mercury: 9821319.

In 2004, Donna hosted/sang on British television special *DiscoMania*, where pop acts of the day covered classic disco tunes. Irish boy band Westlife, big business in the UK and other territories, teamed up with Donna for a rendition of 'No More Tears (Enough Is Enough)'. As Donna pointed out, this was the first time she had sung it with a man (band member Mark Feehily took the lead). It was probably also the first time she had sung it with a gay man, because a year later Feehily came out. Is this the Donna Summer conversion therapy in full effect? The rather good Donna/Westlife (straight/gay?) duet appeared on the compilation *DiscoMania*, produced by WIP, released in the UK in June 2004. Also included on the CD was 'The Donna Summer Eternity Megamix' ('Hot Stuff', 'I Feel

Love' and 'Bad Girls' all in 3:44 minutes!) produced by Clive Scott and hi-NRG legend Ian Levine. Other disco remakes came courtesy of Rachel Stevens, Atomic Kitten, Geri Haliwell, Girls Aloud and more. A television performance of Donna and Westlife duetting is also available online.

'Let It Be' (on *Later ... with Jools Holland*)

On this BBC music programme Donna chats with host/musician Jools Holland before they perform an awe-inspiring rendition of The Beatles' classic 'Let It Be' ('Mother Mary comes to me'). Donna mentions how this song means a lot to her because her own mother was named Mary.

2005
'Try A Little Tenderness' (Donna Summer and Joss Stone)

In April 2005 Donna was one of the guests joining British soul singer Joss Stone at the *Save The Music: A Concert To Benefit the VH1 Save The Music Foundation* concert. Their tempo-switching rendition of 'Try A Little Tenderness', made famous in 1966 by Otis Redding, deserved a proper release, but that didn't happen. An unofficial *Duets* album by Joss Stone featuring this track was promoed in Europe in 2007.

2005
Night Of The Proms 2005

Sony BMG Music Entertainment: 82876 75468 2

A European musical touring event, this featured Ace Of Base (band member Jenny Berggren later appeared on Donna's 2008 *Crayons* album), The Who's Roger Daltrey and Safri Duo. Donna ended the show/CD with 'MacArthur Park' and 'State Of Independence', the latter also featuring Jenny Berggren and Safri Duo. The original epic 27-minute performance of Donna also performing 'I Feel Love', 'Bad Girls', 'Hot Stuff' and 'Last Dance' can be found online. The *Night Of The Proms 2005* album was released in December 2005. Donna returned for the *Night Of The Proms* event in 2007 adding 'You Are So Beautiful', made famous by Joe Cocker, while the CD release again contained just 'MacArthur Park' and 'State of Independence' (PSE Belgium: 5425020320061).

2009
Nobel Peace Prize Concert

To honour that year's Nobel Peace Prize recipient, US President Barack Obama, Donna performed six songs at the prestigious Oslo event: 'MacArthur Park', 'She

Works Hard for the Money', Charlie Chaplin's 'Smile', 'No More Tears (Enough Is Enough)', 'Bad Girls' and 'Last Dance'. 'I'm honoured that our president has been honoured,' Donna said on the night. She also joined in for a closing group singalong to 'Man In The Mirror' by Michael Jackson who had passed away earlier that year.

2013
Rock 'n' Roll Hall of Fame

A year after her death Donna was finally inducted into the Rock 'n' Roll Hall of Fame. Kelly Rowland, long mooted to portray Donna in a biopic, inducted Donna, calling her 'incomparable'. The award was accepted by husband Bruce, who called it a 'bittersweet moment', and their three daughters. Oscar-winner Jennifer Hudson afterwards belted out 'Last Dance' in glorious seventies afro glory, receiving a standing ovation.

2017
'Time Can't Take It Away' (Twenty Sixty Six And Then)

Getting a proper double CD release after previous vinyl re-releases/single CD reissues was the album *Reflections on the Future* (MIG: MIG 01842 2CD) by prog-rock/Krautrock outfit Twenty Sixty Six And Then. Donna can be heard at the end of 'Time Can't Take It Away' (The Munich Sessions), written by Geoff Harrison and Veit Marvos, if you last that long!

2023
Love To Love You, Donna Summer

Snippets of unreleased material featured in 2023's *Love To Love You, Donna Summer* doco are 'When I Believe In Miracles' (Donna at the piano with daughter Brooklyn), 'Just Say You Don't Love Me' (her 1960s band the Crow), 'Take Your Baby Home' (Donna, husband Bruce and songwriter Danny Peck singing), 'Electricity' (Donna and Bruce in the studio), 'Two Kids Playing In An Alleyway' (Donna at the piano), 'Lost In The Moment' (Bruce solo) and 'Just The Other Day'.

'Could It Be Magic'

'Ordinary Girl'

Donna's unproduced musical, *Ordinary Girl*, was written with husband Bruce Sudano, producer Michael Omartian and songwriter Al Kasha. Donna got to know Kasha through his hosting of Bible studies at his home which Donna, and fellow convert Bob Dylan, attended. The following unreleased songs have been associated with *Ordinary Girl:* 'Bitter End', 'Rain, Rain', 'Arms and Legs', 'Be Rich', 'Gotta Have A Dress', 'My Dream Is For You', 'This Forbidden Fruit', 'I Found A Star', 'Begin Again' (see below) and 'Chairman Of The Board'. Previously released are 'No Ordinary Love Song' (played live and available online), 'Nobody' and the truly dynamic duo of 'My Life' and 'If There Is Music There' (see Chapter 20). Kasha died in 2020.

'Friends Unknown' (Unreleased A–Z)

This is but a fraction of the unreleased Donna Summer material still locked away in various record company vaults. Other titles not readily available but which appear to exist from the nixed *Angel* project include 'Only Words', 'Not A Day', 'Rain On My Shoulders', 'Work It' and 'Til/Till You Get It'. Here's hoping some, if not all, of these finally get properly released and heard by fans.

'Addiction'

A stomping track ('this is your time') cut from *Crayons* which leaked. The original is 12 minutes according to producer Nathan DiGesare. A minimal version is also lurking online.

'All I Ever Think About'

A remix of 2005's 'I Got Your Love' closely resembling the stellar work of Peter Rauhofer.

'Begin Again'

Showstopping ballad kicking into disco bliss from Donna's still unproduced *Ordinary Girl* musical. Extraordinary.

'Freedom'

Well-meaning, if lacklustre, self-empowerment ode written by Donna, Tony Moran and Nathan DiGesare for *Crayons*.

'Half The Battle'

A 49-second extract of this urban ballad about 'learning to say no' was uploaded by songwriter Nathan DiGesare in 2015. A true unreleased treasure.

'If I Could Live Our Love Again'

Donna in vibrant R&B power-ballad mode on a song written by Beth Feldman-Foster in 1986.

'So This Is Lonely'

A sweet acoustic ditty (with Bruce Sudano on guitar) allegedly from a BBC radio session.

'Valley Of the Moon'

Pumping circuit party tune using 'I Feel Love' as its basis and reportedly recorded for the Sony Music *Angel* album in 2000/2001 which never came to fruition.

'We Are Gonna Win/One World'

The fabled, yet gripping, Paul Jabara ballad about the AIDS crisis, recorded in 1983/84 (and reportedly again in 1990/91), which Donna lent vocals to. Never officially released, it leaked some years ago. A special record for a special cause, the 12-minute 'We Are Gonna Win' deserves a proper release if only to help further heal Donna's history with the gay community and repair her own musical legacy.

Bibliography

Primary sources

Summer, D. with Eliot, M. *Ordinary Girl: The Journey* (US: Villard/Random House, 2003)
Summer, D. *Lady of the Night* (Netherlands: Groovy, 1974)
Summer, D. *Love to Love You Baby* (US: Casablanca, 1975)
Summer, D. *A Love Trilogy* (US: Casablanca, 1976)
Summer D. *I Remember Yesterday* (US: Casablanca, 1977)
Summer, D. *Once Upon a Time* (US: Casablanca, 1977)
Soundtrack *Thank God It's Friday* (US: Casablanca, 1978)
Summer, D. *Live and More* (US: Casablanca: 1978)
Summer, D. *Bad Girls* (US: Casablanca: 1979)
Summer, D. *On the Radio: Greatest Hits Vol. 1 & II* (US: Casablanca, 1979)
Summer, D. *Walk Away: The Best of 1977-1980* (US: Casablanca, 1980)
Summer, D. *The Wanderer* (US: Geffen, 1980)
Summer, D. *Donna Summer* (US: Geffen, 1982)
Summer, D. *A Hot Summer Night* (US: Palace Video, 1983)
Summer, D. *She Works Hard for the Money* (US: Mercury, 1983)
Summer, D. *Cats Without Claws* (US: Geffen, 1984)
Summer, D. *The Summer Collection* (US: Mercury, 1985)
Summer, D. *The Dance Collection* (US: Casablanca, 1987)
Summer, D. *All Systems Go* (US: PolyGram, 1987)
Summer, D. *Another Place and Time* (UK: WEA International, 1989)
Summer, D. *Mistaken Identity* (US: Atlantic, 1991)
Summer, D. *The Donna Summer Anthology* (US: PolyGram, 1993)
Summer, D. *Endless Summer: Greatest Hits* (US: Mercury, 1994)

Summer, D. *Christmas Spirit* (US: PolyGram, 1994)
Summer, D. *I'm a Rainbow* (US: Casablanca/PolyGram, 1996)
Summer, D. *VH1 Presents: Live & More Encore!* (US: Epic, 1999)
Summer, D. *The Journey: The Very Best of Donna Summer* (US: UTV/Mercury, 2003)
Summer, D. *Crayons* (US: Burgundy, 2008)
Summer, D. *Love To Love You Donna* (US: Verve, 2013)
Summer, D. *The Ultimate Collection* (US: Driven By The Music, 2016)
Summer, D. *Encore* (US: Driven By The Music, 2020)
Summer, D. *A Hot Summer Night* (US: Driven By The Music/Crimson, 2020)
Summer, D. *I'm a Rainbow: Recovered & Recoloured* (US: Driven By The Music, 2021)
Love To Love You, Donna Summer (US: HBO Max, 2023)

Secondary sources

Brucesudano.com
Discogs.com
donnasummer.com
Donna-tribute.com (truly a gift to Donna Summer fandom!)
SmashHitsRemembered
thedonnasummerfanclub.com
thedonnasummerarchive (doing a remarkable job with Donna's legacy on Instagram)
giorgiomoroder.com
petebellotte.com

Traditional media and digital media

Abbaofficial.com
Allmusic.com
Anthonysmithmusic.com
BBC.com
Beatsource.com
Billboard.com
Bobconti.com
Brendarussell.com
Christies.com
Classic Pop magazine
Daeida.com
Danleysoundlabs.com

Davidfoster.com
Djhistory.com
Donna Summer—Friends Unknown (Facebook)
Donna Summer Tribute 1948–2012 (Facebook)
Donna Summer: The Ultimate Tribute Site (Facebook)
Entertainment Weekly
Faltermeyer.com
Genius.com
Hollywoodreporter.com
Imdb.com
Jimmywebb.com
Johnnyswim.com
Keithforsey.com
Latimes.com
Lightscamerabackbeat.com
Linkedin.com
Markchaitmusic.com
Mcarchives.com
Medium.com
Mercymultiplied.com
Mikestockmusic.com
Mtishows.co.uk
Musicbrainz.org
Officialcharts.com
Neighborhoodarchive.com
NME.com
Nostalgiacentral.com
Pauljabara.com
Petercornish.co.uk
Peterstengaard.com
Pitchfork.com
Popmatters.com
Playbill.com
Popjustice.com
Praisecharts.com
Prince.org
Pwl-empire.com
Recording-magazine.com
Retropop magazine
Rateyourmusic.com
Recordcollectormag.com
Robertchristgau.com
Rollingstone.com

Secondhandsongs.com
Sessiondays.com
Sixonstage.com
Somethingelsereviews.com
Songfacts.com
Songwriting Magazine
Songwriteruniverse.com
Soultracks.com
SoundCloud
Spin.com
Stargayzing.com
Stockaitkenwaterman.co.uk
Sydney Star Observer
Televisionacademy.com
Tennessean.com
The Advocate
The Guardian
The Los Angeles Times
Thestudentpocketguide.com
The Village Voice
Twiggylawson.co.uk
Ultimate70s.com
Variety.com
Vinylpussycat.com
Whosampled.com
Wikipedia
Worldradiohistory.com
YouTube